PLOTTING THE PAST

Purdue Studies in Romance Literatures

volume 12

PLOTTING THE PAST

Metamorphoses of Historical Narrative in Modern Italian Fiction

Cristina Della Coletta

Purdue University Press
West Lafayette, Indiana

00 99 98 97 96 5 4 3 2 1

∞The paper used in this book meets the minimum requirements of American National Standard for Information Sciences—Permanence of Paper for Printed Library Materials, ANSI Z39.48-1992.

Printed in the United States of America
Design by Anita Noble

Library of Congress Cataloging-in-Publication Data
Della Coletta, Cristina, 1962–
Plotting the past: metamorphoses of historical narrative in modern Italian fiction / Cristina Della Coletta.
p. cm. — (Purdue studies in Romance literatures ; v. 12)
Includes bibliographical references and index.
ISBN 1-55753-091-2 (cloth : alk. paper)
1. Historical fiction, Italian—History and criticism. 2. Italian fiction—19th century—History and criticism. 3. Italian fiction—20th century—History and criticism. I. Title. II. Series.
PQ4181.H55D45 1996
853'.08109091—dc20 96-31663
CIP

Ai miei genitori—
Pietro e Wanda

Contents

Acknowledgments

It is a special pleasure to thank the friends and colleagues who provided insight and advice in the making of this book. I am deeply grateful to Lucia Re, whose advice and criticism inspired me throughout the project. I would also like to thank Tibor Wlassics and the colleagues at the University of Virginia for their friendship and support, and Marga Cottino-Jones and José Monleón for their suggestions on the early stages of the manuscript.

I am indebted to the editorial board of PSRL for having graciously accepted this study, and to Peter Carravetta and Mark Pietralunga for providing generous and constructive comments on my ideas. I also thank John Portman and Jennifer Haraguchi for their editorial and bibliographic work. I am grateful to the University of Virginia for the research grants that allowed me to fully dedicate myself to the completion of various chapters during the summer months. Early versions of parts of chapters 2 and 3 appeared, respectively, as "Historical Reconfigurations and the Ideology of Desire: Giuseppe Tomasi di Lampedusa's *Il Gattopardo,*" in *The Italianist* 14 (1994): 96–110, and as "Elsa Morante's *La Storia:* Fiction and Women's History," in *RLA* 5 (1993): 194–99. To the editors of these journals I am obliged for their kind permission to incorporate the essays into this book.

Finally, all my love goes to my husband, Mike Thrift, for his unfailing encouragement and invaluable editorial review of seemingly endless drafts of the manuscript, and to my son, Alexander, for sharing his first months of life with the book's final revisions. Without their devotion and joy, *Plotting the Past* would simply not exist.

Introduction

The Historical Novel and the Dialectics of Genre

Immediately after publishing his historical novel *I promessi sposi* (*The Betrothed*)[1] in 1827, Alessandro Manzoni renounced the entire genre of historical fiction. A best-seller *ante litteram, I promessi sposi,* like the great epic poems of the past, would remain a model to respect, but not to follow. "Ammirami, e fa altrimenti" ("Admire me, and do otherwise"), Manzoni advised in *Del romanzo storico e, in genere, de' componimenti misti di storia e d'invenzione* (*On the Historical Novel and, in General, on Works Mixing History and Invention,* 1850), a controversial essay indicting the historical novel as a flawed combination of facts and fiction that betrays both the homogeneous formal unity that aesthetics demands and the absolute truthfulness to the past that history requires.

In *Der historische Roman* (*The Historical Novel,* 1937), Georg Lukács argued that Italy's political and social fragmentation precluded the development of historical fiction after Manzoni's masterpiece. Lukács believed that Manzoni was the sole great artist who could overcome the "objective unfavourableness of Italian history and . . . create a real historical novel" (*The Historical Novel* 70). Unlike Walter Scott's, Manzoni's theme was not the crisis of national history, but the critical conditions in the life of Italian people caused by Italy's fragmentation and dependence on the intervention of foreign great powers. The nature of Manzoni's theme, however, showed that *I promessi sposi* "had to be an only novel, that it could have been repeated only in a bad sense" (Lukács, *The Historical Novel* 70). From Lukács's humanistic perspective, since art should mirror reality's deep organic wholeness, Italy's political and social fragmentation resisted a unified account and was therefore unrepresentable.[2]

In spite of Manzoni's and Lukács's views, historical fiction has known an almost unbroken development in Italy. Where *I promessi sposi* furnished the classical model for the genre, Manzoni's *Del romanzo storico* provided a polemical, theoretical challenge for those who aimed to revise the genre of historical fiction. In the wake of Manzoni's success, a number of novels simply imitated, without questioning, Manzoni's model of *I promessi sposi,* thus contributing to both the canonization and the conventionalization of the genre.[3] This study focuses on three twentieth-century novels that reshape the genre of historical fiction by directly confronting the aesthetic and philosophical challenges posed by Manzoni's *Del romanzo storico.* These novels are Giuseppe Tomasi di Lampedusa's *Il Gattopardo* (*The Leopard,* 1958), Elsa Morante's *La Storia* (*History,* 1974), and Umberto Eco's *Il nome della rosa* (*The Name of the Rose,* 1980). Because of their innovative and constructive contribution to the genre, these novels constitute Manzoni's legacy. Transformative and revisionist, these "critical" historical novels embark on a discussion of the meaning of writing within the genre of historical fiction, thus participating in the evolution of the genre while also charting its historical development, assessing its aesthetic function, and evaluating its hermeneutical power.

Critical historical novels demonstrate that a given work and the genre to which it belongs are not paralyzed in a fixed and unchanging relationship and thus refute all normative philosophies of genre.[4] These normative philosophies equate genres with literary archetypes endowed with a number of essential attributes elevated to the rank of universal foundational principles. Far from being mere conventional repertoires of themes and motifs—historically mutable forms with a certain temporal persistence due to the simple reason that "they have been tested and found satisfactory" (Guillén 121)—genres are seen as a priori categories that precede the literary historian's codification.[5] In this view, genres quite mechanically establish a number of recurring themes and a set of formal conventions that specific texts strive to reproduce in order to guarantee their belonging to the genre in question. The repertoire of stock themes, stylistic devices, and narrative strategies that form a literary work constitute the stable generic model that shapes and directs the creation of all other literary texts claiming to share certain generic features. In this panorama, variation within the genre occurs only in relation to the number of the prescribed conventions, and deviation from the generic norm refers to the closeness of the imitation of such conventions, which is high in periods of strict generic codification and lower in periods of stronger creative independence.[6]

While rejecting strictly normative genre theories, critical historical novels are also wary of purely typological (i.e., descriptive) perspectives on genre. A typological approach defines a genre by furnishing an inventory of thematic and formal recurrences abstracted from the observation of a body of texts or extrapolated from a work of extraordinary import. Literary genres are seen as self-enclosed and isolated universes, airtight compartments sealed off from all other generic spaces, immutable entities that the literary historian can objectively catalogue and describe once and for all. While this may be partially valid for obsolete genres such as the picaresque novel or the chivalric romance, it certainly does not hold true for genres that are still widely practiced and therefore still developing, such as historical fiction. Even obsolete genres can reappear in a renewed and demystified form and with a novel aesthetic and social function. Examples may include Italo Calvino's ironic and irreverent resurrection of the chivalric tradition in *Il cavaliere inesistente* (*The Nonexistent Knight,* 1962), Sebastiano Vassalli's satirical reworking of the didactic-treatise form in *Tempo di massacro* (*Time of Massacre,* 1970), and John Barth's postmodern revision of the *novellistica* conventions in *Chimera* (1972).

Both normative and descriptive approaches to genre theory conceal a conceptual flaw and ideological bias, as they both assume an interpretative positioning outside of the inherent historicality of the literary structure: an absolute *ante rem,* or an equally absolute *post rem,* with respect to the history of the genre itself. By critically exploiting the genre of historical fiction and by highlighting the historical and cultural specificity of the narrative voice in their novels, authors such as Lampedusa, Morante, and Eco implicitly claim that the only viable approach to genre theory is one that self-consciously places itself within the historical dynamics of a literary system that is in a state of constant change and development. By doing so, these authors do not reject all normative and typological definitions of genre, but rather act within these norms, manipulating them and revealing that both the normative and revisionary acts are historically determined and ideologically charged, and that they thus perform culturally significant hermeneutical functions.

Tempering the prescriptive tones of normative and typological definitions, a genre may be considered a provisional and empirical system furnishing a general "principle of order" (Wellek and Warren 226), establishing a set of "directives" that broadly regulate the production and reception of literary texts (Głowiński, "Les Genres" 81, 86; Fowler 80–81) and offering a "program" constructed on very general rules that writers share with their readers (Corti, *An Introduction* 121). Genres, and all the texts that constitute them, are dynamic units that interact, challenge, and transform one another in the course of time. A genre establishes recurring elements that differentiate its constituent texts from those of other genres. However, each text within a genre, by providing its own peculiarities, promotes changes that affect the genre itself, thus revising the elements that define the genre and preventing it from becoming a rigid receptacle, incapable of evolution and transformation. Moreover, each text within a genre does not exist in isolation, nor does it exist exclusively in a one-to-one relationship with its generic cocoon. Each work establishes a dialogue with the other texts that share the generic space. The genre becomes the surcharged stage where a work participates in "a complex network of relations with other works" (Corti, *An Introduction* 115), and, in turn, the genre itself exists in a situation of constant exchange with the other genres in the literary system.[7] The multivoiced relationships among various texts, among different genres, and between texts and their generic models imply a critical attitude by which the generic models themselves are constantly reassessed, evaluated, and often forced to modify their constituent paradigms.[8]

Broadly defined, a novel belongs to a certain genre because it respects a spectrum of regularities that define the stable elements in a paradigm of variations, thus allowing the readers to recognize the genre to which the text belongs. The regularities constitute the genre's foundational core; they are the traits that differentiate one genre from all the others, making it specific and unique by their ability to persist in time, that is, to remain recognizable (if not unchanged) in the long duration of a genre's evolution. The cluster of a genre's regularities coexists with a mobile array of variations that are responsible for the mutability and vitality of the genre in question. This definition of genre is both synchronically and diachronically justified. While the paradigm of regularities allows for an abstraction of the genre from the specific sociohistorical situations in which it was created, the differences illuminate the particular circumstances that presided over its creation. A genre's regularities, or in Tzvetan Todorov's definition, their "discursive properties" ("The Origin of Genres" 162), arise from different textual levels, as they pertain to the structural organization, thematic choices, stylistic forms, and pragmatic functions (the targeted audience and the practical uses) characterizing specific texts. The differences between one genre and another result from the various possibilities of combination among these discursive properties and can be situated at any of those levels of discourse. In its broadest definition, a historical novel is recognized as such on the level of its thematic properties—identifiable in the combinations of invented characters and historical figures with fictional occurrences and events that actually happened in the past.[9] Variations may occur, of course, within the paradigm of the genre's regularities; however, these variations do not affect the regularities themselves, but only the way these regularities are presented. In the case of historical fiction, for example, historical characters and settings may be depicted with a varying degree of historical accuracy: Manzoni's portrayal of seventeenth-century Milan or of Cardinal Federigo Borromeo, for example, are more historically accurate than are Alexandre Dumas's portrayals of Richelieu, Mazarin, and the siege of La Rochelle.[10]

The history of a genre is not exclusively related to its writers' assimilation and revision of previous models; it also depends upon the public's response to specific literary works. Authors of historical fiction, and of any other literary genre, share with the reading community a certain "generic consciousness."[11] In other words, by providing a model of writing for an author, a genre creates a "set of expectations" for the readers, who know what to expect from a text when they identify the genre to which it belongs (Jauss 81).[12] The genre's regularities work as a set of signals that direct the reading process and condition the meaning and the contextual use of certain themes, as well as the structure these themes assume (Corti, *An Introduction* 117). These signals can be undermined and estranged in order to encourage the reader to critically observe, rather than passively accept, a genre's familiar codes. By transgressing standard generic norms, narrative and formal strategies of estrangement alter a genre's boundaries, thus highlighting the mutability and conventionality of what was uncritically perceived as a natural and irrefutable generic law. In the case of critical historical fiction, estranging techniques may force readers to investigate the implications of combining the forms of fiction with those of history and to rethink their aesthetic as well as epistemological power. Telling, if somewhat extreme, examples are Roberto Pazzi's *La principessa e il drago* (*The Princess and the Dragon,* 1986) and *La malattia del tempo* (*Adrift in Time,* 1987), in which the traditional paradigms of historical fiction are "made strange" by being combined with those of legendary tales and science fiction: historical characters coexist with quasi-mythical heroes, and time as a linear continuum gives way to surprising juxtapositions of different temporal dimensions. Pazzi's historical narratives stretch the genre of historical fiction to its furthest limits, pushing it to the verge of self-destruction and radical transformation.

* * *

The diachronic approach to genre discussed so far has the advantage of stressing the historical dynamics of genres. By situating the literary historian in a specific sociocultural space, the definition of genre has been freed of absolute and prescriptive connotations. A genre's mobility and flexibility, however, do not ultimately prevent all systematizing efforts.[13] These efforts are made with the awareness that all genre systems are provisionary forms and empirical tools that help organize the literary universe while commenting upon the ideological, aesthetic, and cultural circumstances presiding over their structuring act.[14] Genres are literary conventions, "contracts" between writers and their public, their function being to define the proper use of a specific cultural artifact:

> *all* generic categories, even the most time-hallowed and traditional, are ultimately to be understood (or "estranged")

> as mere ad hoc, experimental constructs, devised for a specific textual occasion and abandoned like so much scaffolding when the analysis has done its work. . . . Such classifications in fact prove rewarding only as long as they are felt to be relatively arbitrary critical acts, and lose their vitality when . . . they come to be thought of as "natural" forms. (Jameson, *The Political Unconscious* 145)

Traditionally, the diachronic approaches to genres have been associated with "organic" and "evolutionary" theories. According to the organic theory, a genre, like a living organism, evolves in a steady, regular, and progressive manner through a series of vital stages.[15] Genres are spontaneously "born" and naturally "die": the biological law determining this process does not consider the cultural and historical factors that trigger the emergence and disappearance of a specific genre. This organic model generated the evolutionary one (Wellek 37–53), in which the history of a genre is forced to fit into the teleological scheme of a genre's rise, maturity or culmination, and decadence. The evolutionary system revises the concept of the beginning and the end of a genre (its "birth" and "death" in the organic model) into that of an undivided progression, a growing metamorphosis from an antecedent genre to a following one. As a result, however, the evolutionary theory must abandon the organic model's ability to precisely pinpoint the emergence and, eventually, the disappearance of a generic system. To concentrate on the problem of historical fiction, how does the evolutionary approach justify the appearance of historical fiction as a genre specifically differentiated from others? While it can argue for the unbroken development from the antiquarian novel and other fictional adaptations of historical materials to the historical novel proper, the evolutionary model alone does not explain why this phenomenon occurred in such massive proportions at the beginning of the nineteenth century.[16] Similarly, the biological inevitability of the organic model does not account for the unique and unprecedented events that fostered the critical debate over historical fiction and presided over the publication of so many historical novels in a relatively brief period of time in Italy; nor does it explain the causes that triggered the revisionary trends of current historical fiction.

While both the organic and evolutionary models are acts of critical bad faith, since they squeeze the history of genres into pseudobiological schemes presented as natural processes rather than as artificial constructs and intellectual systematizations, they are still methodologically valuable because they view genres as dynamic systems in a continual state of transformation.[17] In accepting the notion of the diachronic development of genres, the organic and evolutionary models attest to their historical determination, as they define genres within a specific chronological frame of reference. Without falling prey to the biological fallacy of the organic and evolutionary models, the question of the beginning and end of a specific literary genre may be approached by subscribing to a revolutionary theory of genre. The revolutionary model is based on the sudden subversions of preexisting forms rather than on the progressive growth and harmonious changes characterizing the organic and evolutionary systems.

In Michel Foucault's notion of the epistemic change, the liaison to the past is established in antagonistic and oppositional terms. Foucault argues for a philosophy of discontinuity rather than of continuous evolution, one marked by abrupt changes in the configuration and systematization of knowledge. Foucault warns, however, that he has overstressed his concept of historical breaks in order to counter the traditional interpretation of evolutionary progress. For Foucault discontinuity refers to a change from one historical period to another, so that "things are no longer perceived, described, expressed, characterized, classified, and known in the same way" (*The Order of Things* 217). But there is no break so radical and sudden as to appear *ex nihilo.* One could argue that in an evolutionary epistemological substratum there emerge major changes that imply a redefinition of the prior *episteme,* a whole reconfiguration of its constituting elements. In this perspective, the evolutionary and revolutionary models are not mutually exclusive, and become, in practice, not so opposed as they would seem. Taken together, they define a Hegelian dialectics of continuity and discontinuity between the old and the new, an interplay of reversals and preservations that comprehensively defines the concept of genre. The diachronic adventure of a generic ensemble is based neither on continuity nor on discontinuity, but rather on a combination of both. This combination requires a critical reassessment of the forms of the past as a continuation, modification, and rejection of previously established models. Works must be observed in relation to two "simultaneous and yet contrary movements, one tending to the adoption of norms, the other to their rejection" (Głowiński, "Theoretical Foundations" 244). The evolutionary model alone, in other words, illuminates only one side of the issue: while it justifies the development from, say, the antiquarian novel to the historical novel, it does not account for the new elements and the specific changes that triggered such transformation.

Before addressing these transformations, it is important to observe that the rejection of the organic and evolutionary notions of genre also implies a critique of their exclusively progressive chronological orientations. As early as 1919, T. S. Eliot suggested that in the realm of art, evolution follows a course different from the one it follows in the domain of nature. Eliot's synchronic theory modifies and complicates the rudimentary linearity of the diachronic schemes. A literary work exists not only in a sequential framework, as a link in a chain, but also in direct connection with other works belonging to the remote as well as the immediate past. Furthermore, not only do significant existing works influence the production of new ones, but new works that are aesthetically innovative influence the old ones by questioning the genre, altering the canon, and thus producing a change in our understanding of the bulk of literature that preceded them. As we read in "Tradition and the Individual Talent":

> what happens when a new work of art is created is something that happens simultaneously to all the works of art which preceded it. The existing monuments form an ideal order among themselves, which is modified by the introduction of the new (the really new) work of art among them. The existing order is complete before the new work arrives; for order to persist after the supervention of novelty, the *whole* existing order must be, if ever so slightly, altered; and so the relations, proportions, values of each work of art toward the whole are readjusted; and this is conformity between the old and the new. (38–39)

According to Todorov's rereading of Eliot, every literary work participates in a double movement: from the particular work to genre and from genre to the particular work. In the aesthetic sphere, therefore, every work modifies "the sum of possible works, each new example alters the species" (Todorov, *The Fantastic* 6). This implies a consideration of the dynamics of genre that works both progressively and retroactively, and that is both diachronic and synchronic.

A combination of the two models, the evolutionary and the revolutionary, allows us to pinpoint the inception and demise of a specific genre as tied and yet opposed to those that preceded and eventually followed it. Eliot's and Todorov's dynamic models provide a panoramic view of a generic ensemble in which not only the single work conforms to the generic system, but the very system finds itself altered according to the innovations provided by the new work. Thus expanded, the notion of genre does not yet fully explain the reasons behind such inception and demise. Specifically, why is it commonly accepted knowledge that Italian historical fiction "starts" with Manzoni's *I promessi sposi?* Clearly, a merely formalistic approach to the concept of genre cannot fully answer this question. Lukács's extraliterary explanation is still useful, as it sheds light on the sociohistorical occurrences that triggered a new epistemological and discursive approach to historical reality. Contributing to the emergence of historical fiction were the political events of the Italian Risorgimento,[18] the theoretical debates over the romantic current in literature, the popular success of Scott's novels in Italy,[19] and the influence of the historical studies by Sismondi, Thierry, Barante, Michelet, Guizot, Cuoco, Amari, Balbo, and Capponi. The advent of what Harold Bloom would call a "model" of Manzoni's caliber, and the intraliterary relations that he created with his successors, be they simple imitations or revisionist reappropriations, must be equally taken into account (Bloom 5–14). Factors relevant to textual production and reception are also important: in spite of Manzoni's *topos modestiae* regarding his "venticinque lettori" ("couple of dozen readers"), the success of *I promessi sposi* had an enormous impact on the genre's critical approval and its official recognition.

The generic model for historical fiction extrapolated from a body of texts sharing certain similarities, and canonized by Manzoni's influential novel, is not a stable and unchanging entity.[20] The model itself is involved in a dialogic exchange with works that strive to both exploit and revise the thematic and formal demands that the model imposes upon them. If a masterpiece such as *I promessi sposi* gave a fundamental contribution to defining the norm of historical fiction, the norm changed along with the vicissitudes of the masterpiece's reception and the history of its interpretation. In the case of historical fiction, this change started as early as the essay *Del romanzo storico,* Manzoni's surprising attempt to dismantle the genre that only a few years before he had helped to canonize. The shifts and changes within the codes of historical fiction (or any other genre) testify to a change toward the ideological implications and aesthetic requirements of the genre itself. Choosing to write within a genre is never a neutral and value-free choice. Writing historical fiction, in particular, implies applying specific interpretative codes to past reality, and these codes, which affect both the thematic and the formal levels of a text, are inevitably ideologically charged. Imposing specific criteria of selection and organization of the historical world, they establish their own rules on what can be selected from the realm of the real and what can be drawn instead from that of the merely verisimilar. If we see a genre as a "symptom" of a particular culture that creates, distributes, and utilizes it (Corti, *An Introduction* 117), we must also recognize that the changes that affect the genre mirror changes that affect a wider cultural and social body.

In this perspective, genres, as well as their definitions, are not exclusively literary phenomena but also changing entities related and shaped by sociohistorical reality, entities that have a telling story to narrate, that of the history of mentality. According to Horst Steinmetz:

> Genres constitute a system of organization, not only within literature, but also outside it. Every reality becomes lucid, is ordered, by means of classifications into, among other things, genres. Every society, therefore, has at its disposal a categorial system of genres with which reality can be controlled, and without such a scheme would remain chaos. Genres are tools with the aid of which orientation becomes possible; they are a means through which everyday life and non-everyday life can be experienced as meaningful and ordered. (252)

Genre systems, like social systems, are historical phenomena; they are "sediments of consensus" that represent general models of thought and experience. Rooted in a specific historical context, they mirror the ways in which different communities explain and structure the world in which they live.[21] A society enjoys a relatively stable structure as long as the validity of this structure is not questioned. The network of genre organization that orders all the phenomena of reality covers also the area of literature, shaping it in accordance with the interpretation of the world and reality that is accepted in a specific sociohistorical moment (Steinmetz 252). Genres are not only pragmatic organizational systems but demonstrations of the ways in which literature processes and interprets historical reality.[22] Literary genres, then, order the system of literature in accordance with the contemporary interpretations of the world outside of literature. From this assumption Steinmetz deduces that periods of strict adherence to genre conventions are characterized by stable social conditions and, conversely, that modifications in genre conventions show that current interpretations of the world lose authority as "new . . . world-views are developing" (253). Steinmetz's view implies a chronological simultaneity between sociopolitical events, epistemological changes, and literary transformations. This view may not always be accurate, as there may be significant gaps between the social base and the literary superstructure. Literary genres in particular outlast the specific sociocultural situations that contributed to their appearance, and may anachronistically survive in a society that no longer presents the features that fostered their emergence (Krauss 8–9), while single texts may mirror or even prophetically anticipate certain changes in the social fabric.

If genres work as semantic, thematic, and ideological units, then the highest "norm-criterion for the definition and function of a genre is, consequently, its conformity to the system" (Steinmetz 254). In Steinmetz's prescriptive view, the law of genre is one of absolute conformity to the literary system. A problem arises, however, when two systems, such as the literary and the historiographic, are combined. To which of the two systems must the historical novel conform? If the two systems are believed to pose different, often contradictory demands, the historical novel appears as a logical impossibility or a fertile ground for epistemological confrontation. In either case, the notion of genre as normative, exclusive, and prescriptive law must be reconsidered and revised or, as suggested above, made more malleable.

Jacques Derrida argues that whenever the notion of genre is at issue, whether it is a matter of *physis* (gender) or of *technè* (as in literary genre), a norm designating a typology and an interdiction is immediately established. As soon as a genre announces itself, Derrida explains, "one must not risk impurity, anomaly, or monstrosity":

> If a genre is what it is, or if it is supposed to be what it is destined to be by virtue of its *telos,* then "genres are not to be mixed"; one should not mix genres, one owes it to oneself not to get mixed up in mixing genres. Or, more rigorously, genres should not intermix. And if it should happen that they do intermix, by accident or through transgression, by mistake or through a lapse, then this should confirm, since, after all, we are speaking of "mixing," the essential purity of their identity. (204)

However, a logical contradiction emerges from within the limits imposed by the two genres of genre, *physis* and *technè.* In its hybrid ontology, neither natural nor artificial, the notion of genre annihilates and deconstructs the very law upon which it thrives. If the law of genre is that genres must not be mixed, the "law of the law of genre," Derrida argues, implies a counter law of impurity and a principle of contamination that confounds the sense and the order, the noncontradictory logic, of the notion of genre. Derrida calls for a deeper examination of the relationship of nature to history and aesthetics, especially where genre is concerned. Contrary to Steinmetz's views, Derrida claims that there is no room for the concept of genre in a logic that is decisive, critical, and oppositional.

In Derrida's wake, one could dispose of the notion of genre altogether, starting from the assumption that the regulative ordering principle of genre bears within its semantic core the revelation of its hybrid, unclassifiable nature. A part of both *physis* and *technè,* it defies the logic of exclusion and noncontradiction that it apparently supports. If instead we accept the artificial, culturally determined notion of genre, then genre can become a provisionary ordering system, the significance of which resides not in a prescriptive, absolute value but in the practical advantages of a wholly pragmatic use. In this way, the notion of genre loses the principle of totality, of transcendent essence, and becomes context-sensitive. The contemporary rejection of strictly normative standards as well as the revisionary stance toward traditional generic forms do not necessarily presuppose the rejection of genre theory, but a more ambivalent, typically postmodern attitude that implies, at the same time, the application and the subversion of such rules. Rules and their transgressions lead a symbiotic existence. Transgression requires a law to exist, and we are reminded of the existence of the law only through its transgressions (Todorov, "The Origin of Genres" 160). When a transgression is successful, it produces its own revisionary rules, which replace the rules that preceded them. The transgression loses its subversive edge and is eventually reabsorbed into the system's structures, structures that become nevertheless altered in order to host their transgressive guests. Thus, by mutual alterations, a new formal generic type is established. The new generic type activates criticism, and the genre's innovation is sanctioned and institutionalized. A new transgression follows. The history of a genre results from the complex interplay of evolutionary and revolutionary forces, of the compulsion to transgress and the urge to institutionalize that influence the production, theoretical systematization, and readers' receptions of specific literary works.

* * *

Historical fiction constitutes a paradigmatic example of the dynamics of genre. How do critical historical novels relate to Manzoni's two influential models, the canonic and exemplary one of *I promessi sposi* and the prescriptive and censoring one of *Del romanzo storico?* The mutually exclusive nature of the models complicates all unidirectional approaches to the history of genres. Critical historical novels that account for both models are bound to a subtler stance, one that establishes a relationship of continuity as well as a critical revision of both of Manzoni's contrasting paradigms. By accepting the canon, historical novelists implicitly continue the tradition of *I promessi sposi* and critically confront the closing arguments of Manzoni's essay. In *Del romanzo storico,* Manzoni established an exclusive and normative aesthetics that rejected the combination of the two contradictory systems of fiction and history. Contrary to Manzoni, the three authors included in this study embrace the hybrid nature of historical fiction and explore the epistemological problems inherent in the clash between the two cognitive and ideological systems. They also revise Manzoni's literary model by abandoning the teleologically "given" historical framework of *I promessi sposi* and revealing that the narrative frames and structuring devices by which reality is represented and organized are not universal or natural forms but culturally and historically determined strategies that must be evaluated on the basis of their practical and contingent values. However, Lampedusa, Morante, and Eco also follow Manzoni's example, as their historical novels imply a revisionist attitude with respect to the historical records. Invention, therefore, becomes a way to fill in the gaps in the archives and tell the stories of those who did not have a voice in the historical world. In a curious sleight of hand, the realms of invention, creation, and poetry do not highlight art's universality, as Manzoni would have claimed; rather, they stress art's foundations in the historical world and its ties to the sociopolitical reality. Critical historical novels, therefore, relativize all universalist pretensions and emphasize their writers' engagement in "the ethics as well as the historically grounded art of communication" (Bermann 53).

More eloquently than any other genre, then, critical historical fiction such as Lampedusa's, Morante's, and Eco's suggests that genres are ideological units molded by culture and history, and that present ideologies frame and shape the literary representation of the historical past. These historical novels show the ways in which genre works in a dialectics of continuity and discontinuity, and of acceptance and subversion, of the ideological structures that characterize a specific cultural moment. By transcending generic boundaries, this historical fiction relativizes and juxtaposes the categorial demands that are usually applied to historical and fictional systems. It inserts into a dialogical, dynamic confrontation the cognitive and creative tools that history and fiction employ in the act of interpreting and encoding reality and the past.

In spite of its ultimate proscription of the historical novel, Manzoni's *Del romanzo storico* offers a pioneering argument in the debate over historical fiction. Manzoni's discussion concerning the historian's role in the narrative organization of historical facts, and by inference the displacement of the notion of historical truth from an absolute to a relative epistemological base, anticipates current theoretical discussions on the methods of fictional and historical representations. Manzoni's creative historiography explores the cognitive and ideological principles that mediate our comprehension of reality and preside over the formal reconfiguration of the past. It is in the field of historiography that Manzoni anticipates twentieth-century debates regarding historical knowledge and the problems of representation, referentiality, and truth. Manzoni, however, does not give up the universal framework defining poetic language—the realm of the verisimilar—which for him demarcates a nonhistorical plane allowing for the intuitive apprehension of ideal universal truths. The insurmountable discrepancy between his idealistic aesthetic philosophy and his empirical historiographic approach forces him to dismiss historical fiction as an impossible marriage, a doomed contradiction in terms.

Giuseppe Tomasi di Lampedusa's *Il Gattopardo* revises traditional criteria of historical narrative by juxtaposing a historical reconstruction based on the causal connection of factual events with one that sees facts as embedded in subterranean patterns of cyclical recurrence and repetition. The textual reconfiguration upon which *Il Gattopardo* depends questions and expands the structuring principles that organize our understanding of the past. While depending on the laws of necessity, causality, and probability, the formal structure of *Il Gattopardo* also counteracts the strict logical order, promoting the formal encoding provided by memory and desire as a legitimate alternative method of making sense of reality and the past. By reshaping reality into patterns of recurrence rather than into patterns of progression, metaphorical and analogical strategies become significant rivals to logic in the process of historical representation. These processes also question the reactionary or at least conservative worldview with which they are traditionally associated and reveal their force in combining historical becoming with the preservation of the cultural and historical heritage of both individuals and communities.

In Elsa Morante's *La Storia,* the Manzonian tenet of narrating the story of simple *gente meccaniche* becomes the starting point for writing histories that are significantly different from those that official records narrate. The female narrator of *La Storia* not only confronts the issue of subjectivity in the historian's reconstruction of the past, she also develops a feminine voice that challenges a number of traditionally accepted historiographic demands. Neither impersonal nor omniscient, the narrator's feminine voice emphasizes her subjective and emotional participation in the events she narrates. Polyphonic and diverse, *La Storia*'s narrator takes up different personas and speaks with multiple voices, thus disrupting the patriarchal notion of the unitary subject and expressing experiential areas that orthodox historiography had confined to oblivion.

Umberto Eco's *Il nome della rosa* tests the intelligibility and the epistemological validity of historical reconstructions of the past. In Linda Hutcheon's sense, *Il nome della rosa* is a type of historiographic metafiction, a self-reflexive practice that examines the value and the limits of its own narrative strategies (105–23). Narrative in general and the apocalyptic narrative model in particular are accepted as transhistorical modes of giving order and meaning to reality and the past. However, their validity as well as absolute values are questioned in the novel, as they finally emerge not as foundational certainties but as strategies, methodological tools that can be used, exploited, and eventually discarded. Finally, the founding norms of historical discourse—identity and causality—are evaluated within and against the citational framework and the polyphonic structures and linguistic games created by *Il nome della rosa*'s carnivalesque discourse.

The responses to Manzoni's *Del romanzo storico* provided by Lampedusa, Morante, and Eco function as powerful rebuttals to the assessment that we live in the age of the death of the author and the end of ideology.[23] Their historical novels show a renewed commitment to writers' ideological responsibilities toward their creative materials. In particular, by conceiving a constructive ideology and aesthetics that has notable current import, their novels demonstrate how historical fiction can involve more than a mere decorative use of the past or a nostalgic withdrawal from present commitments and more pressing preoccupations. Critical historical fiction defines the past in terms of the unrealized potential it entails by narrating the stories that official documents have neglected, by subjecting the extant cognitive modes of apprehension of the past to criticism and revision while at the same time elaborating new ones, and finally by proposing narrative voices that strive to define the values of literature and the self in their potential to rewrite the past in order to serve the present.

This book does not approach the critical historical novel simply as a study in literary history alone, nor as the result of the vicissitudes of a particular genre, historical fiction. Rather, it focuses on the analysis of the ideological frames and conceptual categories with which we necessarily approach the literary object. By emphasizing the complex dialogue with the Manzonian archetype and proscription, critical historical fiction offers an emblematic instance of the cultural and historical dialectics of all literary genres. These novels highlight what Fredric Jameson defines as the "mediative function" of the notion of genre: "the coordination of immanent formal analysis of the individual text with the twin diachronic perspective of the history of forms and the evolution of social life" (*The Political Unconscious* 105). Finally, critical historical novels show that all genres (including historical fiction) are implicated in the literary history and formal production that these genres were supposed to categorize neutrally and objectively (*The Political Unconscious* 107). Critical historical narratives engage in a self-conscious discussion of their ideological implications and lay bare the provisionary nature of their forms, thus becoming historically reflexive analyses not only of a specific genre, but of the mechanisms of genre definition and formal categorization in general.[24]

Chapter One

Alessandro Manzoni's *J'accuse*

Literary Debates, the Essay *Del romanzo storico,* and a Theory of Creative Historiography

Romanzieri, fa d'uopo finalmente disingannarsi: per questa via non v'è speranza di lode: se volete vivere, bisogna inventare.

Paride Zaiotti
"De' romanzi storici"
See appendix 1

In spite of Francesco De Sanctis's influential dismissal (349–50), Manzoni's essay *Del romanzo storico* is as much a touchstone for the theory of historical fiction as his novel *I promessi sposi* is for its practice. Although the essay eventually rejects historical fiction as a logical impossibility and a self-destructive contradiction in terms, it nevertheless raises questions about the theory of historical representation that are of pressing interest today. Manzoni's essay explores, albeit in an often problematic manner, the ways in which historical and fictional realities are given narrative form. *Del romanzo storico* meditates on the hermeneutical value of these reconstructions and discusses the epistemological significance of both fictional and factual truths. Thus, Manzoni's essay inaugurates modern critical discussion on the status of fictional and historical knowledge.

Manzoni's new form of creative historiography explores the cognitive grids, ideological filters, and linguistic systems that mediate our perception of reality and direct our understanding of the historical past. As a result, Manzoni anticipates, without embracing, the antidogmatic and pluralizing epistemologies of modern philosophical thought. *Del romanzo storico* inaugurates a debate on the ideological value of literature and the sociopolitical implications of writing within the genre of historical fiction. The essay demonstrates how historical fiction problematizes our relationship with the historical referent and yet refuses to abolish it altogether, thus asserting art's connections to the historical and the political.

The Background of Manzoni's Essay *Del romanzo storico*

Theoretical discussion of fiction—and particularly of the historical novel—was a matter of topical interest in 1827, when Manzoni published the first edition of *I promessi sposi.* The Italian intelligentsia had been divided between *Classicisti* and *Romantici* since 1816,[1] and the major literary magazines were hosting an increasingly heated debate on the virtues and faults of the novel. In spite of pressure from both sides of the dispute, Manzoni refused to engage in the literary polemics. Although he had been planning *Del romanzo storico* since 1828, he did not publish it until 1850.[2] Perhaps because of this delay, Manzoni critics have generally interpreted *Del romanzo storico* as the creation of a "solitary thinker" (Derla 112) or, at best, have considered it a response to Goethe's and Lamartine's opposing interpretations of *I promessi sposi.*[3] While Goethe criticized the historical redundancies of the third part of the novel,[4] Lamartine regarded this section as the best in the book and encouraged Manzoni to abandon the historical novel in order to make of history itself "un genre neuf."[5] The importance of these two authoritative observations can hardly be dismissed, but Manzoni's essay responded to more immediate intellectual exchanges. By 1827, in fact, the inflamed *querelle* between Classicists and Romantics had transformed the initial dichotomies into a more diversified agenda that included the *questione del romanzo* among the most discussed topics. Fiction and the status of Italian literature were among the most frequently addressed subjects in the major literary magazines of the time. Milan in particular became the crucible of an intense cultural and ideological controversy. There, the classic foundation of Italy's aesthetic tradition came to terms with the new literary movements arriving from beyond the Alps. The ideology of the Enlightenment and the democratic enthusiasm that followed the creation of the Cisalpine Republic (1797–1802) had soon to be reexamined in terms of the political disillusionment that subjected Italy to Napoleon's despotism and Austria's reactionary rule. The debate on the novel as a viable literary form was not merely a matter of rhetorical norms and aesthetic merits, but was colored with ideological and political connotations.

The classical rhetorical norm ("genres cannot be mixed") and the dogmatic moralistic clichés that the conservative literary clique exploited to dismiss the historical novel were soon developed, by Classicists and Romantics alike, into a dispute on the epistemological significance of a genre that mixes the opposite categories of history and fiction, truth and the verisimilar, the real and the ideal, and the material and the spiritual. The purely rhetorical quandary revealed its far-reaching implications, as mixing (or not mixing) genres implied, in the final analysis, accepting or rejecting the combination (or contamination) of aesthetics with ideology and of fiction with politics. The essay *Del romanzo storico* shows its truly innovative character in the context of the response it provides to these issues, as it concludes the debate that engaged the Italian intellectual world between 1816 and 1850, the years in which the historical novel reached the peak of its popularity in Europe.

* * *

Pietro Borsieri's *Avventure letterarie di un giorno, o consigli di un galantuomo a vari scrittori* (*One Day's Literary Adventures, or a Gentleman's Advice to Various Writers,* 1816), one of the earlier manifestoes of the romantic era, staged a pioneering discussion on fiction between an anonymous *Classicista,* an unidentified *buon compagnone,* and three intellectuals of the romantic journal *Il Conciliatore:* Silvio Pellico, Carlo Gherardini, and Borsieri himself. This discussion reveals that the historical argument concerning the cultural, epistemological, and aesthetic functions of the novel was originally oriented through ethical channels, guiding the Classicists' charges against the novel and the Romantics' rebuttals against these accusations. In *Avventure,* the Classicist *Oratore* argues that novels belong to periods of moral decadence and social confusion. Summoning the authority of the classical tenet of *utile dulci,* he dogmatically embraces an antirealistic moralism and contends that novels provide neither instruction nor amusement, but only a reproachable portrait of human passions.[6] With an unexpected philosophical shift, he concludes his tirade by approaching history from a realistic perspective, arguing that, unlike fiction, historical texts are useful because they are entirely founded upon truth (357).

The Romantics' claims do not swerve from the moral guidelines imposed by their Classicist opponents, as they agree that novels thrive in periods of moral crisis and social corruption. Their antidotes, however, differ from those of the Classicists. Gherardini empirically claims that since "the good old innocence" is lost forever, corruption must be fought with its own weapons; and the portrayal of current customs must be used to introduce useful truths into "indolent souls" (359). Pellico, instead, approaches the problem from an idealistic point of view and maintains that the novel has ethical value because it is a corrective to the truth of the historical records. History is indeed morally blind:

> mi sovviene . . . che l'immortale Bacone . . . afferma che la Storia vera narrando le riuscite delle cose e degli eventi quali avvennero in fatto e senza riguardo alcuno alla virtù od alla scelleratezza di chi operava, ha bisogno di essere corretta colle invenzioni della finta; e ch'essa accortamente può presentare ai lettori felici od avversi rivolgimenti di cose, secondo l'intrinseco valore delle azioni, e i dettati d'una giustizia vendicatrice. (361; see appendix 2)

Pellico justifies the shift from "objective" reality to fictional representation only in terms of content, through a moral imperative. Fiction, then, does not paint reality "as it is," but as "it should be," ideally correcting history's shortcomings. The aesthetic evaluation of the novel is completely subsumed under the category of its moral justification. The mixture of *vero* and *verosimile*[7] characterizing the novel is evaluated in purely rhetorical and/or moral terms. While the Classicists invoke the laws of ancient rhetoric to censure the "amphibious genre," the Romantics accept the Classicists' terms of the debate and fail to plot an original defense. Like the Classicists, they rely on past authorities and insist that Tasso himself had taught poets to "weave ornaments" upon historical truth (358). Pellico's passing reference to the "high truths" of philosophy (360) that the novel translates into an instructive and enjoyable form constitutes the germ of a discussion where epistemology slowly incorporates ethics in the attempt to assess the value of the different types of "truths" that history, fiction, and historical fiction provide.

Borsieri's dialogue set the tone for the ensuing debate on the historical novel, as empirical and idealistic viewpoints were manipulated, by Classicists and Romantics alike, to either condemn or acquit the new genre. While the dialogue denounces the Classicists' blind dogmatism and narrow moralism, it also, involuntarily, reveals the limits of the Romantics' position. At the dawn of the age of the historical novel, the Romantics had not yet built a consistent theory of fiction. While they rejected the Classicists' abstract generic norms in the name of a literature whose sole duty is to portray current customs, they had not yet provided a reasoned argument regarding the cognitive and aesthetic value of fiction independent of moral qualifications.

* * *

Classicist Paride Zaiotti was one of the leading literary critics in the Milan of the Restoration period. A loyal agent of the Austrian government, in 1824 he was appointed Consigliere del Tribunale Criminale di Milano (Counsel to the Criminal Court of Milan) and later became one of the most influential participants in the court proceedings against the members of Giuseppe Mazzini's revolutionary patriotic organization, the Giovine Italia (Romagnoli 18–19). Portraying himself as a champion of both good taste and morality, Zaiotti directed his civilizing crusade against falling literary standards, which he viewed as a direct consequence of a wider societal decay. His prescriptive moralism was especially aimed at fiction in order to discourage Italian novelists from emulating foreign romantic models, of which Scott's were the chief example. While making unfavorable generalizations about the current state of fiction, Zaiotti endorsed a form of didactic, idealistic criticism acclaiming the beauty of "pure truth." His conservative crusade against philistinism concealed an ambition to regulate literary production and consumption. With Zaiotti, criticism became a prescriptive, monitoring act that defended the value of high art against popular forms of literary entertainment like the novel.

Zaiotti published two significant essays on fiction in the *Biblioteca italiana.* The first appeared in 1827 and was entitled

"Del romanzo in generale, ed anche dei *Promessi sposi,* romanzo di Alessandro Manzoni" ("On the Novel in General, and also on *The Betrothed,* a Novel by Alessandro Manzoni"). The second was published three years later under the title "De' romanzi storici" ("On Historical Novels").[8] Examined together, Zaiotti's two essays reveal a significant ideological shift in his discussion of fiction and a hasty defensive retreat by the end of the three crucial years during which the historical novel achieved climactic success in Italy. Unlike other, extemporaneous reviews on newly published works, these essays demonstrate Zaiotti's effort at methodological rigor, his penchant for philosophical analysis, and his aim to provide synthetic definitions and organized systematizations through a sweeping, bird's-eye view of the whole range of literary history. The essays also show his normative compulsion and his unyielding reliance upon traditional rhetorical categories and aesthetic models, as well as his tentative efforts to account for the new genre of the novel. Most of all, the articles reveal that Zaiotti's prescriptive and systematizing drive did not ultimately reconcile his conflicting views regarding the status of fiction vis-à-vis that of history. Fiction, and the historical novel in particular, raise a set of closely related problems for him. These problems involve rhetoric and literary history, as Zaiotti strives to reckon with the newly born historical novel while still subscribing to a fixed generic theory that does not accept innovation and shuns the mixture of genres. They also include epistemology and ethics, as he attempts to illustrate the type of knowledge that fiction provides and assess the moral value of such knowledge.

Zaiotti's 1827 study opens and closes with a praise of truth. In the essay's opening paragraphs, he argues that it is truth, and not invention, that provides "the intellect's supreme gift" and "the soul's prime food" ("Del romanzo" 322). Bombastically proclaiming humanity's longing for truth, Zaiotti espouses the idealistic notion of a universal truth that lies beyond human reach and only fleetingly manifests itself in the phenomenal world. Elsewhere in the same essay, however, he refers to empirical truth as the goal of humanity's intellectual pursuits. History, which Zaiotti classically sees as the objective and transparent account of the deeds of the great, is the realm of such truth. The essay's final words emphasize that the truth of history is both epistemologically and morally superior to the mere verisimilar offered by fiction:

> Ci valgano i romanzi a tenerci l'animo gentile, e a staccarne qualche volta dalla noja dolorosa della vita reale, ma non ci sfugga mai dagli occhi, che siamo nati alla ricerca e al conoscimento del vero. Bella è la corona che il romanziere può aspettarsi in Italia, ma quella dello storico sarà sempre più gloriosa, e diremo anche più eterna. Felice intanto Alessandro Manzoni che ha oramai raccolto la prima, e solo che il voglia può raccor la seconda. ("Del romanzo" 372; see appendix 3)

Given these premises, and these conclusions, fiction should be relegated to an inferior position among the liberal arts, but the bulk of the essay demonstrates significant shifts and a fundamental contradiction on this issue. Because of the novel's growing popularity, Zaiotti cannot utterly dismiss the *problem* of fiction and must address the predicament of fiction's generic placement. He resorts to anthropological, psychological, and philosophical arguments to answer the questions posed by the existence of fiction.

Zaiotti's first approach is to equate the novel with fiction in general: "Romanzo o novella . . . è quel racconto favoloso, in cui gli avvenimenti siano esposti con quella larghezza che lasci campo a rappresentare i caratteri e i costumi, e ad esprimere il movimento delle passioni" ("A novel or a *novella* is . . . that imaginary tale in which events are narrated with a breadth that allows the representation of characters and customs, and the expression of the movement of passions") ("Del romanzo" 362). Zaiotti thus circumvents the problem of having to account for a generic form that, in the classical theory of genres to which he subscribes, is a non-genre and, in the case of the hybrid forms of historical fiction, is a "monstrosity." Zaiotti's discussion implies an underlying definition of fiction as a "mode" present in innumerable genres, from Boccaccio's *novelle* to chivalric romances and gothic tales. This psychological approach to fiction allows him to account for the novel without being forced to renounce his normative theory of genres.

Zaiotti identifies fiction's origins in humanity's need to narrate, invent stories, and create tales. Fiction, in other words, emerges from the primary desire to fantasize, dream, and embellish the real through imaginative flights. The term *romanzo,* then, must be extended to all those works that "presentano un mondo diverso dal reale, o il mondo reale medesimo ne offrono attraverso ad un prisma, che tutto lo tramuta di allegri colori" ("present a world that is different from the real one, or offer the real world itself through a prism that transforms it with cheerful colors") ("Del romanzo" 326). This need is present in different forms and varying degrees in every time and in all civilizations. Here, however, Zaiotti specifies that the desire to create fictions belongs to the weaker stages in the development of individuals and societies: youth and old age, the dawn and stagnation of a nation. Maturity and adulthood strive for action and do not demand a sugarcoating of reality. History, therefore, is the highest intellectual expression of a mature culture ("Del romanzo" 328–29).

Zaiotti resorts to another philosophical reason to justify the existence of fiction. Fiction is the necessary evil of a fallen, imperfect world. Since it is part of humanity's flawed nature to be unable to grasp truth in its entirety, we must be content with its partial and fragmentary approximations. Zaiotti's attitude is crudely empirical: we must accept fiction as long as we dwell among "Romulus's scum" rather than in the ideal Republic from which Plato banished all creators of fictions ("Del romanzo" 323).[9] Arguably, if fiction is useless in the ideal world where truth is unmediated, it fulfills a significant function in the real one because, by furnishing copies of the ideal, it allows us to approach the ultimate truth. Fiction acts as a mediator between the real and the ideal, between humanity and truth, thus contributing to the betterment of human nature. By raising fiction into a superior sphere, Zaiotti implies that the knowledge fiction provides is different, in quality and degree, from the knowledge provided by the mere chronicle of factual occurrences. He stops short of openly claiming the superiority of fiction over history, thus bringing to the forefront the essay's unresolved inconsistencies.

In Zaiotti's first essay the fictional system is still in a fluid, contradictory state: when he embraces an idealistic view of fiction, he praises the unique ability of "good" fiction to approximate the ideal. When he acclaims the value of historical truth, fiction seems caught in an insurmountable *impasse:* if novels depict a "better" version of the world, they obviously subscribe to an idealistic system and are no longer as faithful to the real facts of life as history is; if they do "mirror" empirical reality and adopt a realistic tone, they risk focusing on reality's cruder aspects and becoming morally reproachable. History never incurs this danger; the kind of history Zaiotti prefers is, in fact: "quella che merita di essere chiamata con questo gran nome, quella che ricorda fatti memorabili, uomini illustri, avvenimenti che determinarono in qualche modo la sorte de' popoli" ("that which deserves to be called by this great name, which remembers memorable facts, illustrious men, events that in some ways determined the fates of peoples") ("Del romanzo" 370). He advocates a concept of political or military history that was already being dismantled by current historiographical debates in France.[10] Moreover, by concentrating exclusively on memorable historical events, he utterly dismisses the historian's role as interpreter as well as the relationships between past and present that historians, from their vantage point in the present, establish. Behind Zaiotti's simplistic assertion of the facts that "come to the universal cognition of men" ("Del romanzo" 370) there resides an empirical attitude, the idea that there is an unmediated grasp of the deeds and destinies of the great.

In spite of the apparent breadth of his literary analysis ranging from classical authors to contemporary English novelists, Zaiotti ultimately evaluates fiction in strictly moralistic terms. A good novel prevents indolence, provides moral guidance, and, by embellishing a harsh reality, offers consolation and pleasure. A bad novel betrays both empirical and transcendental truths and becomes an offense to the laws of morality, religion, and "healthy politics" ("Del romanzo" 339), fostering excess, lawlessness, and sin. Zaiotti's anthropological definition of the *romanzo* as the literary mode responding to humanity's need to invent and narrate is a strategic maneuver to avoid the problem of its generic placement. However, the broadness and apparent pliability of this definition conceals his aim to classify and label the whole of literature under opposite moral categories. The acceptance of the novel among the literary genres implies careful monitoring, strict regulation, and severe censorship: the establishment, that is, of a controlling and paternalistic authority that regulates what falls "into the hands of the masses" and eliminates what might "damage them":

> Il vero morale non dev'essere perduto di mira un istante, e per questo solo che se ne scorga in un romanzo il difetto, pare a noi che la pubblicazione ne debba esser vietata. Il volgo ha una grande riverenza per tutto ciò che vede stampato, e troppo è facile che si lasci deviare a credere naturale effetto d'una passione quello che n'è quasi la parodia. Anche i giovani non esperti ancora del verace movimento degli affetti, corrono il rischio di modellarsi a quelle idee sregolate, ed entrano nel mondo dannosamente persuasi che irrefrenabile è il corso delle onnipotenti passioni. ("Del romanzo" 342; see appendix 4)

Concentrating on historical fiction proper, he reiterates the Classicists' clichéd notion of the dangerous mixture of truth and invention that mars the pleasures of fiction as well as the usefulness of history. Zaiotti is convinced that a shrewd combination of history and fiction not only gives the novel a historical quality but, conversely, gives history an unacceptable fictional hue. By bluntly associating invention with falsity, he adopts a realistic stance and argues that the imaginary parts of a historical novel do not provide access to the ideal world, as he had previously claimed when discussing the novel in general, but rather hinder the faithful representation of the real world. He stresses the dangers of a type of history that is made untrue by fiction, and aristocratically shuns the cognitive potential and ideological implications of a kind of fiction that shares the referential power of history while addressing characters and events that official history has always ignored:

> tutti i casi o pubblici o privati, quando vennero una volta alla cognizione universale degli uomini, debbono essere sottratti per sempre all'arbitrio della finzione. . . . Ma chiameremo noi storia la miserabile cronaca d'un oscuro villaggio, le dubbiose memorie d'un'antica famiglia, le vecchie leggende che non uscirono mai di mano alla plebe? ("Del romanzo" 370; see appendix 5)

In this essay, Zaiotti is not primarily concerned that historical fiction may betray the idealistic notion of art's autonomy and the universality of its truth. Rather, he is alarmed that it may question the ability of history to faithfully record what really happened in the world, as if by holding a mirror that reflects the events of the past. In other words, Zaiotti fears that the historical novel may dismantle the idea of history's absolute objectivity while bolstering the opinion that the writing of history implies subjective reconstructions, personal selections, and creative reconfigurations of an elusive past. Depriving the truth of history of its absolute value means replacing a normative philosophy with a philosophy of doubt:

> Non è maraviglia che una filosofia, la quale dubita di tutto, e converte gli assiomi in problemi, si sforzi di combattere la verità nella sua più salda trincera insinuando la finzione, ove non avrebbe dovuto mai penetrare. Ella spera forse che dal rendere storico il romanzo si passerà a credere romanzesca la storia, e se tanto le riesce tien sicuro l'infelice trionfo de' suoi sistemi, perchè avrà resi dubbiosi ed incerti i fatti, soli nemici ch'ella vede di non potere coi sofismi distruggere. ("Del romanzo" 358; see appendix 6)

Historical fiction represents a danger for the classical taxonomy and separation of literary genres as well as for the classical philosophy of history, which demands the direct transcription of past events into the pages of the historical record. Zaiotti is aware of the potential epistemological turmoil caused by historical fiction. By combining opposite genres, the historical novel denies a purely idealistic approach to fiction—thus challenging art's absolute autonomy—and also questions the realistic faith that historical experiences may be immediately translated into the written word. Thus, historical fiction is a potential manifestation of a decentered philosophy based on the coexistence of relative, provisional, and even contradictory epistemological systems rather than on the quest for unconditional and conclusive truths.

If, in his 1827 essay, Zaiotti emphasizes the dangers of a type of history that is rendered "untrue" by being combined with fiction, he does not discuss the potential problems of a kind of fiction that shares the referential power of history. Despite his reticence on this subject, Zaiotti's viewpoint emerges through his definition of historical fiction. He distinguishes between historical novels that portray real historical figures as props to the narrative line and what he calls descriptive historical novels, borrowing James Fenimore Cooper's distinction. Zaiotti praises descriptive historical novels, where an accurate "antiquarian" description of places and customs supports a totally imaginary action; he condemns historical novels proper, where the narration of real historical events is combined with the invention of private occurrences. In this first essay, he praises Cooper over all historical novelists. Cooper appeals to Zaiotti's taste in spite of the historical quality of his novels. According to Zaiotti, in fact, Cooper's novels use history as a background, a *scenario*. Thus, Zaiotti praises Cooper's pictorial ability to portray characters and places, but utterly fails to recognize the utility of history as an instrument of change and a catalyst for closely related personal and social transformations. For Zaiotti, novels such as Cooper's do not highlight the connections between the past and the present, and do not consider history as "a process . . . as the concrete precondition of the present" (Lukács, *The Historical Novel* 21). Zaiotti endorses a kind of antiquarianism "for which the past does not have to justify its claim of interest on us," a form of historiography that, by focusing on memorable facts and famous individuals, solves "the problem of the relationship between present and past by the simple gesture of abolishing the present as such" (Jameson, *Ideologies* 152). By limiting the referential power of historical fiction to the "curiosities and oddities of the *milieu*" (Lukács, *The Historical Novel* 19), Zaiotti deprives the genre of any ideological import and of any political interest with respect to the present world, thus relegating it to the uncontroversial realm of mere escapist literature.

But these were not Zaiotti's final words. When he returned to the subject in 1830, his views on historical fiction appeared significantly different. To properly understand the changes in his ideas, we must consider the transformations that affected the cultural landscape between 1820 and 1830, culminating in the three years that separate Zaiotti's essays. The proliferation of novels imitating Scott's models, the translations of Scott's works, the increase in the publications in installments of popular historical novels, and the unprecedented success of novels such as Carlo Varese's *Sibilla Odaleta* (which was quickly republished twelve times) were initially regarded by the intellectual elite as marks of a mere fad (De Castris 8–9). The increasing popularity of the historical novel among the wide reading public only served to confirm the conviction that historical fiction was a subgenre relegated to the margins of the literary establishment—the nineteenth-century Italian counterpart of dime novels or pulp fiction—and therefore constitutionally unable to challenge the official, established literary forms.[11] It was not the popularity of historical fiction that finally attracted the interest of the official culture but the fact that a highly respected and universally acclaimed authority such as Manzoni had decided to measure himself with the new genre. In 1830 the success of *I promessi sposi* had become a fait accompli, and the ideological implications connected to the "boom" of historical fiction now far exceeded the transience of a fad. As Zaiotti wrote, "La sola notizia che l'autore dell'*Adelchi,* il poeta degl'*Inni sacri* scriveva un romanzo, nobilitò la carriera, e trasse alcuni chiari intelletti ad entrarvi" ("Only the news that the author of *Adelchi,* the poet of the *Inni sacri* was writing a novel, ennobled the [novelist's] career, and drew some bright minds to pursue it") ("Del romanzo" 369). Fiction, solely by virtue of its association with Manzoni's prestigious name, took center stage in the literary arena. There, however, the genre had to either perform according to the demands of high literature or defy its laws, modify its course, and finally revise an entire set of aesthetic, ideological, and cultural prejudices against the novel as a genre.[12] The usual charges against historical fiction could no longer be brought against *I promessi sposi.* Manzoni's novel was neither historically inaccurate nor morally reproachable. The abundance of documentary evidence, the careful citations of historical sources, and the accurate depiction of historical details had been a constant preoccupation for Manzoni, who strove to differentiate his novel from more superficial forms of writing about the past. In a letter to his friend Claude Fauriel, Manzoni articulated the difference between his quest for truth and what he called the "spirit of romance":

> je fais ce que je peux pour me pénétrer de l'esprit du temps que j'ai à décrire, pour y vivre. . . . Quant à la marche des événements, et à l'intrigue, je crois que le meilleur moyen de ne pas faire comme les autres est de s'attacher à considérer dans la réalité la manière d'agir des hommes, et de la

> considérer surtout dans ce qu'elle a d'opposé à l'esprit romanesque. (*Opere* 7.1: 271; see appendix 7)[13]

Manzoni's *I promessi sposi* was, in many ways, a direct challenge to the Classicists' accusations that historical fiction promoted falsity and immorality. The novel's success could not be ascribed to what were considered the dangerous elements of the historical novel: history was not falsified, and passion was the novel's most notable missing trait. Manzoni's chaste description of love did not result from mere personal reticence, but rather from his demand for historical accuracy[14] as well as his desire to defend fiction's ethical value.[15]

Zaiotti's 1830 essay is marked by an increasingly defensive tone and a guarded aristocratic attitude toward the ever expanding diffusion of popular fiction. Proclaiming himself a Classicist, he identifies the role of the critic as that of the moral censor and defender of superior art against its degenerations. A critic, Zaiotti argues, must "mettere un argine all'arditezza e all'imperizia della plebe scrivente, e sollevare le buone lettere a un punto che faccia disperato alla mediocrità il poterle raggiugnere" ("hold in check the boldness and unskillfulness of the writing populace and elevate good literature to a point where mediocrity will despair to be able to reach it") ("De' romanzi storici" 146). In a cultural era characterized by a multitude of insipid novels that, more numerous every day, "si va calando come una nuvola d'insetti su' bei campi della nostra letteratura" ("descend like a cloud of insects on the beautiful fields of our literature") ("De' romanzi storici" 152), criticism becomes a policing act that must protect high literature against contamination by lesser fare intended for mass consumption.

The invasion of literary markets by innumerable mediocre historical novels was a cultural phenomenon that puzzled and disturbed Zaiotti. His analysis did not consider the social and cultural circumstances that contributed to such wide diffusion and enthusiastic reception of fiction in general, and of the historical novel in particular. Napoleon's reform of the elementary school system with the consequent increase in the general literacy level, the distribution of affordable texts (often in cheap, pirated versions, as well as their publication in installments in popular magazines), and the unprecedented growth of the publishing business in Milan had a significant impact on the phenomenon.[16] Zaiotti exclusively blamed the "imitative spirit" that encouraged so many ungifted writers to follow in Scott's and Manzoni's footsteps. In Zaiotti's view, Manzoni had indeed a serious responsibility. With *I promessi sposi* he had provided a novel of indubitable aesthetic quality, but had also inspired pedestrian imitators who, because of their number and the inferior quality of their works, had shaken the solidity and damaged the moral strength of the literary citadel. Repeatedly supporting his points with the authority of the soon-to-be-published dismissal of the historical novel by Manzoni, Zaiotti revised his 1827 views on fiction ("De' romanzi storici" 170–73).

In 1830, Zaiotti apocalyptically viewed the novel as the visible sign of a deep cultural crisis, the monstrous offspring of a time when doctrine was confused and laws and principles were uncertain, of an age in which knowledge was replaced by doubt, truth had become controversial, and private individuals were bold enough to challenge the authority of the centuries ("De' romanzi storici" 150, 165). In this essay, he directs his crusade against fiction in two directions. He confirms the prejudices against the novel and defines it as an inferior genre. Then, he proceeds to offer what he considers a much needed definition of "literary truth." Abandoning all realistic positions, he embraces a strictly idealistic view of art. There is a definite semantic shift in his use of the word *truth* from the former to the latter essay. While in 1827 he refers also to factual truth, in 1830 he exclusively calls for an absolute truth that he couples to the concept of ideal beauty. The unity of ethics with aesthetics allows Zaiotti to define the work of art as the concrete, sensible rendition of universal truth. Beauty is then the necessary manifestation of truth; the worthy reflection of divine unity in the ordered and organic totality of the harmonious work of art:

> Il Bello nelle arti vuole unità, perché vuole armonia; e l'impressione che deriva da esso, se ha da produrre tutto l'effetto di cui è capace, non dev'essere interrotta da nessun contrario, ma giugnere inviolata all'anima nostra. ("De' romanzi storici" 178; see appendix 8)

In this illusion of formal unity, he claims, readers may temporarily dwell in the superior reality of an ideal world. Zaiotti's refusal of all realistic systems, and his philosophical adjustment, is a strike against the historical novel, which constitutes an unacceptable combination of the real and the ideal. By connecting fictional and historical systems, the historical novel is neither unitary nor harmonious; it has no aesthetic value (beauty), and therefore it can only be a "vicious genre" deprived of all moral significance (truth). Unlike the historical novel, fiction *per se* is not false, because it concedes its own artifice, and its truth is the general truth of "the human heart." Differentiating itself from factual truth, Zaiotti claims, the moral truth of fiction idealistically defends the autonomy of the work of art, as it represents a superior form of knowledge. He ultimately fails to acknowledge the discrepancy between his ranking the novel as an inferior genre and his contending that the novel is endowed with superior epistemological powers.

To be effective, the novel's moral truth must conform to strict ethical standards, and Zaiotti's are paradigmatic, normative, and in conformity with the authority of religious and secular laws. It is a domesticated, escapist truth meant to spare readers the painful experiences of the real world, make their souls kinder, and (implicitly) encourage their acceptance of the status quo in a more resigned and acquiescent manner ("De' romanzi storici" 190). There is no place for the real in Zaiotti's idea of the novel, which, deprived of concrete ideological appeal and political influence, perfectly fulfills its antihistoric and consolatory mission. Anticipating Manzoni, Zaiotti addresses the issue of the readers' response to historical fiction. Given that the goal of fiction is to allow its readers to dwell in a kinder and purer reality ("De' romanzi storici" 179), historical fiction destroys this aim by forcing its readers to repeatedly descend into the real world, stifling the pleasures of the imagination. Not only are readers immersed in the crude material reality, but their critical spirits are alerted as they are forced to discriminate historical from fictional facts. The critical spirit destroys the pure enjoyment of the novel, which is founded on unity of impression and, one may add, on the passive, acritical diversion offered by a work that creates alternative worlds built upon the moralistic precepts of a central censoring authority.

Zaiotti's idealistic retreat is clearly a defensive reaction to the new historical novel, which in its popular forms was seen as a means of political propaganda, a forum for patriotic statements, and a way to cultivate a new historical consciousness. If, in the previous essay, Zaiotti was mainly concerned that historical fiction challenged the truth of history, now he is alerted to the dangers of the historical novel's referential powers, to the degree of historical verifiability pertaining to its thematic contents. The inner contradiction of the historical novel results from the confusion of two philosophic postures: a realistic one, demanding confirmation of the factual world, and an idealistic one, content with the intuitive perception of a superior reality. The historical novel, a hybrid genre, fails to satisfy either one. The flaw lies less in the genre than in the interpretative systems that the genre is expected to satisfy:

> In questo genere di romanzi ogni sforzo per conservare la verità dee riuscire impotente o avere ad effetto che l'indole del componimento si snaturi del tutto. L'alternativa è tale che nessuno arriverà mai a sfuggirla. Se i personaggi ed i fatti sono storici e restano come li descrive la storia, il racconto romanzesco rimarrà affatto indipendente da essi, ed in vece d'avere un romanzo storico si avrà un romanzo e una storia che cammineranno vicini come due linee parallele, ma senza toccarsi giammai. Che se i casi veri ed i finti verranno scambievolmente ad ajutarsi, e gli uni serviranno a vicenda a formare e sciogliere il nodo degli altri, ecco necessariamente tradita la verità. ("De' romanzi storici" 170; see appendix 9)[17]

Therefore, if the historical novel creates an aesthetic unity, it commits an ethical violation. If, on the other hand, it keeps factual and fictional systems separate, it prevents the reader from having a unified experience of the work, which is a basic demand of the fictional system founded on a unitary experience.

By attempting to educate and regulate literary taste and to set aesthetic standards and establish the "proper" grounds of high literature in the pages of the official literary magazine of the time (the *Biblioteca italiana*), Zaiotti became the spokesperson for governmental supervision in literary matters.[18] The idealistic choice along with the strong assertion of the absolute autonomy of the aesthetic sphere was clearly a defensive move by the literary institution itself, at the time quite influenced and even economically supported by Austria's antiliberal government. Logically, a reactionary government cannot overlook the ideological implications of a type of fiction addressed to a wider public, a fiction that claims direct reference to objective reality and that aspires, like Manzoni's masterpiece, to the realm of high art, as opposed to mere entertainment for mass consumption.

Zaiotti's essays not only foreshadowed many of the points that Manzoni developed in his essay, but also exhibited the uneasy and often confused coexistence of realistic and idealistic interpretations. The emergence of the novel gave enormous impetus to a progressive erosion of the concept of the autonomy and universality of the work of art. The fictional world was evaluated in terms of its dialectical relation with factual reality. The referentiality rather than the self-sufficiency of the novel gave it a potentially tremendous social and ideological force. The kind of diffusion that novels gained ensured their ability to influence the reading public. At the same time, a strong idealistic background and a fetishized notion of art prevented the rise, in the area of high art, of a conception of the novel as a "neutral" rather than "aesthetic" copy of reality. The historical novel became, in its hybrid form, a response to both idealistic and realistic frameworks. But its very novelty and force of impact also became its Achilles' heel. While its composite unity could satisfy a need for art's independence *and* for its commitment to actual reality, rejecting the possibility of a synthesis between independence and commitment meant sentencing the historical novel to death. Zaiotti chose to idealistically defend the superior knowledge that art affords. This stance disguised a defensive attitude toward the force of the "real." It represented, therefore, a conservative maneuver designed to protect the literary institution from any form of ideological commitment except, of course, the metaphysics of aesthetic intuition.

Zaiotti did not combine his 1830 impassioned defense of the novel with an explicit revision of his 1827 evaluation of history. However, praising fiction's ability to touch upon the ideal implied modifying the higher rank that history had filled in 1827. Still an objective rendition of meaningful deeds, history becomes—in tune with Aristotle's precepts in his *Poetics*—a plain chronicle of discrete events, methodologically unable to afford poetry's superior syntheses. Among the Classicists, it was Ferdinando Orlandi who addressed this issue in an essay entitled "Dissertazione sopra il romanzo storico" ("Dissertation on the Historical Novel," 1839).[19] The portrayal of historically accurate occurrences and individual characters, Orlandi contends, is, overall, less instructive than the invention of exemplary figures created from the observation of innumerable models subsequently combined into an ideal synthesis (109–10). A writer should not be forced into a pedestrian imitation of history, and critics should not praise descriptions that contain a merely factual instruction, lacking the merits of invention (111–12). Orlandi's rejection of history does not involve a discussion of the different theories of representation pertaining to fiction and history, but concentrates instead on the Classicists' moralistic concerns. If one were to limit oneself to the genuine and inclusive exposition of material facts, Orlandi asserts, one would be forced to insert all the scandalous instances that plague the historical annals. History is never instructive unless it is corrected by a philosophical analysis directed toward "reflection" (i.e., idealization). Historical novels favor the historical chronicle; novels of pure invention, instead, are able to leave factual reality aside and provide "sovrumani modelli di un bello morale" ("superhuman models of moral beauty") (126). With orthodox subservience to the Classicists' positions, Orlandi concludes that historical fiction is a contradiction, an illicit mixture of history and invention. The consequences inferred from the amalgam of invented and historical facts have no legitimacy and damage both learned and ingenuous readers. The former must renounce the pleasures of illusion and sift true from invented circumstances, properly cataloguing what was illegitimately coupled. The latter remain dupes of the text, forced to blindly roam among the historical counterfeits of the land of unfiction (113–14).

* * *

For the Romantics, the novel represented a new genre free from the jurisdiction of rhetoric, independent of preexisting models, and open to the unmediated illustration of historical reality. "[I]l romanzo storico è la moda del giorno," Varese enthusiastically wrote in the introductory essay to *Preziosa di Sanluri* (1832), "ma questa che voi chiamate moda, è appunto la misura delle inclinazioni del secolo, cioè di quelle modificazioni che il concorso di una folla di circostanze politiche e civili fa nascere" ("Historical fiction is the fashion of the day . . . but what you call a fashion is indeed the measure of our century's tendencies, that is, the sign of those changes that are born from the concurrence of a multitude of political and social circumstances") (ix). The early romantic theories of historical fiction focused on the genre's practical functions and extraliterary applications. For many, the historical novel was a forum for political education, promoting a utilitarian usage of literature for disseminating revolutionary ideological propaganda. It was also a pedagogical genre inspiring the study of history proper and allowing the circulation of historical materials that would otherwise remain obscure, abstruse, or downright tedious. In its most mature and self-conscious expressions, the historical novel was seen as a literary genre endowed with thematic originality, epistemological significance, and aesthetic excellence. But to reach this point, the romantic theoreticians of historical fiction had first to defend themselves against the Classicists' accusations of the genre's falsity and immorality.

In the prefaces to his historical novels, Varese insisted on the "indisputable truth" of the narrated facts (*Sibilla Odaleta* i), claiming that he had no interest in offering a picture of "ideal beauty," but wanted to faithfully present "la società privata coi molti suoi vizii, i più numerosi suoi difetti, e le poche sue virtù" ("private society with its many vices, more numerous flaws and few virtues") (*La fidanzata ligure* ii). For Varese, the truth of historical representation results from the accurate and objective reconstruction of the past and from inventive inferences based on the laws of the verisimilar, so that characters act and speak "come probabilmente, e dietro le norme del carattere che si desume dalle loro azioni veramente storiche, avrebbero agito e parlato in circostanze simili a quelle inventate dal poeta" ("as they would have probably acted and spoken, according to the laws of character inferred from their real historical actions, in circumstances similar to those invented by the poet") (*Preziosa di Sanluri* lx). Varese's rebuttal to the Classicists' accusations of the historical novel's falseness is orchestrated in purely realistic terms (characters are presented as they are and not as they should be) and according to the criteria of a strictly reflectionist theory. The morality of the novel ultimately depends on the inclusiveness and accuracy of the historical picture.

The discussions of the historical novel's pedagogical function developed into a more mature awareness of its thematic autonomy as compared with that of history proper. In its most superficial theorizations, historical fiction was regarded as an incentive for readers to pursue "real" historical studies.[20] By making history more accessible and enjoyable, the historical novel was able to translate history's moral exempla and circulate them among the general public: historical fiction had an integrative function, as it completed the historical records in a democratic and populist direction by addressing the average reader and depicting common people in everyday situations.[21] The Anonimo's juxtaposition of the history of "Prencipi e Potentati, e qualificati Personaggj" ("Princes and Powers and such qualified Personages") and his own history of "gente meccaniche, e di piccol affare" ("Mechanical Folk and of but small Account") in Manzoni's foreword to *I promessi sposi* is a case in point. Unlike traditional historiography, the historical novel traces a history of mentalities and captures a period's moral and intellectual climate by analyzing cultural phenomena such as private customs, domestic habits, and shared opinions. It examines how this historical substratum affects political changes and, conversely, how political changes modify the sociocultural landscape. Thus, historical fiction furnishes, in critic Sansone Uzielli's words, "[un] vero supplemento alla storia" ("[a] real supplement to history") (125). The shift in what constitutes a historical topic involves a change in the narrative perspective from which the subject matter is approached, together with a more sophisticated awareness of the narrative techniques specific to the craft of fiction. In the introduction to *Falco della Rupe* (1829), Giambattista Bazzoni contends that:

> La storia . . . si può chiamare un gran quadro ove sono tracciati tutti gli avvenimenti, collocati i grandi personaggi, e la serie d'alcuni fatti esposta con ordine, ma dove la moltitudine delle cose v'è negletta o appena accennata in confuso e di scorcio, e sole le azioni più straordinarie e gli uomini sommi vi stanno dipinti isolatamente e quasi sempre nella unica relazione dei pubblici interessi. Il Romanzo storico è una gran lente che si applica ad un punto di quell'immenso quadro: per esso ciò ch'era appena visibile riceve le sue

> naturali dimensioni, un lieve abbozzato contorno diventa un disegno regolare e perfetto, o meglio un quadro in cui tutti gli oggetti riprendono il loro vero colore. Non più i soli re, i duci, i magistrati, ma la gente del popolo, le donne, i fanciulli vi fanno la loro mostra: vi sono messi in azione i vizi, le virtù domestiche, e palesata l'influenza delle pubbliche istituzioni sui privati costumi, sui bisogni e la felicità della vita; che è quanto deve alla fin fine interessare l'universalità degli uomini. (27–28; see appendix 10)

Political engagement, realistic agenda, pedagogical ambition (both as integration and popularization of traditional historiography), and narrative distinctiveness: these were the main topics around which the Romantics structured their defense of the historical novel. But these were, after all, peripheral issues: the unresolved predicament at the core of the debate concerned, of course, the legitimacy—this time on strictly epistemological rather than rhetorical terms—of the mixture of genres, and discussion concentrated on the ideological consequences of the illicit alliance between history and fiction.

A plea for interdisciplinarity and the organic solution of opposites, coupled with an interesting revision of the concept of truth in historical fiction, characterizes Giuseppe Bianchetti's response to Zaiotti's controversial essays. In "Sopra i romanzi storici" ("On Historical Novels"),[22] Bianchetti, much like Zaiotti, petitioned Manzoni to use his authority to intervene and resolve the polemics over the historical novel. Manzoni broke his noncommittal silence only to decline the challenge and apologize with a courteous but scarcely believable letter, explaining that he had not and was not going to read Bianchetti's essay because of his decision to abstain from anything that dealt with "controversies of Italian literature" (*Opere* 7.1: 606).

Enthusiastically supporting the new genre, Bianchetti argues that truth can be conveyed through different media. History reports and delivers truth to posterity, moral philosophy analyzes it to determine ethical norms, and poetry filters it through emotions and imagination to make it pleasant and accessible. The symbolic, or mediated, nature of fictional truth and its instructive function associate Bianchetti's views to Zaiotti's. But, unlike Zaiotti, Bianchetti is convinced that there is no intrinsic difference between the truths of poetry, history, and moral philosophy; the only differences reside in the media that convey them. In other words, the material form that truth assumes may vary, but its moral essence and intrinsic value remain unchanged.[23] The inventions of poetry are simple exterior ornaments that do not affect the work's "truth" (89).

If the substance of truth does not change, different vehicles of expression may be more or less effective in conveying it. The historical novel, by organically combining aspects of history, moral philosophy, and poetry, results in a genre "di maggiore e più universale utilità che gli altri tre" ("of higher and more universal usefulness than the other three") (93). The historical novel provides a synthesis in which truth differs in degree, rather than in kind, from the truth conveyed by the separate disciplines. With a similar argument, Bianchetti explains that the imagined characters of a historical novel epitomize an era's general traits; they represent the overall tendency of the ways of thinking, feeling, and acting in a specific time and place (105). They are, in Hegel's definition, "world historical individuals" that embody the spirit of an age, according consciousness and direction to a historical movement (Lukács, *The Historical Novel* 39–40).

The imaginative freedom of the historical novel not only considers single characters and specific events, but also regards the way in which the historical sequence is manipulated, supplemented, and altered: it involves, in other words, issues of representative technique and formal structuring that demand the writer's most refined organizing skills. Real and invented circumstances are combined in the creation of a plot that, instead of passively mimicking the linear course of history, reveals history's necessary truth:

> Ma la storia avendo per fine di raccontare il vero, e però dovendo narrare i casi in quel modo e in quell'ordine con cui sono accaduti, non è in arbitrio, come, mediante le invenzioni, è il romanzo, di disporre, tirare, allungare ed accorciare le fila del racconto in quella guisa che la mente di ogni volgar lettore sia condotta necessariamente, irresistibilmente alla conclusione in cui è bene che vada. (Bianchetti 106; see appendix 11)

Unlike historians, who are limited to reproducing the chronological sequence and superficial appearance of the events they report, novelists can organize these events in a manner that discloses the deeper order of reality, thus providing a powerful tool of instruction and moral education.

In spite of his schematic and overly simplified definitions, Bianchetti realized that the epistemological significance of historical fiction did not exclusively depend upon thematic choices, but entailed a work's formal structures as well. Representing the historical truth was no longer a matter of providing a carbon copy of the material world; it involved the philosophical quest for history's ultimate reasons, the aesthetic challenge to accurately interpret and depict history's profound order, and the ideological commitment to make this order accessible and profitable by revealing what is essential and significant in the historical process.[24]

Bianchetti's intuition of the substantial identity, yet formal difference, between real and ideal truths takes a different turn in Giuseppe Mazzini's systematic analysis of the types of knowledge afforded by history, philosophy, and the historical novel.[25] For Mazzini, material and moral truths, and real and ideal worlds, do not constitute separate systems, as Zaiotti had claimed, but coexist one within the other. They are related as if by synecdoche or metonymy, material truth being only a part or an aspect of moral truth. Facts, Mazzini argues, are composed of two faces, "l'una interna, razionale, immutabile, l'altra esterna, materiale, contingente" ("one internal, rational, immutable, the other external, material, contingent") ("Del dramma storico" 275). The ideal exists within the real, the moral world is not an abstract intellectual construct but part and parcel of the sensible world, and the universal principles that guide historical becoming are constantly translated into practical actions. Although interdependent and dialectically related, the real and the ideal do not occupy the same hierarchical space: Mazzini conceives a binary metaphysics founded on the qualitative difference between material truth, which remains provisional and contingent, and ideal truth, which is eternal and necessary.[26] Coexistence, in other words, does not mean amalgamation and the loss of all distinctions in a synthesis of opposites: the real and the ideal, variety and unity, and contingency and necessity remain discrete elements within the historical scene; their interplay has cognitive value only insofar as the ideal term of the equation is granted superior standing.

The same hierarchical difference separates history from philosophy. Like Bianchetti, Mazzini has a reductive view of the writing of history, which he identifies with the mere compilation of chronicles. The historian gathers facts, records them in the order of their chronological succession, and consigns them to posterity. Unlike Zaiotti, Mazzini questions the absolute objectivity of the chronicle. Chroniclers, traditionally subject and subservient to the partisan views of their sponsors, have interpreted facts in the light of ingrained beliefs, sectarian prejudices, and superstitious religious views. Limited in their research by their subordinate social and economic status, hampered by material restrictions imposed upon the diffusion of knowledge and free dissemination of information, historians had to rely on scant, partial, and imprecise records. Far from being oracles of truth, historians have provided, at the most, a translation of a translation ("Del dramma storico" 272–73). Like modern historians such as Marc Bloch and Lucien Febvre, Mazzini is aware that historical documents, while collecting and relating historical events, tell the story of the institutions and attitudes that guided the interpretation of these events. Unlike Bloch and Febvre, Mazzini does not attach any hermeneutical value to this discovery: the second-degree discourse, which reveals the specific intellectual methods and material conditions of historical reconstruction and shows that historical meaning is ideologically constructed across a number of institutional sites and practices, is only evidence that all historical reconfigurations are misinterpretations. According to Mazzini, since the science of history as objective and neutral observation of facts is impossible, historiography does not constitute a viable method of historical research.

Historiography presents an even more fundamental problem for the philosopher of history who addresses the nature of historical knowledge by assessing the truth that history provides. Apart from the social, economic, and ideological drawbacks of its interpreters, the *historia rerum gestarum* is intrinsically unable to fully grasp the very object of its research: *res gestae.* As plain selection and compilation of facts, historiography is inescapably tied to the particular: it is a short-sighted gathering of single and isolated relics. History, therefore, is only the foundation of a higher intellectual activity aimed at discovering the inner laws and universal ordering principles of historical becoming ("Del dramma storico" 278–79). This intellectual activity pertains to philosophy.

Philosophy delves into the multiplicity of material facts, grasps the unifying principles within the apparently casual and contradictory course of historical events, and interprets them in order to disclose their inner meaning. Facts are necessarily tied to one another, and their connections are universal and inalterable. As Mazzini contends:

> La religione superstiziosa e minuta de' fatti ha consumato il suo tempo: ora noi siam maturi per la religione de' principii. . . . Fino ad oggi si raccolsero fatti: si schierarono come il tempo li dava, o s'ordinarono a gruppi come suggeriva l'osservazione isolata d'un anno, d'un secolo, o d'una gente. Si rintracciò la connessione esistente tra' fatti che componevano i diversi gruppi, senza pur badare se un vincolo superiore unisse l'un gruppo all'altro: si dedussero conseguenze parziali. . . . È tempo ormai di . . . stabilire una serie di formole generali de' procedimenti dell'intelletto: —trovar modo di verificarle nella storia. ("Del dramma storico" 274; see appendix 12)

The philosopher's search does not linger on chronological inventories of phenomena: it prompts an inductive process that examines concrete facts in order to discover the general laws that express the intellectual foundations of a specific historical period. Anticipating Foucault's definition of the *episteme,* Mazzini argues that these laws define the political, social and religious physiognomy of an era. They constitute the codes that determine the empirical orders and social practices of a particular culture. It is Mazzini's contention, however, that these laws must come to terms with the transhistorical moral laws that guide history's course, ultimately determining its inner truth. The dramatic clash between historical and transhistorical laws marks the moments of historical crisis,[27] while their alliance marks those of emancipation and progress. Unlike history, philosophy can identify both the historical and transhistorical principles that, when directed toward the same goals in the concrete historical praxis, allow humanity's material and spiritual advancement ("Del dramma storico" 274).

Literature combines history with philosophy. Poets and philosophers interpret the facts that history gathers in order to discover their arcane rule. This kind of interpretative act, Mazzini argues, does not imply violating or manipulating history, because it does not impose subjective ordering principles upon the chaos of historical facts. It means discovering that the same rational categories that order our intellectual procedures also order historical becoming. Like Bianchetti, Mazzini believes that the novelist represents the variety, with all its anomalies and contradictions, of the historical world in order to disclose the unitary principle shaping nature's apparent chaos; he thus reveals the secret connections that give a meaning to life by anticipating its goal. By theorizing the intrinsic ties between the real and the ideal, Mazzini eliminates all obstacles to the coexistence of history and fiction. Behind the axiomatic statement that in the historical novel, "un *principio* [è] spiegato da un *fatto:* la *verità* insegnata colla *realità*" ("a *principle* is explained by a *fact, truth* is taught by *reality*") ("Del dramma storico" 307), Mazzini recasts the humanistic faith that by applying rational principles to the study of the universe, we may indeed discover its operating laws. Once again at the center of the universe, "man" enjoys the certainty that the world is understandable and decipherable, the observation and interpretation of the past is the best way to infer the laws of the future, and the principles that "generarono ciò che fu, dominano quel che è, e creeranno quel che sarà" ("generated what was, rule over what is, and will create what shall be") ("Del dramma storico" 305) shape the exhilarating tale of humanity's "magnificent and progressive destinies." Heir to Descartes and the Enlightenment, Mazzini champions reason as the "source of progress in knowledge and society, as well as the privileged locus of truth and the foundation of systematic knowledge" (Best and Kellner 2).

In this optimistic panorama, fiction, and the historical novel in particular, share with philosophy the moral responsibility of heralding humanity's spiritual advancement and material progress. Taking the cue from Zaiotti's blunt distinction between thought and action, Mazzini concurs that fiction belongs to that reflexive, individualistic stage of social development that replaces the age of public and communal action. For Mazzini, however, the advent of fiction does not imply either resigned contemplation of past glories or self-absorbed withdrawal into introspection. It is the necessary preliminary to action and a spur to change: the foundation of a new, revolutionary praxis. Literature, Mazzini agrees with Zaiotti, has a pedagogical and moral function. This function, however, is not merely preventive (a lesson in avoiding harmful experiences), or consolatory and escapist (a picture of a kinder, better world), but truly inspirational. Mazzini sketches a prophetic and optimistic picture of a literature that by fostering hope, incites people to act for a brighter future. "National, free and popular," this literature, unlike Zaiotti's, is closely tied to the sociopolitical realities of the contemporary world: it monitors and reflects the intellectual progress of the people ("Del dramma storico" 258). Interpreter of public opinions and prophet of the future, the novelist foresees the destinies of humanity and helps to bring about significant social changes ("D'una letteratura europea" 181).

Mazzini's insight regarding the coexistence of the ideal within the real allowed him to reckon with historical multiplicity and vitality without renouncing the rational order of a totalizing systematization of history. His unifying philosophy acts as a bulwark against the endless dispersion of meaning, the "thousands of different interpretations" ("Del dramma storico" 271) that would hinder the pursuit of truth. Mazzini attacks, like Zaiotti, all philosophies of doubt based on epistemological relativism, vehemently rejecting the skeptical view that "nulla è di certo . . . la verità è chimera . . . e noi dobbiam rassegnarci ad una guerra perpetua di pareri, e sistemi, che si divorin l'un l'altro, come gli armati di Cadmo" ("nothing is certain . . . truth is a chimera . . . and we must resign ourselves to a perennial war of opinions and systems devouring one another like Cadmus's soldiers") (rev. of "Del romanzo" 38). By building his totalizing system on the belief that reality is ordered according to laws that the human intelligence can grasp, Mazzini justifies, as self-evident, the ideals of totality, continuity, genesis, and teleology. Mazzini's rationalist myth craftily places itself both within and beyond ideology and history. Its being within the real avoids the danger of antihistorical abstractness and conservative idealism *à la* Zaiotti; its reaching beyond material reality to identify history's founding principles justifies its claim to truth and universality, while exorcising the specters of fragmentation, disorder, and incoherence that haunt the intellectual edifices of liberal humanism.

The sacrificial victim in Bianchetti's and Mazzini's systems, historiography acquires a new status with Niccolò Tommaseo, who discussed the historical novel in the pages of the moderate Florentine journal *Antologia*.[28] Subscribing to an evolutionary theory of literature, Tommaseo argues that every cultural period produces specific literary discourses that, if examined from a diachronic perspective, tell the story of the progress of the human spirit.[29] The historical novel reveals humanity's increasing need for factual truth and is a genre of transition, the connecting ring and intermediate stage between imaginative literature and history proper.[30] Historical fiction has replaced the traditional systematic historiography that sacrificed the multiplicity of historical events to a set of abstract unifying principles and shunned the rich details of manners and customs in favor of a dry catalogue of axiomatic pronouncements. Novels such as Manzoni's, Tommaseo claims, have popularized a different narrative practice founded on the dialectic exchange between real facts and ideal reasons, and particular events and universal principles, thus providing the most instructive example of the ultimate unity, as well as a fascinating variety of truth ("Del romanzo storico" 42–44).

Like Mazzini, Tommaseo insists that universal truth remains an empty concept if it does not acquire a sensible appearance by permeating the concrete objects that, in turn, reflect the principles originating the heterogeneity of the physical world (rev. of *I Lombardi* 9). Tommaseo, however, narrows Mazzini's hierarchical distinction between real and ideal truths and, like Bianchetti, argues that while the *idea* of truth is unique and singular, its embodiment within a variety of material forms makes it knowable and enjoyable. By depicting the countless facets of historical reality, fiction captures a kind of truth that is alien to both speculative philosophy and traditional historiography. Historical fiction spreads information about memorable characters and events, and furnishes a psychological and moral study of an epoch by observing the minute circumstances, both public and private, that official history overlooks. In this approach to the historical novel, historical truth and fictional invention are mutually dependent: fiction integrates history, revealing, by means of informed inference, the material variety, psychological physiognomy, and intrinsic design of a particular period; history keeps invention in check, limiting its freedom within the boundaries of the reasonably verisimilar. The two systems, the fictional and the historical, do not need to be organically fused in the historical novel. Rebutting the Classicists' attacks on the "amphibious" genre, Tommaseo polemically states that a novel can be "beautiful" even while combining heterogeneous discourses ("Del romanzo storico" 56), thus implying a premodernist interpretation of the concept of aesthetic beauty that depends on neither the classic tenet of the separation of genres nor the romantic concept of the organic principle directing the harmonious blending of a work's individual parts.[31]

While Tommaseo does not renounce those generalities that "senza guastare l'individualità del fatto, lo spiegano anzi, e ne mostrano il carattere intrinseco" ("without destroying the individuality of a fact explain it, and demonstrate its intrinsic character") (rev. of *Sibilla Odaleta* 88), he also contends that the ultimate unity gathers a diversity of truths that are relative to specific circumstances of time and place, and to the changing traits of the human mind in different social strata, specific cultural circumstances, and unique historical moments. In a note accompanying his historical novel, *Il duca d'Atene* (1837), Tommaseo rejects the objective despotism of the historical record while stressing the subjective nature of all historical discourses:

> ma questo, come tutti gli altri argomenti, può essere ritrattato in nuova forma, secondo il variare de' prospetti che si viene facendo nella varietà degli ingegni e de' tempi. . . . L'esperienza nuova che facciasi o da un uomo o da un popolo o da un'età può ad un tratto diffondere luce novella su fatti antichi notissimi, e rischiararli di nuova moralità. (230; see appendix 13)

The *locus* of historical truth is thus displaced: it does not belong to the historical object but is relativized as part of the changing perspectives of its interpreters, colored by their ideological views, and evaluated with the ethical codes that they derive from their own historical time. The rising awareness of the historians' contributions in shaping and representing the historical world induced Tommaseo to praise historical novels designed as allegories of the present and charged with subliminal or explicit political messages ("Del romanzo storico" 58–59).[32]

The critical bonds between Tommaseo and Manzoni are particularly evident in their historiographic theories.[33] Eclectic and comparative, Tommaseo's ideal historiography derives from the experiences of the historical novel and foreshadows the methods of historians Raymond Aron, Jacques Le Goff, Pierre Chaunu, and others by combining different research fields such as those of anthropology, ethnography, linguistics, art history, and even geology ("Del romanzo storico" 45). Stressing the historian's interpretative operations, Tommaseo raises to historiographic dignity the art of conjecture and hypothesis, coupling the practice of archival research with creative inferences and verisimilar reconstructions of a past whose relics have been destroyed by the ravages of time or overlooked by conventional historiographical studies. Formally, Tommaseo combines poetic digressions and analogical proceedings with the illustration of the causal paradigm highlighting the connections between historical phenomena, while the historian's traditionally impersonal and univocal style is replaced by a citational framework merging the voices, and exegetical methods, of modern and ancient interpreters ("Del romanzo storico" 45).

Like Mazzini, Tommaseo participated in the romantic quest for absolute truth. He subscribed to a totalizing philosophy aimed at the discovery of unifying rational principles that order and explain both material and spiritual realities. At the same time, Tommaseo anticipated twentieth-century relativism in his discussion of the ideological specificity and interpretative plurality of all historical reconstructions. He foreshadowed new aesthetic forms founded on the coexistence of multiple and separate discursive systems, and thus sketched the perspectivist and relativistic approaches that, originating with Nietzsche and culminating in poststructuralist and postmodernist critiques, argue that all cognitive representations of reality are historically, linguistically, and ideologically mediated—that there are no objective truths, only diverse hermeneutical procedures resulting in the dissemination of meaning rather than the construction of unified philosophical structures.

* * *

Even if polarized by moralistic drawbacks, rhetorical biases, and political misappropriations, the debate on the historical novel produced an engaging investigation of the epistemologies of fiction and history. The two arguments that emerged from the discussions can be summarized as follows: one, idealistic in nature, defends the separation of aesthetic knowledge from historical knowledge and either accepts the historical novel as providing a synthesis that allows a superior cognitive form (Romantics) or rejects it as unable to provide this synthesis (Classicists). The other argument emphasizes the need for empirical truth and sees the historical novel either as a transitory form used to make empirical truth more palatable (Romantics) or as a hindrance to the discovery of objective truth because it confounds truth with spurious fictional elements (Classicists). It is not enough to argue that the *questione del romanzo* was one of the issues of the battle between the two camps. It is necessary to stress that both Classicists and Romantics adopted the same philosophical systems, one empirical, the other idealistic. Both systems were, paradoxically, manipulated to reach opposite results, that is to either defend or condemn the historical novel. Interestingly, while the Classicists originally defended the value of historical knowledge, they subsequently retreated into idealistic positions praising fiction's ideal truth and debasing history to a mere chronicle unable to achieve fiction's superior syntheses. The Romantics maintained a more eclectic approach and, caught between the appeal of both empiricism and transcendentalism, agreed on fiction's moral truth but were unable to present a united front regarding the form and the significance of historical knowledge, as demonstrated by Tommaseo's and Mazzini's opposite views on this topic.

Manzoni's Essay *Del romanzo storico*

When Manzoni finally decided to break his noncommittal silence with his long-awaited essay on the historical novel, he lucidly outlined the terms of the debate, identified the debate's shortcomings and intellectual dead ends, and plotted a new course that would leave behind the contradictions of the historical novel while directing its formal and thematic achievements into an innovative method of historical writing. Manzoni constructed his essay with an eye to the classical tradition of the dialogues, in which a number of interlocutors are dialectically involved in an epistemological debate. The direct references are, significantly, the philosophical debates staged by

Plato's Socratic dialogues and Aristotle's adaptation of the genre for didactic purposes. In the Italian tradition, writers as diverse as Petrarch, Pietro Bembo, Baldassar Castiglione, Galileo Galilei, and Giacomo Leopardi experimented with the genre of the dialogue. In Manzoni's times, the dialogue, together with the epistolary form, was one of the favorite ways of tackling contradictory issues: serving the purpose of polarizing divergent opinions, it was adopted by Borsieri, Pellico, Ermes Visconti, and Vincenzo Monti in the pages of the *Biblioteca italiana,* the *Attaccabrighe,* the *Giornale delle dame,* and the *Conciliatore.* Manzoni deliberately exploits a form that derives its meaning from the philosophical problem of a dialectical search for truth, using it for the definition of a specific type of truth, not universal and aprioristic in kind, but related to historical and fictional interpretations of the real. Implicitly, therefore, Manzoni intends not only to dismantle the historical novel; he also offers a *pars construens* that establishes the originality of his contribution to the current discussions on fiction and historical writing. By adopting the mixed genre of a *dialogo/ discorso,* Manzoni places himself within and at the end of a debate. In other words, he demands for himself the privilege of having the last word. In this sense, Manzoni also exploits the sophistic legacy of Protagoras's antilogies, the oratorical debates in which two antithetical discourses were resolved, trial-like, by a third authoritative party (Perelman 75). *Del romanzo storico,* then, is a *discorso sui generis,* as it ironically combines dialogical exchange with the argumentative and monological definition of the treatise and the disquisition.

The juxtaposition of the essay's three voices combines the evaluation of the historical novel (the "negative" part in Manzoni's own terminology) with a constructive discussion in which a new form of historiography is appointed (the "positive" part, again to quote in another context Manzoni himself). In this way, Manzoni's essay may indeed, as De Sanctis observed, mark the death knell of his creativity, but at the same time it redirects that creativity toward the reevaluation of the historiographer's role, methodology, and field of analysis. The first interlocutor in Manzoni's essay embraces the Classicists' concerns and, like Zaiotti in his first essay, raises ethical rather than aesthetic questions, accusing the historical novel of not making a clear-cut content distinction between the *vero* (what actually happened and who really existed) and the *verosimile* (the realm of invented characters and events). Like Mazzini, this accuser offers a value judgment asserting art's cognitive superiority over historiography. In orthodox Aristotelian terms, in fact, he claims that while history offers only a chronological account of political and military events (a mere chronicle, that is), a novel focuses instead on a smaller scale and delves deeper into the facts, discovering the private effects of public occurrences, following relations, deducing results, and establishing a chain of causation between discrete events. Going a step further than both Zaiotti and Mazzini, this speaker argues that this aesthetic construction does not reveal whether it is "una manifestazione reale dell'umanità, della natura, della Provvidenza, o solamente un possibile felicemente trovato da voi" ("a real expression of humanity, nature, Providence, or only a possibility happily found by you") (*Opere* 5.3: 291). Fiction, for the first speaker, must be strictly evaluated in terms of its analogy to and difference from the objective world, and the issue of truthfulness applies to both the factual area ("what" is narrated) and the formal one ("how" it is narrated). While the contents of fiction may differ from those of reality, the question remains open, as a result, as to whether the forms of fiction mirror those of reality or are man-made artifacts. Moreover, this speaker implies, when fiction is perceived as fiction (i.e., human construction), it can enjoy some kind of independence as a self-sufficient unity. When it establishes a stricter relationship with reality (i.e., the historical novel), it faces two moral demands: to distinguish between true and invented facts and to establish a link between the form of life and that of fiction. From the essay's opening remarks, it is clear that unlike his predecessors (with the notable, yet sketchy, exception of Bianchetti), Manzoni directs the theoretical inquiry on the nature of aesthetic and historical knowledge toward a discussion of the concrete methodological problems concerning the modes of writing history and fiction.

The second interlocutor in Manzoni's essay expresses aesthetic rather than ethical concerns and establishes the grounds for answering the first speaker's open question. Summarizing some of Zaiotti's claims in the 1830 essay, this speaker sees "unity" as the gist of the literary work. Unlike Tommaseo, he claims that the "racconto" is based on continuity of impression and the confluence of its parts to create a total effect. He argues, on the content level, that wanting to separate factual from fictional truth is harmful for the unity of the whole (*Opere* 5.3: 292). Unlike the first speaker, the second rejects an empirical, atomistic, and analytic approach in favor of a systematically unifying one. Advancing beyond Zaiotti's claims, he suggests that while the "narrative form" (i.e., a chronicle) is the proper and natural form of history, the "narrative form" applied to "invention" creates a conventional structure arranged around the unity of "racconto." Thus he suggests the distinction that the Russian formalists adopted later between *fabula* as basic narrative materials and *sjužet* as the way in which these materials are organized in a plot (Erlich 240). While a chronicle faithfully mirrors the sequential unfolding of historical events, a fictional plot manipulates the chronological order, creating an artificial structure that does not reproduce the laws of historical becoming. The form of the historical novel is a paradox, since in its double nature it claims to be both natural and artificial as well as both reflective and creative of the forms of reality.

Manzoni's first-person intervention develops the other two speakers' points. He borrows the concept of the organic principle of art to explain that trying to divide true from invented facts is contrary to the very notion of organic form. On the other hand, he agrees that a narrator who intervenes to separate factual from fictional events would effectively direct the two responses required from the readers.[34] One response resides in the acceptance of the narrative pact through the suspension of disbelief. The other response demands instead documentary confirmation of the empirical reality of narrated facts. But in this way, Manzoni argues, the unity called for by the second speaker is dissolved, for the historical novel forces together materials that must remain separate. The historical novel thus conceived forces critics to maintain a dualistic approach, and a harmonious interpretation becomes unfeasible. The historical novel:

> è un componimento nel quale riesce impossibile ciò che è necessario; nel quale non si possono conciliare due condizioni essenziali, e non si può nemmeno adempirne una,

> essendo inevitabile in esso e una confusione repugnante alla materia, e una distinzione repugnante alla forma; un componimento, nel quale deve entrare e la storia e la favola, senza che si possa nè stabilire, nè indicare in qual proporzione, in quali relazioni ci devano entrare; un componimento insomma, che non c'è il verso giusto di farlo, perchè il suo assunto è intrinsecamente contraddittorio. (*Opere* 5.3: 300–01; see appendix 14)

The pressing question, at this point, is whether the materials themselves are really separate or the interpretative systems used to organize these materials force them to be separate. The continuous references to the reader's response in Manzoni's essay seem to direct us toward the latter interpretation. The key point of Manzoni's mock trial of the historical novel is his emphatic argument that the genre stages the battle between two epistemologies and two aesthetic ideologies. One ideology renounces referentiality altogether in the name of the idealizing quality of aesthetic mimesis, thus proclaiming the autonomy of high art and the legitimacy of the superior truth that art affords.[35] The other stresses the referential value of fiction and therefore explores the ways in which novels may encode objective reality. This latter approach redefines the literary institution in anti-idealistic terms. The theoretical options it allows for are either a full representation of the real (the kind of "objective art" that even the Italian realists of the second half of the century were unable to fully and convincingly theorize) or the favoring of fragmentation over unity (a course that, suggested by Tommaseo, was fully explored only by the historical avant-garde, which gave up the organic principle with all its implications). Manzoni, however, decides on a different alternative: he chooses historiography rather than the novel as the literary form capable of solving the problems that had plagued historical fiction. For Manzoni, historiography, and not fiction, can explore the ways to endow reality with a coherent, unitary form without falling into the trap of claiming for itself a sterile, transtemporal autonomy. Manzoni's contribution to the debate lies exactly in his defining a new form of historiography that incorporates the methodologies of the novel in order to better represent the variety and complexity of historical reality. With Manzoni, the writing of history reaches a higher formal sophistication, as it "makes use of fiction" (Ricoeur, *Time* 3: 185) to refigure the past by imitating, in its own writing techniques, the types of narrative structures pertaining to the literary tradition.[36]

Manzoni's Aesthetics

Del romanzo storico justifies the classic tenet of the separation of genres from ethical and epistemological points of view and discusses the imperatives that the organic principle imposes upon two narrative systems deemed to be unreconcilable. In this essay, Manzoni explores the nature and assesses the limits of aesthetic knowledge. Although he champions the uniqueness of the knowledge that art affords, Manzoni is well aware of the ideological drawbacks of a system built on the belief of the absolute autonomy of the aesthetic sphere.

Manzoni exploits the romantic notion of the organic principle to explain the formal coherence of the literary work. At the core of this concept, as it developed in Germany, England, and the United States in the early 1800s, is a reexamination of the relationship between art and nature. Art is asked to find its direct referents in the natural environment and not in its approximation to other artistic forms. Commenting on Shakespeare, S. T. Coleridge distinguishes between the mechanical, predetermined, artificial form that is imposed on the artistic material and the organic form that is innate as "it shapes itself from within . . . such as the life is, such is the form" (46). This idea is developed also by August Wilhelm von Schlegel and other German Romantics, and in its extreme applications it fosters a notion of intuitive creation. The work of art molds itself from the force of the poet's seminal idea, which necessarily determines its appropriate expression. Believing in the inner harmony and spontaneous organization of the natural world, the American transcendentalists base their rediscovery of the relationship between art and nature on the simple Neoplatonic assumption that art mirrors the forms of reality, and that those forms are in turn a projection of the Divine Mind (Matthiessen 133). The intuitional framework that informs this aesthetic concept makes technical dissection of the artifact impossible: factual truth and universal truth become interchangeable in the immediate, intuitive, harmonious synthesis of the aesthetic, empirical, and metaphysical planes. As witnessed by Mazzini's aesthetic theories, choosing to synthesize the ideal with the real means accepting the historical novel as the form that facilitates transcending all ideological dichotomies not in rational terms but in the form of an inspired, creative sublimation.[37]

Manzoni borrows the romantic concept of the organic principle, but at the same time redirects it by questioning the transitivity between art, nature, and the ideal world. Favoring the analysis and dissection of the work of art, Manzoni is keener on logical distinctions than on intuitive syntheses. As early as 1822, Manzoni argues that what he calls "racconto" often has "une unité artificielle que l'on ne trouve pas dans la vie réelle" ("an artificial unity that is not found in real life") (*Opere* 7.1: 271).[38] In an interesting shift, the organic principle comes to represent, in the Italian highly classicized background, the very opposite of what it had originally meant: it stresses an interest in form as autonomous and self-sufficient rather than as reflective of material and spiritual realities. Therefore, dealing with structure proper means facing art in its permanent, self-determining nature. The kernel of the problem lies right here: the historical novel challenges this autonomy, and Manzoni questions whether a stylized and conventional formal unity is ethically acceptable in a literary genre that requires referential comparison with the forms of historical reality. Thus, Manzoni rejects *in anticipo* the structuralist manifesto of Viktor Šklovskij, according to whom "the forms of art are explainable by the laws of art" (Hawkes 61).

Translated into twentieth-century structuralist terminology, one could argue that Manzoni does not deny the *literariness* of the literary work, but rather is puzzled by the necessity and difficulty of reconciling this concept with art's relationship to actual social and historical reality. While Manzoni revises in formalistic terms the notion of the organic principle in art, thus granting art's autonomy, he is aware of the historical loss implicit in a philosophy of art that established universal beauty and truth as final objects of the artistic experience. The truth that is art's ultimate subject matter, Manzoni argues, is a permanent and timeless entity that cannot be altered by historical change or defaced by the ravages of time:

> L'arte è arte in quanto produce, non un effetto qualunque, ma un effetto definitivo. . . . Il verosimile (materia dell'arte)

> manifestato e appreso come verosimile, è un vero, diverso bensì, anzi diversissimo dal reale, ma un vero veduto dalla mente per sempre o, per parlar con più precisione, irrevocabilmente: è un oggetto che può bensì esserle trafugato dalla dimenticanza, ma che non può esser distrutto dal disinganno. (*Opere* 5.3: 298–99; see appendix 15)

Subtracted from the realm of chance and relativity, the unique knowledge that art affords defies rational categorization: the truth of fiction is "qualche cosa di non ancor definito; nè il definirlo mi pare impresa molto agevole, quando pure ella sia possibile" ("something which is still to be defined, and defining it does not seem to me an easy task, if it is even possible") (*Opere* 5.3: 250).

Like Tommaseo and Mazzini, Manzoni does not renounce an aesthetic system founded upon metaphysical unity and is fascinated by the intuitional appreciation of the ideal in art. At the same time, he explores the mutable and multiple realms of historical truth. Truth is thus relativized as partaking of both historical becoming and the subjective systems applied to its codification. Ideal beauty is then sacrificed to the laws of factual accuracy: "il y a dans la vérité un intérêt si puissant, qu'il peut nous attacher à la considérer malgré une douleur véritable, malgré une certaine horreur voisine du dégoût" ("there is such a powerful interest in truth, that we strive to consider it in spite of genuine suffering, in spite of a certain horror akin to repulsion") (*Opere* 5.3: 95). Manzoni reaches the point of disclaiming poetic invention as a naive form of knowledge and favoring a nonfictional, essaylike form of narrative inquiry: "l'exposé des faits a pour la curiosité très raisonnable des hommes un charme qui dégoûte des inventions poétiques qu'on veut y mêler, et qui les fait même paraître puériles" ("a factual account has, for people's very reasonable curiosity, a charm that leads them to reject the mixing of poetic inventions with facts, and that makes the inventions even appear puerile") (*Opere* 7.1: 227).

Taking these comments out of their specific context and time references means highlighting an inner tension always present in Manzoni's thought, a contradiction that emerges in the clash between his unwillingness to overcome an idealistic notion of art and his will to embrace a historical method as well. Manzoni's refusal to reconcile the two philosophical systems in the intuitional framework of the Romantics' synthetic approach brings him to the impasse staged in *Del romanzo storico* and the condemnation of the historical novel. In this sense, *Del romanzo storico* contains neither the negation of poetry (Negri) nor its reappraisal as a form of supreme knowledge (Bosco); it paradoxically states both. Art is indeed a superior epistemological form, and as such, Manzoni pays tribute to it. Because it is an *aesthetic* mimesis of the real, it must be granted its autonomy. Historiography, at this point, becomes for Manzoni the "neutral" ground where he can explore the ways in which the historical past can be granted narrative form.

Manzoni and the Historical Imagination: Between Fiction and History

Manzoni the historiographer tackles the issue of how to represent reality and the past, this time without the screen of fiction. Is history, for Manzoni, a worn-out fabric that the historian has to resew following dim traces of thread or is it a chaotic sequence of events that the historian creatively forges into an intelligible and meaningful form? Manzoni rejects all artificial structuring devices, as he believes in the natural order that lies underneath the superficial confusion of the historical scene. Certainly, the historian gathers the individual events that make up the historical continuum into a historical "system," but, for Manzoni, this system is neither conventional nor artificial. The historiographer overlays a critical and interpretative grid upon past reality in order to map out a pattern that is already present in it, albeit *in nuce.* Like Mazzini, Manzoni believes in the coincidence between the mind's ordering structures and those of reality. For Manzoni, however, it is the historical text that provides a truthful orchestration of facts arranged according to the universal rational principles (cause and effect; space and time) that reflect the inner logic of historical becoming. As Manzoni explains in his *Lettre à M. Chauvet,* the historian represents a series of events by emphasizing their necessary connections. These connections are not arbitrary, but are founded in "nature" and "truth": they exist, in other words, in the logic of historical progress, and the human mind discovers and reproduces them rather than subjectively inventing or creating them *ex nihilo:*

> C'est, en effet, une des plus importantes facultés de l'esprit humain, que celle de saisir, entre les événemens, les rapports de cause et d'effet, d'antériorité et de conséquence, qui les lient; de ramener à un point de vue unique, et comme par une seule intuition, plusieurs faits séparés par les conditions du temps et de l'espace, en écartant les autres faits qui n'y tiennent que par des coïncidences accidentelles. C'est là le travail de l'historien. Il fait, pour ainsi dire, dans les événemens, le triage nécessaire pour arriver à cette unité de vue; il laisse de côté tout ce qui n'a aucun rapport avec les faits les plus importans; et, se prévalant ainsi de la rapidité de la pensée, il rapproche le plus possible ces derniers entre eux, pour les présenter dans cet ordre que l'esprit aime à y trouver, et dont il porte le type en lui-même. (*Opere* 5.3: 77–78; see appendix 16)

The order of history surpasses the sequential arrangement of the chronicle, and the historian's task is to acquire and transmit a cognition of real facts that is as truthful and as coherent as possible.

The methodological consequences of Manzoni's argument are that historiographers perform functions that previously belonged only to the artist's craft. Mere chronological reports are replaced by a systematic narration of facts, which is not only faithful to the truth of the document but also discloses the historiographer's organizing intervention. The historian selects and arranges the events of the past in order to reveal, in an exemplary manner, all the relations that tie them together in an intelligible design. The historical imagination has a "representative function" (Ricoeur, *Time* 3: 185) through which a given series of happenings is exposed, in Manzoni's case, according to the providential scheme of a teleologically oriented view of history. While Manzoni's totalizing philosophy of history differs from the relativistic and skeptical approaches of twentieth-century thinkers, he anticipates modern discussion of the historiographer's methodology. For Manzoni, historians *are,* in a way, storytellers, as their success as historians results from their ability to build a story out of a variety of apparently unrelated historical facts. Similarly, R. G. Collingwood argues that:

> Each of them [the historian and the storyteller] makes it his business to construct a picture which is partly a narrative

> of events, partly a description of situations, exhibition of motives, analysis of character. Each aims at making his picture a coherent whole, where every character and every situation is so bound up with the rest that this character in this situation cannot but act in this way, and we cannot imagine him as acting otherwise. (245)

Like Collingwood, Paul Veyne rehabilitates the concept of historical narrative by relating it to the Aristotelian notion of plot as the intellectual construction that makes events hold together in a harmonious totality (32–34). Hayden White argues along similar lines that historiographers, like novelists, "make stories" through an operation that he calls "emplotment" (*Metahistory* 5–11). In other words, historical events are transformed into a story "by the suppression or subordination of certain of them and the highlighting of others, by characterization, motific repetition, variation of tone and point of view, alternative descriptive strategies . . . in short, all of the techniques that we would normally expect to find in the emplotment of a novel or a play" (H. White, "The Historical Text" 47).[39] Manzoni differentiates himself from twentieth-century thinkers such as Martin Heidegger, Jean-Paul Sartre, Claude Lévi-Strauss, and the narrative historians (Arthur C. Danto, William H. Dray, Louis O. Mink, Veyne, White, etc.) who connect fictional and historical narrative techniques in order to assert the fictive character of all historical reconstructions. For Manzoni the narrative strategies applied to the representation of history serve to emphasize its necessary rather than conventional order. If Manzoni would have agreed with "narrativist" historians that historical understanding depends upon narrative activity, and "what is called explanation is nothing but the way in which the account is arranged in a comprehensible plot" (Veyne 87), unlike most narrativist historians, Manzoni held the optimistic belief that the logic of the plot reproduces the inner logic of history or, in other words, that history has an intrinsic narratable order.

Manzoni's transcendental realism justifies the overall "truth" of historical representations founded upon teleological schemes. The problem of historical truth also involves, however, the minute details that are enclosed within those schemes. For Manzoni the writing of history implies the rediscovery of forgotten and unwritten events: it becomes an inverted *res gestae* that encompasses what has been traditionally excluded from historical texts. Manzoni chooses to represent a broader picture, one inclusive of social reality in all its undocumented expressions during a very specific, unrepeatable historical moment. Anticipating Nathan Wachtel's *Vision of the Vanquished,* Manzoni consigns to posterity the experiences and perspectives of the multitude of people who "passa sulla terra . . . inosservata, senza lasciarci traccia" ("pass on the earth . . . unobserved, without leaving any traces") (*Opere* 4: 44). This historical project implies a revision of the "truth" of history as mere testimonial accuracy and transcription of what was stored away in archival documents.

Manzoni combines the antiquarian search for historical records with an inventive and creative effort on the historiographer's part. The historiographer's conjectures and deductions are necessary, Manzoni feels, for a reasonable integration of the material facts. Collingwood's definition of "constructive imagination" (242) parallels Manzoni's notions of historical conjecture as the ability to infer as well as discover or report facts. Manzoni's creative "truth" is thus legitimized through its moral and ideological implications. The exhumation of neglected histories lived by those who did not hold a monopoly on official historical discourses denotes Manzoni's suspicion concerning the "guardianship of history by the inventors and the beneficiaries of the discourse pronounced on the front-stage of history" (Ricoeur, *Contribution* 47). The seventeenth-century manuscript of Renzo and Lucia's adventures is worth rewriting, Manzoni implies, because the Anonimo is an anomalous historian for his own times, having renounced the erudite and annalistic antiquarianism of baroque historiography for the narration of two peasants' adventures under the Spanish domination.

By rejecting the traditional forms of historiography referred to in Zaiotti's essays, Manzoni embraces the Romantics' denunciations of the short-sightedness of classic historiography and opts for "una storia più ricca, più varia, più compita di quella che si trova nell'opere a cui si dà questo nome più comunemente" ("a richer, more varied, more complete history than that found in works that more commonly go by this name") (*Opere* 5.3: 289–90). In agreement with Tommaseo's views, for Manzoni the writing of history becomes an encyclopedic act, addressing formal as well as philosophical, sociological, and psychological issues. Rich with the experiences of the historical novel, historiography can incorporate all those narrative materials and formal techniques that, in the *Lettre à M. Chauvet,* Manzoni had delegated to poets in their responsibility to "compléter l'histoire, [et] en restituer, pour ainsi dire, la partie perdue" ("complete history and restore, so to speak, its missing parts") (*Opere* 5.3: 126).

Unlike fiction, historical writing represents the medium that can provide a reconciliation between formal unity, historical accuracy, and socioideological commitment. The *Storia della Colonna Infame* is the most striking example of this total commitment. In this sense, Manzoni foreshadows some of the findings of twentieth-century historiography, namely, the French school of the *Annales d'histoire économique et sociale.* These historians, and Fernand Braudel in particular, elaborate a theory of historiography as the study of the full human phenomenon, stressing social, economic, political, and cultural conditions. This implies that the history of the "individual" is replaced by a notion of social history in which "groups, categories, classes, town and country, bourgeois, artisans, peasants, and workers become the collective heroes of history" (Ricoeur, *Contribution* 10).

By abandoning the writing of the historical tragedies for the rich plurality of voices of the novel, Manzoni makes a choice similar to that of the *Annales* historians, a choice that stresses the mutual relations and the dialectical exchanges among the various levels of historical, social, and even geographical realities. The essay *Del romanzo storico* is not simply a critique and rejection of *I promessi sposi* in particular and historical fiction in general. The essay theorizes the methods of historical representation that are already implicit within the pages of Manzoni's great novel. Indeed, the two texts must be viewed not in opposition to each other, but rather in a relation of dialogic exchange. Within the teleological framework of *I promessi sposi,* Manzoni explores a variety of specific interpretative historical systems as well. The past may be stored away in an antiquarian fashion, and Manzoni offers an implicit comment on it through the ironic portrayal of Don Ferrante and his library. History may also be grasped through a deterministic scheme, and Gertrude's story, with its merciless logic of evil, is the prime example. The deterministic pattern can be overturned by providential *coups de théâtre,* or by mere chance occurrences, as revealed by the fiancés' changes of fortune after the Unnamed's conversion. While Renzo's adventures in the riots of Milan demonstrate the interaction between an individual person and dramatic historical events, Lucia's private story in the closed spaces of the convent and the Unnamed's castle relate the clash between public circumstances and private sufferings.

Providence, in Manzoni's view, takes the place of the ancient *merveilleux* by opposing a simply deterministic historical development and by defining a teleological framework that rejects all negative determinism in the novel. Lucia's simple philosophy at the end of the novel, endorsed by both Renzo and the "Moralist" as representing "il sugo di tutta la storia" ("the very essence of the whole story") (*Opere* 2.1: 673), is a quintessential expression of a teleologically oriented philosophy of history.[40] This philosophy states the belief in a divine master plan and in a "'positive' future or 'end of history' in whose name you might be expected to be willing to sacrifice your own present" (Jameson, *Ideologies* 154). For Manzoni, Providence itself, as the expression of a divine will, is transhistorical, but one can only experience its intervention in historical reality—that is, in the ways it bears on and is borne upon by human free will. Although in his novel Manzoni exploits a concept of Universal History that he directly inherited from Giambattista Vico's idea of an "ideal eternal history traversed in time by the histories of all nations" (6), this abstract concept becomes "history" for him only by coming to terms with human choices. In other words, there might be a universal pattern, an ideal plan for actual events, but such a pattern does not predetermine human action. What finally counts is the subject's choice among a variety of possibilities. In *I promessi sposi,* Manzoni juxtaposes different possibilities of systematizing the past, and thus highlights the historiographers' interpretative responsibilities and the constructive options regarding the organization of the raw materials of history. What is finally accessible to us, for Manzoni, is neither the providential plan, which can only be inferred, nor history as master text or master narrative, but rather history in its textual and narrative form—in other words, what we approach by way of "textualization or narrative (re)construction" (Jameson, *Ideologies* 150). Although Manzoni does not discard the teleological orientation of Universal History, he is firmly committed to studying the particular time span of individuals' historical intervention and their margin of free choice in the providential framework. This also implies examining the free play of chance and relativity within the boundaries of this framework and exploring the ways in which fortuitous happenings and the contradictions of history affect the lives of individuals, provoking suffering and changes in the conditions of their material existence before being solved in the long span of providential time.

In the foreword to *I promessi sposi,* through the parodistic imitation of the redundancies and convoluted similes of seventeenth-century narrative style, Manzoni expresses his idea of historiography as follows:

> L'Historia si può veramente deffinire una guerra illustre contro il Tempo, perchè togliendoli di mano gl'anni suoi prigionieri, anzi già fatti cadaueri, li richiama in vita, li passa in rassegna, e li schiera di nuovo in battaglia. (*Opere* 2.1: 3; see appendix 17)

Historians are indeed the custodians of the past. Unlike Zaiotti, Manzoni endorses a form of historiography according to which "*historicity* as such is manifested, by means of the contact between the historian's mind in the present and a given synchronic cultural complex from the past" (Jameson, *Ideologies* 157). This historiography initially stresses the "difference" or gap between past events and present sensibilities that, according to Jameson, is the source of "aesthetic appreciation and recreation" (*Ideologies* 157). However, Manzoni's use of a convoluted and archaic style also performs a sort of "estranging" function in Šklovskij's sense of the term (Hawkes 62–63). This style defamiliarizes the past by dissociating current from prior expressive modes, while the perception of the past as unmediated otherness demands a heightened awareness on the reader's part.

A provocation of the reader's curiosity establishes the first contact between present interpreter and past situation. By subsequently abandoning the archaic style, Manzoni exorcises this past strangeness through the more familiar forms of nineteenth-century discourse. The stylistic change stages the move from absolute otherness to sympathetic reappropriation. Similarly, Collingwood theorizes a notion of historiography as reenactment of the past, a way to close the gap between past and present, to establish a connection between these two poles (215). At the same time, Manzoni makes it very clear that it is discourse itself (in its two forms of seventeenth- and nineteenth-century stylistic options) that allows for the contact between past object and present subject. As Michel de Certeau observes, language "'authorizes' the historian's writing, but, for the same reason it becomes history's absent figure" (2). The stylistic change in Manzoni's foreword to *I promessi sposi* stages the way in which the present historiographer subsumes the uncanny otherness of the past into some form of identity, thus originating a dialectical exchange between two historical worlds.

Manzoni also recognizes that once antiquarianism is abandoned for the juxtaposition of past cultural objects and present subjective interpretations, "[e]ach pole of this experience is . . . at once open to complete relativization" (Jameson, *Ideologies* 159). One option would be stressing the logic of the historical object alone, the other highlighting instead the subject's experience of this object. The first choice brings us back to antiquarianism, or to a simple reflectionist theory. The other risks losing the object (the past does not exist) in order to exclusively emphasize the subject's representation or reconstruction of that past, resulting in what Paul Ricoeur terms the logic of "unreal constructions" (*Contribution* 7). Bringing this interpretation to its logical extremes means agreeing that there are as many "pasts" as there are subjects who reformulate them. Although this critical posture leads to absolute relativism, it does take into consideration the sociopolitical dimension in which the historian operates and, therefore, the impact of the historiographer's interpretative forms on the reconstruction of past events.

Accepting the fact that the past is available only by means of written records (Manzoni's ironic rewriting of the Anonimo's manuscript) means concluding that the historiographer works exclusively on a body of *texts*. Indeed, according to de Certeau, the "violence of the body reaches the written page only through absence, through the intermediary of documents that the historian has been able to see on the sands from which a presence has since been washed away" (3). Historiography itself becomes a metacritique, a writing of texts that interpret and translate other texts. Historiography, then, may end up appearing as a negative ontology of the past, in which the past only becomes the "relevant absent" (de Certeau 3–6). Facts exist only in and through plots in which they take the importance imposed upon them by the historiographer's logic. Once this extreme is reached, all links with lived experience are cut, and history becomes "a bookish, not an existential, notion" and an "intellectual activity that, through time-honored literary forms, serves the aims of mere curiosity" (Veyne 72, 81). Significantly, while stressing the different layers of textuality between past and present, in *I promessi sposi* Manzoni is eager to maintain an existential tie between past events, the Anonimo's story, and its *raccomodamento* by the nineteenth-century narrator. This tie is represented by the insertion of Renzo's first-person oral narration, which immediately shortens the distance between the lived past and the texts that narrate it. The moral force of history resides, for Manzoni, in its links with lived experiences, in the degree of verifiability of the historical referent, and in the indestructible distinction between the *true* and the *verisimilar:* in sum, the profoundly ethical belief that history is something more than the artificial construction of plots.

In essence, Manzoni's ambitious historical inquiry achieves two goals. In his creative efforts, and especially in *I promessi sposi,* Manzoni stages the issue of historiography's methodologies and their ideological implications by means of their dialogical coexistence and juxtaposition in the novel. *I promessi sposi,* by combining a variety of options to encode and make sense of the past, demonstrates the mind's ability to impose different kinds of formal order upon the historical process. The novel's overall structure, however, depends upon a paradigm of historical comprehension based on the harmonization of the parts of the whole and on the solutions of all contradictions in a plan under which nothing is ultimately fortuitous or arbitrary. White's comments on Herder's organicist philosophy may be directly applied to Manzoni's:

> *the plot structure* or underlying myth which permitted Herder to bind together the themes and motifs of his story into a

> comprehensible story of a particular sort was that which had its archetype in Comedy, the myth of Providence, which permitted Herder to assert that, when properly understood, all the evidence of disjunctions and conflict displayed in the historical record adds up to a drama of divine, human, and natural *reconciliation* of the sort figured in the drama of redemption in the Bible. (*Metahistory* 79)

The purifying rain that ends the drought and halts the spreading of the plague, Renzo's purgatorial forgiving of Don Rodrigo, and Father Cristoforo's freeing Lucia from her vow of chastity achieve exactly the three-tiered reconciliation that coronates the comedy's optimistic conclusion.

On the theoretical grounds of the essay *Del romanzo storico,* Manzoni opts for the narrow path between, on the one hand, a positivism seeking to eliminate the historian in the name of objective history (a history already written in the documents or, in Jameson's terms, history as master narrative) and, on the other, a radical subjectivism that would claim that "there is no history; there are only historians."[41] For Manzoni, the truth about the past is necessarily twofold: it is composed of both past evidence and evidence about the historian. In this sense, the historian is neither a parasite nor a demiurge. Like contemporary historian Henri-Irénée Marrou, Manzoni claims that history is knowledge insofar as it clarifies the relationship between the experiential past and the historian's interpretative grids. These interpretative grids are the means by which the experiential and documentary past is configured into a historical narrative, and they conduct the hermeneutical effort to approach two levels of truth.

The first level is absolute, as it identifies the overarching providential scheme that justifies, in transcendental terms, the course of human history. The second level, instead, is relative, as it portrays the variety of the documentary and experiential pasts with the colors of the historians' specific times and cultures. In his polemical progression from fiction to history, then, Manzoni implies that the historian's reconstruction of the past has an epistemological value as long as it highlights what de Certeau calls "deviation" and Ricoeur terms "deductive modification" (*The Reality* 22–23). By stressing the historian's intervention—that is, the area of the *discours* over the narrated *histoire*—Manzoni emphasizes his awareness of the dialectical interplay between past factuality, present hermeneutics, and reader responses and interpretations. At the same time, he explains the ideological necessity to keep the level of *discours* separated from that of *histoire*.[42] With one voice and tense (third person, past tense) historians produce the objective plot of history, while with another voice and tense (first person, present tense) they provide all those personal conjectures, comments, and judgments that define the subject's interpretative freedom within a teleological scheme that remains untouched by ideological relativism and the transformations of historical understanding.

Like Tommaseo, Manzoni both recognizes the relativity of historical reconfigurations and keeps this relativity in check by posing a limit to the otherwise endless proliferation of interpretative models and narrative discourses through his belief in a totalizing historical law. This law accounts for the connection between ethics and epistemology. It is the historian's moral duty, Manzoni feels, to illuminate the course from relativity to totality, making the intellectual leap (or, in another perspective, the intuitional act of faith) from mere historical chance to providential fatality. Free of all fictional and conventional webs that had entangled the novel, Manzoni's new historiography exploits the novel's narrative strategies to explain the multifarious variety as well as the "true" order of history. Historiography, with Manzoni, gains not only philosophical status, as it did with Tommaseo, but also aesthetic excellence. The experience of the historical novel allowed Manzoni to establish a connection between ethics and aesthetics. The Anonimo's "bella storia" proves that, among the many possible ways of emplotting the past, some are formally better, and morally truer, than others. Philosophical speculation applied to narrative practice becomes a discussion on the ethical and ideological significance of formal experimentation. Manzoni's sophisticated craft of fiction (and history) makes him a theoretician/practitioner of the stature of Henry James and T. S. Eliot, and the precursor to the self-conscious narrative investigations of twentieth-century writers.

The twentieth century's decline of metaphysical certainties and totalizing philosophical systems has restored legitimacy to the genre of the historical novel. Rejecting the faith in an apodictically certain mode of historical reconfiguration, contemporary writers are aware that there are multiple, and contending, *formalizations* that both fictional and historical narratives may exploit to make sense of the past, while knowing that these strategies have no absolute epistemological guarantee (none of them is truer or more realistic than the other), and that our choice will ultimately have to be made on aesthetic and/or moral grounds (H. White, *Metahistory* xii). Manzoni's reflection upon the ideological, ethical, and aesthetic significance of narrative discourse as form of historical representation constitutes the legacy that he bestowed upon writers as diverse as Lampedusa, Morante, and Eco.

Chapter Two

Historical Reconfigurations and the Ideology of Desire

Giuseppe Tomasi di Lampedusa's *Il Gattopardo*

Quand par les soirs d'été le ciel harmonieux gronde comme une bête fauve et que chacun boude l'orage, c'est au côté de Méséglise que je dois de rester seul en extase à respirer, à travers le bruit de la pluie qui tombe, l'odeur d'invisibles et persistants lilas.

Marcel Proust
Du côté de chez Swann
See appendix 18

In a letter dated 2 January 1957 to his friend Guido Lajolo, Giuseppe Tomasi di Lampedusa denied that *Il Gattopardo* was a historical novel. Although the novel refers to Garibaldi's landing in Sicily and depicts an episode from the Unification of Italy, Lampedusa suggested that *Il Gattopardo* provided more of a semiautobiographical narrative than a truthful depiction of nineteenth-century characters and situations (Vitello 229–30).[1] Rather than negating the novel's historical setting, Lampedusa's claim that *Il Gattopardo* is a kind of *autobiografia romanzata* demonstrates that historical fiction inevitably reveals its author's choices—both aesthetic and ideological—in the shaping of past reality and stresses the continual interrelationship between past stories and present discourses. Lampedusa does not offer a chronicle-like, naturalistic reproduction of the past; rather, he discloses the subjective filters and processes of construction and selection that organize current renditions of historical events. *Il Gattopardo* is not an antiquarian novel, capturing the exotic lore of bygone times and the uncanny remoteness of the past. Unlike antiquarian fiction, *Il Gattopardo* does not solve the problem of the relationship between past and present by abolishing the present and presenting the textualized past as the neutral and unproblematic translation of lived history.

Il Gattopardo is a truly historical novel engaged in a dialectical exchange between historical events and present interpretations. The novel self-consciously addresses the nature of present ideologies in the shaping of past realities while pointing to the role of subjectivity in the reconfiguration of the past. Historical knowledge, Lampedusa argues through *Il Gattopardo,* does not exist within the historical object, but is constructed and continuously transformed by present interpreters: the historical text constitutes a testimonial about the historian as well as a tribute to the past. Far from being inscribed once and for all in the materiality of the historical document, the truth of the historical past is not an absolute notion but, rather, is embedded in the historicity of its multiple interpreters, subject to the changes of institutions and individuals, and disseminated among a variety of hermeneutical practices and conscious and even unconscious responses to the historical scene.

Il Gattopardo explores the combination of fiction and history, particularly in relation to the ways in which history is emplotted and fictionalized. The novel's complex structural order, with its use of analogical schemes and patterns of repetition, can be read as a writerly response, alternative to the exclusively causal logic of traditional historical writing. *Il Gattopardo* explores the epistemological value of its own textual reconfigurations and highlights their ideological significance. Thus, Lampedusa demonstrates that a novel's ideology is not simply entrusted to its thematic content but pertains to its structural order as well. This is particularly significant as *Il Gattopardo,* one of Italy's *casi letterari,*[2] elicited a number of contradictory and polemical responses ranging from being praised as ideologically progressive to being attacked for delivering reactionary messages (Lucente, "*Scrivere*" 220–30; Gilmour 185–93).

Neorealism, Neo-avantgarde, and *Il Gattopardo*

Long after the odyssey of the manuscript's rejections[3] and eventual publication by Feltrinelli in 1958,[4] *Il Gattopardo* continued to puzzle its critics, provoking polemical and often tendentious arguments among its interpreters. Italian Marxist critics and the literary left rejected the novel's apparent denial of progress and dismissed it as a reactionary text cynically acquiescing in the status quo. Catholic intellectuals equally disliked *Il Gattopardo*'s pessimism and its distressing spiritual emptiness (Gilmour 186).[5] Like Italo Svevo's novels, *Il Gattopardo* found its approval abroad. The 1959 French edition received an "enthusiastic reception" (Gilmour 188), as did the British edition later in the same year.[6]

Il Gattopardo fostered so much critical disagreement because it came to light in a period of transition. Throughout the 1950s, the fate of realism in art was being assessed by the leading Italian intellectuals. These critics called into question the future of the novel, and redefined from multiple ideological perspectives the duties and limits of sociopolitical commitment in art and criticism. While critics carefully sifted the achievements and the failures of neorealism, the "objective flux" (Calvino, "Il mare" 9) of the French *école du regard* and the *nouveaux romans* of Michel Butor, Alain Robbe-Grillet, and Nathalie Sarraute intrigued Italian critics and novelists alike.[7] The rising neo-avantgarde, unlike its historical predecessor, did not theatrically reject all of the past, but rather subjected the past to a critical, if often harsh, reconsideration.[8] At the same time critics closer to the neorealist arena were involved in a similar reevaluation, which failed, however, to offer convincing solutions to many of the pressing issues of the day. While the neo-avantgarde challenged the value of objectivity in art and examined the ideological import of artists' selective choices in their aesthetic reshaping of experience, neorealist intellectuals seemed mired in an unpromising and often pedantic revisitation of traditional realist aesthetic principles. Such interpretative turmoil brought some confusion to the literary debates of the time, but this was a time of transition, of assessment of past experiences, and of groping experimentation with new forms and new themes. Almost inevitably, as in every attempt to draw a balance, shades and details were lost in favor of the broader picture. The debates that filled the magazines of that decade demonstrate that critical and ideological positions tended to be radicalized against those of opponents.

In spite of a widespread tendency to quickly dismiss the neorealist era as dead and gone, the intellectuals of the 1950s were forced to come to terms with its legacy. One of the most controversial topics was the problem of writers' political commitment as expressed in their literary works.[9] In the 1956 issue, entirely devoted to the future of the novel, the magazine *Ulisse* included, among others, an article by Armanda Guiducci entitled "La problematica politico-sociale nella nostra narrativa" ("The Sociopolitical Problems in Our Fiction"). According to Guiducci, the neorealist era had fostered an intensified awareness of the ideological, cultural, and sociopolitical dimensions of modern literature. After neorealism, Guiducci argues, a literary work can no longer be produced as if in a vacuum, but must directly express its ideology. This political elaboration of the novel, Guiducci continues, is built around the two opposing structures of Marxist and bourgeois interpretations of reality. Reflecting either of these structures, the modern novel is an ideologically oriented exploration of a number of significant relationships: people and reality; society and the state; moral, political, social life and art. Despite the strong premises in her argument, Guiducci simplifies the problem of ideological commitment in art because of her own biased reading of twenty years of Italian literature as the ordered and progressive *presa di coscienza* (witness the fall of Benedetto Croce's idealism and the rise of Antonio Gramsci's materialism) of the socio-ideological nature of artistic representations, marking the inexorable growth from the self to objective reality and from objective reality to the historical world (987–97). In spite of her one-sided Marxist interpretation, Guiducci's essay is significant for illustrating the kinds of problems that Italian intellectuals faced during the 1950s and early 1960s and that contributed to the critical turmoil surrounding *Il Gattopardo.*

If Guiducci concentrates on what she considers the exclusively political nature of the novel, Pier Paolo Pasolini addresses the writer's opposing needs for aesthetic freedom and political responsibility, and in an important article published in the magazine *Officina* in 1958, he defines his own position in what he terms the "neo-experimental" arena.[10] Experimentalism, in Pasolini's terms, becomes a form of ideological independence, a way of facing reality free of predetermined ideological grids:

> Il suo fine . . . è di abolire alle origini ogni forma di "posizionalismo," in una verifica continua, in una lotta continua

> contro la latente tendenziosità. . . . Questo stesso spirito filologico presiede dunque anche all'atteggiamento politico, al nostro difficile, doloroso e anche umiliante atteggiamento d'indipendenza, che non può accettare nessuna forma storica e pratica di ideologia, e che insieme soffre, come d'un rimorso, d'un indistinto e irrazionale trauma morale, per l'esclusione da ogni prassi, o comunque, dall'azione. ("La libertà" 346; see appendix 19)

Pasolini's *anti-posizionalismo* as a form of ideological noncommitment causes literature to become the choice of an "ethos" rather than a well-defined political ideology, thus promoting cultural independence and aesthetic autonomy from the political sphere. In this regard, Angelo Romanò explains that such autonomy has been generally obstructed in several neorealist works by the artists' refusals to reshape aesthetically the pressing ideological content of their writing (174–75). Romanò expresses the need for a stronger stylistic and formal elaboration in art, and Pasolini maintains that this goal is achieved by the fusion of post-hermetic stylistic freedom with neorealist sociopolitical commitment ("Il neo-sperimentalismo" 170).

The discussion of political engagement in literature, and conversely of purely ideological interpretations of literary texts, arises directly from the critical assessment of the neorealist era in Italy. However, the debate during the same period involved a much wider arena. In 1956 in the *London Magazine,* Philip Toynbee published an article significantly entitled "Experiment and the Future of the Novel." In the United Kingdom the Jamesian tradition of the "craft of fiction"—of formal analysis, that is, delving into questions of narrative techniques and creative craftsmanship—was so widespread that Toynbee felt compelled to remind his fellow critics that exclusively methodological issues should not hide other concerns of an ideological, moral, philosophical, or psychological nature. Toynbee believed, in other words, that for the critic the analysis of "how to do something" must be subordinated to the "what to do" and "why to do it."

The record of critical interpretations of *Il Gattopardo* reveals that Italy's critical world during those years was at the opposite pole from England's. Yet the comparison between Toynbee and Pasolini is worth making because, in spite of their different backgrounds, they shared similar views regarding the issue of the artist's commitment. Toynbee, in fact, found it necessary to argue for a subtle distinction between "engagement" and "concern":

> Engagement demands that the novelist should be left-wing, and preferably communist in his views; that he should expound such views in his novels; . . . that his books should be intelligible to those who are totally uneducated in the history and development of the novel. (52)

Concern comes to represent, therefore, an intellectual openness toward reality: an interpretative attitude that is still interested in "the present situation of ourselves, our neighbours and our society" (Toynbee 52) but which is not narrowly limited by a predetermined ideological bias. The move from engagement to concern implies, in Toynbee's view, a shift from traditional techniques and subject-matters to "new methods, new ideas, new sensitivities and new material" (53). Without Pasolini's ambivalence toward *anti-posizionalismo,* Toynbee defines experimentalism as the creative combination of ideological "concern" and formal innovation, and sees in J. D. Salinger's *The Catcher in the Rye* (1951) one of its most successful manifestations. In the wake of these discussions, Angelo Guglielmi, who became one of the major exponents of the neo-avantgarde, advocates the need to speak "a tu per tu con la realtà" ("face to face with reality") ("Il nuovo 'realismo'" 9). Guglielmi argues that, especially in the highly idealized Italian tradition, direct contact with reality is systematically prevented by preestablished sets of ideological and aesthetic screens. Like Toynbee, Guglielmi underscores the close relationship between formal innovation and ideological freedom. The novelty of form becomes therefore a prerequisite for liberating content from all ideological, stylistic, and sentimental predefinitions.[11]

In spite of the critical turmoil over the issue of commitment in art and the consequent call for a more pliable ideological attitude, a survey of the criticism of *Il Gattopardo* reveals largely political readings of the text. "È una Sicilia senza astratti furori, e senza sindacalisti" ("It is a Sicily without abstract furies and without trade-unionists") (248), Franco Fortini complains, making an obvious reference to Elio Vittorini's *Conversazione in Sicilia* (*In Sicily,* 1941) and reducing the whole novel to the political bias of its protagonist, Fabrizio Corbera, Prince of Salina, whom he identifies with the author himself. Since *Il Gattopardo* praises recurrence rather than historical change, Fortini argues, it can only be considered a reactionary creation of the right (248–51). "Non siamo più agli attivi, eroici furori" ("We are no longer dealing with abstract, heroic furies"), Geno Pampaloni immediately retorts, reading the novel as the ideological product of a cynical society that is desperately observing its own conformism and is self-consciously aware of its indifference toward the movements of history ("Destra e sinistra" 90). Louis Aragon argues instead that *Il Gattopardo* is the deliberate, and therefore political, representation of the aristocracy's decadence. This representation results from a writer engaging in a pitiless critique of his own class, and this critique, Aragon concludes, can only be "di sinistra" (224).[12] The arguments over what Pampaloni aptly calls "destra e sinistra in letteratura" ("right and left in literature") (88) are, in the case of *Il Gattopardo,* practically innumerable. Suffice it to say that the history of Lampedusa criticism reveals the emergence of two related problems: the first discloses a critical attitude that is exclusively bound to define a novel ideologically, and the second demonstrates that this ideological definition is limited to a content reading of the text in question. This results in a blindness or, at best, a superficial approach to the ideologies of form.[13]

Inverting Toynbee's claim, one might easily argue that the kind of formal analysis that the Russian formalists had introduced in the 1920s was quite alien to Italian criticism in the late 1950s and early 1960s. Formal concerns, however, are by no means symptoms of ideological indifference. As Terry Eagleton points out, "the true bearers of ideology in art are the very forms, rather than abstractable content, of the work itself" (24). The specificity, in other words, of the art product is maintained in the fact that "We find the impress of history in the literary work precisely *as literary,* not as some superior form of social documentation" (Eagleton 24). In arguing for the dialectical relationship between content and form, Eagleton defends the independence of the literary discourse as well as its ties to the contemporary social reality. This kind of dialectical reading, however, was never practiced by critics of *Il Gattopardo,* who showed, as Tom O'Neill aptly puts it, an "extraordinary lack of sophistication" (181).

* * *

The one-dimensional ideological discussion of *Il Gattopardo* originated a series of critical fallacies. The ideology of the novel was generally identified with that of its protagonist, Prince Fabrizio of Salina, and that of Prince Fabrizio with the author's. Moreover, a number of facts related to Lampedusa's social and literary background engendered a biased and distorted interpretation of his novel, branding it as the solitary achievement of a reactionary aristocrat, one totally estranged from the social reality of his time. Lampedusa has traditionally been regarded as oblivious to discussions of an ideological or aesthetic nature. A Sicilian aristocrat from a formerly prosperous noble family, Lampedusa was for temperamental as well as obvious geographical reasons quite isolated from Italian intellectual society. His sole appearance at a literary conference, at San Pellegrino Terme in July 1954, astonished the northern literati, who observed a "bizarre trio" (Lampedusa, his cousin the poet Lucio Piccolo, and a servant) awkwardly trying to mingle with the crowd. Exactly like its author, *Il Gattopardo* could, at least at first, excite amused curiosity for its oddness rather than sympathetic interest for its modernity. If Lampedusa's personal estrangement from the contemporary literary world cannot be disputed, it is intriguing to consider whether *Il Gattopardo*—generally regarded as the casual creation of a literary novice—may indeed offer a valuable response, albeit indirectly, to the literary queries of that period.

Recent studies, revising previous interpretations, have demonstrated that Lampedusa was much more than a snobbish amateur. He had an impressive literary background; was well read in French, German, and English, and later Spanish and a little Russian; and by his mid-fifties he regretted that "he had read almost everything" (Gilmour 107). If he despised complicated theoretical criticism, he was nevertheless very interested in the theory of fiction, especially in issues dealing with the handling of fictional time, point of view and characterization, narrative voice, and literary style. Lampedusa's first passion, however, was history, not literature, and he closely followed the French historiographers of the *Ecole des Annales.* From the *Annales* historians, Lampedusa derived the belief that the knowledge of historical facts is inevitably enmeshed with the knowledge of the historian's analytical and interpretative procedures. Fernand Braudel inspired Lampedusa with his notion of the plural character of historical times. The traditional time of history—the time of the individual and of the single historical event—must come to terms, in Braudel's theorization, with the "long duration" of social groups, the "gentle rhythms" of cultural attitudes, and the almost unchangeable "geographical time" that marks the relations of innumerable generations with their surroundings (3–4). As we shall see, *Il Gattopardo* is, in its fictional elaboration, an exploration of different layers of experiential and narrative times, ranging from the time of single historic occurrences to the protagonist's personal time of memory, and from the geographic time of a changeless, almost mythical Sicily to the very specific time of the text—the overt narrator's a posteriori reconstruction of the story.[14]

Because he never directly concerned himself with the most vexing literary issues of his day and remained estranged, both in theory and in practice, from the debates involving the fate of "social realism" and the future of neo-avantgarde experimentalism, Lampedusa was subject to an odd critical fate. On the one hand, his novel was dismissed as an ill-timed occurrence, belonging to a time past and utterly unrelated to current literary productions; on the other hand, *Il Gattopardo* became the pretext for several partisan discussions regarding the issues of commitment in art and the future of the novel. Unfortunately, all of these discussions ignored the specificity of Lampedusa's text as an original response to the much-debated issue of the ideology of aesthetic representation within the framework of historical fiction.

* * *

By the 1950s, Marxists were faced with the failure to establish a socialist society in Europe. The technological developments of neocapitalism, the massive economic support offered by the United States, and the resulting economic boom, demanded a reexamination of Marxist ideology and a new critical awareness of changing socioeconomic realities after the harsh years of postwar reconstruction. The ideological crisis was accompanied by concern, among intellectuals, with the failure to establish a durable cultural hegemony. For some of the prominent Italian Marxist critics, however, this *esame di coscienza* did not translate itself into a revision of their aesthetic views, which for the most part remained anchored to Lukács's principles of aesthetic composition. The Marxist critic Mario Alicata, in particular, in an article significantly entitled "Il principe di Lampedusa e il Risorgimento Siciliano" ("The Prince of Lampedusa and the Sicilian Risorgimento") written for *Il Contemporaneo,* accused Lampedusa of failing to objectively represent the Italian Risorgimento. In the wake of Lukács's literary theories, Alicata claimed that *Il Gattopardo* lacked "ampiezza di visione storica" ("broadness of historical view") (340–41). Instead of offering a critical interpretation of the Risorgimento's historical process, Lampedusa had provided an arbitrary, unilateral, and finally unacceptable deformation that only stressed its limits:

> Una cosa è . . . rifiutarsi di trasformare la storia del Risorgimento nell'agiografia e oleografia di un "miracolo dell'Italo patriottismo," un'altra cosa ignorare, puramente e semplicemente, la somma di idee, di sentimenti, di passioni che quella storia contribuirono a realizzare, e, in primo luogo, delle idee, dei sentimenti, delle passioni legati alla formazione di una coscienza nazionale. (342; see appendix 20)

More specifically, Lampedusa was accused of not including in his historical representation a number of significant events, including the peasants' rebellions and repressions in the inland regions, the political problems caused by Garibaldi's "dictatorship" and by the Savoy government, the internal fights within Garibaldi's army, the diplomatic intrigues involving Mazzini's and Cavour's emissaries with English agents and Bourbon spies, and the final inability of the Partito d'Azione to give a Jacobin appearance to the "Italian revolution." In choosing to filter the historical events through the subjective consciousness of his protagonist, Alicata argued, Lampedusa had inevitably sacrificed the realistic creed of inclusion to a very idiosyncratic, highly selective, ironically detached, and incurably pessimistic historical interpretation. Alicata thus implicitly rejected Giorgio

Bassani's view of *Il Gattopardo.* In his preface to the first edition of the novel, Bassani asserted, without elaboration, that *Il Gattopardo*'s value resided in its "ampiezza di visione storica unita a un'acutissima percezione della realtà sociale e politica dell'Italia contemporanea" ("broadness of historical view combined with an acute perception of the sociopolitical reality of contemporary Italy") (11).

The dismissal of *Il Gattopardo* in the pages of *Il Contemporaneo* paralleled a wider analysis of the problem of realism in fiction and a discussion of the relation between Marxism and literature that involved both Alicata and Carlo Salinari. Accepting the inevitable fact that realism—especially in the form of "militant humanism"—was undergoing a profound crisis, Salinari attempted to revive a positive form of realism in the face of what he took to be its degeneration. While rejecting the anarchic, anguished, apocalyptic, and despairing expressions that ended up either in an absolute subjectivism or in a mysticism of the object, he nevertheless defended what he termed "rational realism," and in accordance with Alicata he supported an impartial view of reality, that is, an integral view of contemporary times.[15] In this sense, however, both Alicata and Salinari did not diverge much from a traditional Lukácsian critical perspective. According to the Hungarian critic, in fact, a literary work must provide an objective representation of reality as an integrated totality in its profound organic wholeness. The structural harmony and the narrative completeness of great realist masterpieces faithfully mirror the inner order of reality itself.[16] The realist writer delves beyond the superficial and the accidental and reaches the core of specific social situations, selecting and organizing them into a total form. But, in spite of these premises, neither Alicata nor Salinari reached the heart of the matter: namely, whether Italian literature was, at that particular moment, able or willing to fulfill that requirement and, eventually, what kind of different solution an atypical book like *Il Gattopardo* could have achieved.

Raffaele Crovi took a bold view when he stated, in an article dedicated to the neo-avantgarde, that postwar Italian fiction had failed to complete the historical exploration that it had set out to do. Sharing both Alicata's and Salinari's Lukácsian views, Crovi maintained that most literary works dealing with the war and the Resistance had not provided a "historic" (i.e., objective) representation of these events but had offered, instead, their celebrative, didactic, and pamphletary distortions (262). *Il Gattopardo* no doubt constituted an obvious, if late, exception to this trend, since it contributed to the demystification of both the Unification of Italy and, by analogy, the Reunification as resulting from the Resistance's popular and collective fight.[17] Surprisingly enough, Crovi chose not to mention Lampedusa's successful novel: to a shaky leftist intelligentsia the criticism of a pessimistic monarchist was, clearly, not welcome.

The change that Crovi, together with Salinari and Alicata, promoted was not so much a revision of current realistic theories of aesthetic representation, as a more superficial correction, on the mere content level, of those "realistic" illustrations coated with naive utopian optimism that had characterized Italian literary production of the mid-1940s.[18] Salinari argued for a "rational art" that would integrate "modern desperation" with all of the other aspects of reality (Manacorda 243). Again in the wake of Lukács's humanism, Salinari subsumed the subjective, psychosocial category of the individual's alienation under the broader philosophic and aesthetic category of its sublimation into a harmonious picture of the whole of modern times. While the relationship between subject and history in a particularly critical moment, and the reconfiguration of this relationship in the aesthetic form of a novel, are in fact the key issues of *Il Gattopardo,* these points were neglected because the novel was prematurely crushed by two destructive critiques. First, *Il Gattopardo* was found guilty of giving the *coup de grâce* to neorealist fiction, replacing the hagiographic portrayals of the heroic moments of Italian history with their skeptical deconstruction; and second, as Alicata's comments demonstrate, *Il Gattopardo*'s rendering of the historical facts was dismissed as incomplete, one-sided, pessimistically cyclical, and cynically contrary to the notion of history's progressive course.

Salinari expressed his opinions on *Il Gattopardo* in *Vie nuove.* While he argued that the novel's thesis about historical change ("if we want things to stay as they are, things will have to change") was in itself simplistic, borrowing Leonardo Sciascia's own term *qualunquistica,* he was also aware of the subtle ironic manipulation of this thesis in the pages of the novel (46). A discussion of the use of subjective irony in a historical narrative could have established the modernity of *Il Gattopardo* by relating the aesthetic solutions it provided to the literary concerns of those years, yet Salinari chose not to develop his interesting point. This was partly due to the weight of Vittorini's influential dismissal of Lampedusa's novel. According to Vittorini, *Il Gattopardo* provided a mere reflection of society, without attempting either to change or to criticize it, but, worse, crystallizing it into a pessimistic pattern of circular repetition. In other words, Vittorini contended, Lampedusa had given an inert and mechanistic reproduction of a specific segment of social reality, which had failed to become typical (in Lukács's meaning of the word) and which was neither comprehensive nor, ultimately, instructive (9).

Intervening in the debate, Marxist critic and writer Aragon reacted against those who were, in his words, merely deceived by the "appearance of the novel," insisting, rather, that *Il Gattopardo* did not simply portray the decadence of Sicilian aristocracy but gave a conscious and political image of that decadence. In the tradition of Engel's comments on Balzac, Lenin's arguments about Tolstoy, and Lukács's on Scott, Aragon warned his readers against a mechanical superimposition of authors' ideologies over the artistic truth they manage to achieve (226).[19] Despite Aragon's comments, however, the debate over *Il Gattopardo* soon stalled over an unresolved *querelle* between those who considered it an example of social realism and those who claimed that it was a subproduct of decadent bourgeois realism.

More recently, Gregory Lucente has reopened the question in the same terms: "does *Il Gattopardo* merely describe the period of the Risorgimento in Sicily without seriously examining or questioning the ideologically determined, class-oriented motivations of historical characters and events, . . . or does the novel provide not only a narrative of nineteenth-century history and historical processes but also a running critique of that history . . . and then demonstrate a commitment to, or at least a challenge regarding historical change?" ("*Scrivere*" 226). While the question is well posed, the history of Lampedusa criticism shows that the answer was thwarted by a reading of the book as a mere political phenomenon, subjected to broad ideological generalizations that made it either a reactionary creation of the right or a subversive achievement of the left. If the opposing interpretations were in fact rooted in a basic disagreement over two contrasting ideologies of historical representation in the text (i.e., critical or decadent realism), the response was reached only through a superficial content reading of the book.

Il Gattopardo's formal complexity, as well as its ideological implications, were never recognized nor taken into serious consideration by Italian critics in general. However, from the perspective of a dialectical interplay between the formal organization and its ideological import, *Il Gattopardo* had much to say in the debate over the future of the novel and the evolution of historical realism. While *Il Gattopardo* is, for obvious reasons, quite unlike the experimental achievements of the neoavantgarde, it is certainly not bound to a simple reflectionist theory. In its unclassical form *Il Gattopardo* represents an attempt to combine the causal and chronological narrative frame of a traditional historical account with the subjective and analogical patterns of mnemonic reconfigurations of the past. At the same time, the creation of memorable characters and the linear and progressive reconstruction of significant historical events (Prince Fabrizio and the Unification of Italy) are dramatically juxtaposed against broader historical and social trends. These trends include the progressive fall of the aristocracy and the rise of the middle class, set against the background of Sicily as both a sociogeographic reality and a mythical, immutable natural landscape.

* * *

Before embarking on a discussion of the ways in which formal structures direct the ideology of a novel and, more specifically, before analyzing the ways in which historical realities are filtered through subjective channels in *Il Gattopardo,* one should note that even the most insightful critics of traditional realism overlooked Lampedusa's innovations. Shortly before the publication of *Il Gattopardo,* Remo Cantoni attempted to overcome the crisis of the Italian novel by reformulating the concept of realism in literature. According to Cantoni, the switch from the well-made novel to avant-garde experimentalism was the inevitable result of trying to adapt new expressive methods to new perceptions of reality. If modern civilization is undergoing a crisis in its values and institutions, Cantoni argues, if reality appears distorted and contradictory and lacks fixed meaning, and if the self is also part of material reality, then the unrelated, chaotic rendering of an interior flux, unmediated by secondary interpretative grids or by external ideological structures, is in itself a form of realism. Paradoxically, in order to overcome the crisis of realism, Cantoni makes of realism itself an all-encompassing label, including, for example, both the social chronicles of Malraux and Dos Passos and the personal chronicles of Joyce and Kafka (968–77). This attempt at reconciliation is flawed, as it completely overlooks the different ideological positions at the bases of these authors' formal representations of reality.

One ideology promotes the view that literature's ultimate goal should be the restoration of a full humanism wherein human beings are, once again, able to comprehend and master material reality. Consciousness is regarded as an active force that penetrates beneath superficial experiences and allows the understanding, and representation, of the categories that direct and explain the course of history. This critical perspective, deriving from Hegelian and Lukácsian aesthetics (Eagleton 27–31), rejects neo-avantgarde experimentalism because it is based on the absolute degradation of the human condition: rather than disclosing the sociohistorical causes of modern alienation, neo-avantgarde writers consider alienation a universal state—an eternal, and therefore inescapable, human infirmity. According to its detractors, the neo-avantgarde has renounced all forms of historical analysis and has concentrated, instead, on an atypical reality of neurotic situations and traumatic events (Crovi 261).

On the other side, the followers of neo-avantgarde experimentalism argue that, since modern society has depersonalized the individual, human consciousness is nonreflective and dispersed into mechanical actions rather that constructed through self-analysis. The era of technology is responsible for this alienated state. Trying to provide images of human wholeness is an act of bad faith. By depicting a mediocre and semiconscious human condition, steeped in the unrelieved materiality of everyday routines, literature does not seek to provide unreal constructions, escapist dreams, or metaphysical sublimations.

Literature's only value is, therefore, a shock value—its only message, the awareness that objective reality is, indeed, an unintelligible chaos; and its only truth, the revelation that individuals are deprived of authentic selfhood, moral conscience, and historical awareness (Barilli, "Le strutture" 43–47).

Following the example of several other literary journals, Luciano Anceschi's avant-garde publication *Il Verri* dedicated a whole issue to the fate of Italian fiction in February 1960, and included Renato Barilli's "*Cahier de doléances* sull'ultima narrativa italiana" ("*Cahier de doléances* on the Most Recent Italian Fiction"). Barilli's famous article attacks neorealist fiction as unimaginative and uncritically conforming to the modes of experience accepted by the public at large. But the article's value does not reside in the harsh and polemical dismissal of all neorealist fiction. Rather, it must be sought in Barilli's attempt to draw a connection between ideological progressivism and formal innovations. The recurring claim in Barilli's critical production is that it is not enough to have progressive political views; in addition, one has to change the manner of conceiving time and space, of perceiving objects, of identifying and naming feelings, and of articulating the syntax of desire ("Le strutture" 43). By emphasizing and even expressionistically exaggerating the aspects of modern alienation and by devising new forms of representation centered on discontinuous and contradictory realities, neo-avantgarde intellectuals mediated and developed the lesson of Bertolt Brecht's experimental theater (Eagleton 63–67). Neo-avantgarde writers sought to dismantle crystallized modes of ideological perception by systematically frustrating readers' conventional expectations and, through shocking contents and unclassical forms, forced readers to critically analyze, rather than hypnotically absorb, their literary works. Neo-avantgarde experimentalism found one of its most significant expressions in Edoardo Sanguineti's *Capriccio italiano* (*Italian Caprice,* 1963), in which, significantly, the logical chains of traditionally linear narrative discourse are substituted by oneiric patterns of recurrence, analogy, and temporal simultaneity.

On this front, only critical silence was granted to *Il Gattopardo.* The radical deconstruction of traditional fictional forms attempted by the avant-garde did not deal with the more subtle experimentalism of Lampedusa's text. *Il Gattopardo,* however, is far from a return to nineteenth-century fiction. Only Luigi Blasucci had a notion of its originality. Instead of the *narrazione continua* typical of the well-made novel, Blasucci perceived that *Il Gattopardo* proceeds through a number of temporal cuts, thus juxtaposing different periods of the protagonist's existence (119). Blasucci called for an analysis that would discuss the combination of both psychological and historical narrative techniques in the novel. This analysis, however, was never completed.

Maria Corti indirectly foreshadows the reasons behind such silence when she claims that the two opposite experiences, neorealism and the neo-avantgarde, reveal similar views about subjectivity. Both engage in what Corti terms a refusal of the self:

> Nel movimento neorealistico quel processo che l'avanguardia chiama la "riduzione dell'io" non era sconosciuto, anzi considerato inconfondibile segno del nuovo di fronte alla prosa dell'anteguerra; . . . [nel neorealismo] la coscienza del singolo era emblematica della coscienza sociale. Nella neoavanguardia il problema della riduzione dell'io si fa più sottile e complesso, anche perché si prescinde a priori dal vissuto personale. . . . L'aspetto contestante qui è rivolto contro il soggettivo come categoria poetica. (*Il viaggio testuale* 120–21; see appendix 21)

Awkwardly set between the fall of neorealism and the rise of the neo-avantgarde, *Il Gattopardo* takes up the problem of the relationship between subject and reality in a moment of both personal and historical turmoil. But *Il Gattopardo* rejects both the inevitable fragmentation and dissolution of the subject that the neo-avantgarde sees as inscribed into the modern condition, and the positive, dialectical exchanges between subject and object and inner and outer worlds that neorealist critics advocated in their attempts to emphasize the links between individuals and the social whole.

Repetition and Desire as Modes of Narrative Emplotment

Il Gattopardo fits right into the median territory that stretches between neorealism and the neo-avantgarde. Arnaldo Bocelli defines this area in the pages of Bompiani's *Almanacco letterario* in 1959. Attempting one of the many overviews of postwar fiction, Bocelli quickly surveys eighteen years of Italian literature from 1941 to 1959, drawing a broad differentiation between what he labels "memorial realism" and "surrealist realism." According to Bocelli, memorial realism has degenerated into mere propaganda, ideological rhetoric, and pure social criticism of either a Marxist or a Catholic stamp. By giving up the utopian concept of objectively reproducing reality, surrealist realism, instead, has stressed the subjective shaping force inherent in the dialectical exchange between subject and object. Expressed in works such as Cesare Pavese's *Paesi tuoi* (*The Harvesters,* 1941), Elio Vittorini's *Conversazione in Sicilia* (*In Sicily,* 1941), Guido Piovene's *Lettere di una novizia* (*Confessions of a Novice,* 1942), and Romano Bilenchi's *La siccità* (*The Drought,* 1944), surrealist realism establishes itself in a central area without degenerating into either sterile subjectivism or an alienated cult of the object. This new realism, Bocelli concludes, manages to convey a reality filtered through memory, distorted in its temporal frame, even made magical in a timeless space, full of mysterious links between subject and nature, all stretched not toward the real but rather toward the ineffable essence of the real (229). In this way, Bocelli retrieves the writers' powers to shape the forms of objective experience, and to refract, deform, and even construct reality rather than symmetrically duplicate it in their literary works.

Although he addresses Lampedusa's attempt to combine the traditionally linear patterns of historical reconfiguration with the labyrinthine plays of memory and desire as alternative methods of representation, Bocelli overlooks the fact that this representation is entrusted, in the novel, to a double subjectivity. On one hand there is the narrator's subjective voice with an omniscient point of view that, from the vantage point of temporal distance, organizes a slice of history according to a very specific narrative order. This constitutes the superior aesthetic organization that the novel, by means of an overtly omniscient narrator, imposes upon the flux of existence. On the narrator's level, therefore, memory and desire become tools for effectively emplotting the historical past. On the other hand, there is also the protagonist's own focus on events and situations. This level marks the subject's attempt to make sense of and cope with objective reality in a moment of crisis. From the protagonist's perspective, memory and desire constitute ways of exorcising traumatic changes and of facing history at one of its most dramatic turning points.

Lampedusa critics have often and repeatedly confused the voices and points of view of the author and the protagonist of *Il Gattopardo.* In a typical remark, Pampaloni observes:

> Il punto di riferimento è sempre il personaggio nascosto che dice io, lo scrittore, che si arricchisce in un certo senso di tutta l'esperienza trascorsa tra i fatti narrati e il *suo* presente. . . . Il personaggio nel corso del racconto . . . perde a poco a poco le sue caratteristiche di personaggio storico, per acquistare il rilievo e il dramma paradigmatico di uomo travolto dal tempo, di uomo solo di fronte al destino. ("*Il Gattopardo*" 80–81; see appendix 22)

Pampaloni does not separate the author (or more precisely the explicit narrator in *Il Gattopardo*'s case) from the main character. Maintaining a differentiation between *Il Gattopardo*'s narrator and its protagonist is not only demanded from a methodological point of view, but is essential for separating Don Fabrizio's failure to discover an order and a plan in the flow of inchoate historical events from the narrator's willful aesthetic reconstruction. The narrator, in fact, is the one responsible for reshaping and structuring, according to specific formal criteria, a complex relationship involving the novel's protagonist and a fast-changing historical world. The main character is dramatically plunged into the course of history and, unlike the narrator, is unable to give a stable form to his relationship with a reality that is too rapidly evolving. *Il Gattopardo* provides a picture both of "history in the making," with the extemporaneous and partial attempts at organization made by Don Fabrizio, and of the "making of history," with the narrator's a posteriori aesthetic reorganization of historical events. This reconstruction validates two different ways of accounting for historical experiences. The one sees them embedded in a logical pattern of causal progression, the other discovers instead subterranean schemes of recurrence and repetition in the chain of discrete and progressive events. Thus, while the narrator's vantage point speaks for an emplotment of sorts, the protagonist's denounces instead the crisis of both an individual and a social class in a moment of historical transition. This crisis emerges in the protagonist's frustrated desire to give permanent shape to a reality that is perceived as chaotic, lacking both direction and fixed meaning. Reversing the neorealist notion of the "positive hero," Don Fabrizio experiences in the first person and with acute self-awareness the fracture between a self yearning for permanence and the inevitability of historical change.

* * *

In the years of neorealism, it was "history in the making" that polarized writers' concerns. The urgency of experienced history sought immediate transposition into the literary text, while the aesthetic organization of bare facts was reduced to a minimum. According to Aldo Garosci, the reemergence of historical fiction at the wane of the neorealist season represented nothing more than the degeneration of that great tradition. Once the epic vein is tapped out, Garosci explains, and once the direct link between the individual and history is severed, writers abandon the narration of immediate events to go back into past stories. The result, according to Garosci, is pictorial, idyllic, and descriptive rather than epic:

> il romanzo storico è proprio dei periodi in cui la storia riposa e non c'è una sua continuità popolare, ma una ricerca del passato delle classi colte. Gli spiriti epici si rivolgono allora con la fantasia al passato, perché hanno bisogno di grandi scenari per impiantarvi personaggi di statura adeguata ai loro sogni, alla loro immagine del mondo. Ma chi non ha avuto l'accento epico per raccontare quel che accadde accanto a lui . . . come lo avrà nel descrivere oscure vicende, che sono o sembrano epiche semplicemente perché lo affermino le tesi degli storici marxisti? (1019; see appendix 23)

One way of answering Garosci's query is to question the epic form itself as a legitimate method of accounting for a specific historical epoch. *Il Gattopardo* challenges, in fact, on the level of content, the literary renderings of the Unification of Italy as epic saga.[20] The novel starts on May 13, 1860, when Garibaldi's

Mille landed in Sicily. The way in which this traditionally heroic moment is addressed deconstructs the epic code altogether. By choosing as the novel's protagonist one of the last scions of the Sicilian aristocracy, Lampedusa opts for a decisive decentralization away from the perspective of the makers of the Unification—the northern Italian enlightened aristocracy and the entrepreneurial middle class. Lampedusa's account of the Unification of Italy rejects the epic transformation of the world it describes into "an absolute past of national beginnings and peak times" (Bakhtin, *Dialogic* 15). Rather, this time of undeniable transition is accounted for from the perspective of a man who observes the defeat and the bitter end of his own social class. It is the narration of a concluding chapter, rather than of a bright beginning.

Il Gattopardo abolishes the "epic distance" that for Mikhail Bakhtin allows the mythic transfiguration of the past. The shifts between the time of narrated *histoire* and the emerging time of the narrator's *discours* create in fact an unsevered tie between past and present. Furthermore, Don Fabrizio hardly fits into the Hegelian definition of the epic hero that Lukács borrows to describe the "world-historical individual" that he sees at the centers of Scott's modern bourgeois epics. As Hegel remarked, the heroes of the epic are total individuals who "magnificently concentrate within themselves what is otherwise dispersed in the national character, and in this way they remain great, free and noble human characters" (Lukács, *The Historical Novel* 36). Certainly, Don Fabrizio is hardly representative of the transformative forces behind the sociopolitical development in one of the most significant phases of modern Italian history. He has no active role in the process, his sole function being that of coping with and eventually succumbing to upcoming events: "il povero principe Fabrizio . . . stava a contemplare la rovina del proprio ceto e del proprio patrimonio senza avere nessuna attività ed ancora minor voglia di porvi riparo" ("poor Prince Fabrizio . . . [watched] the ruin of his own class and his own inheritance without ever making, still less wanting to make, any move toward saving it") (21; 17). In this sense, the epic stature that characterizes Don Fabrizio reveals the narrator's ironic voice, a voice that differs from the traditional narratorial tone toward epic materials.[21] According to Bakhtin, the epic narrator expresses an attitude full of veneration and awe regarding the greatness of the past and the superhuman attributes of its heroes. *Il Gattopardo*'s narrator contends that, in spite of his being at the center of the plot for most of the novel, Don Fabrizio is no hero in the Lukácsian sense of the word. *Il Gattopardo* reverses both the realist "positive hero" and the definition of an absolute epic past as the sole source of all the good for times to come: "dopo sarà diverso, ma peggiore" ("after that it will be different, but worse") (219; 190–91).

Don Fabrizio's marginalized perspective, however, grasps a part of the historical process that is as significant as any other. The actual experience of the Unification is divested of its heroic rhetoric and is presented as a time of compromise, fragmentation, stagnation, and self-interest. During a sullen October night in 1860, the "other" Italy is born in a remote village of the Sicilian interior. This Italy, Don Fabrizio contemplates, has come to light under the spell of an evil fairy rather than the augurs of propitious gods. Tainted by fraudulent and ultimately unnecessary maneuvers to eliminate the very few "noes" in the Plebiscite for the Unification, Italy's new order—and newly constructed national identity—is symbolized by Don Fabrizio consigning his "yes" into the rapacious hands of Don Calogero Sedàra, the "new man" epitomizing the rising, unscrupulous middle class. Don Fabrizio, as representative of the defeated southern aristocracy, exemplifies the point of view of those whom history has silenced, as he tells a story that is not admitted into the new nation's institutionalized memories. In Manzoni's wake, albeit with an interesting reversal of social class, *Il Gattopardo* gives voice to those who did not succeed in inscribing the public records of official History.

* * *

A number of interpreters contended that *Il Gattopardo* marked a nostalgic return to the great masterpieces of nineteenth-century bourgeois fiction. The literary critic Leone Piccioni, for example, described *Il Gattopardo* as an ill-timed example of traditional "horizontal" storytelling (following, that is, a chronological organization of events) in an era when "vertical" narration was becoming more and more popular (132–34). When compared with a classic nineteenth-century "well-made" novel, however, *Il Gattopardo* immediately differentiates itself by the complex formal organization that lies beyond the superficial (and by no means comprehensive) chronological framework. Piccioni's account of *Il Gattopardo* takes into consideration only one aspect of the text, that of its fifty-year linear progression. The emplotment of Lampedusa's novel exploits other structuring techniques that disrupt and complicate the simple temporal continuum and render the novel much more than a simple "horizontal" narration.

According to Ricoeur, a plot is "the privileged means by which we re-configure our confused, unformed, and at the limit mute temporal experience" (*Time* 1: xi).[22] Ricoeur reinterprets Aristotle's theorization of the plot, taking into account the temporal dimensions at work in the act of narrative reconfiguration. It is Artistotle's contention that the notion of plot is not simply based on the succession of separate episodes but is mainly related to the inevitable, logical connection between the plot's parts: "The accent, in the analysis of this idea of a 'whole,' is therefore put on the absence of chance and on conformity to the requirements of necessity or probability governing succession" (Ricoeur, *Time* 1: 39). What makes the plot a "whole," in other words, is the chain of cause-and-effect relationships that the text establishes among its discrete elements.[23] The textual representation of experiential time, however, can bring into play a number of structuring principles that are not limited to the principles of necessity, probability, and causal connection. *Il Gattopardo*'s novelty emerges precisely in the confrontation of multiple structuring elements at work in the depiction of historical and personal pasts.

Il Gattopardo is divided into eight chapters and covers a time period of roughly fifty years, from 1860 to 1910. The novel immediately provides a first temporal level that is structured around a chronological pattern. Time as chronological development, however, is not presented as a narrative continuum. While most of the events occur in two years (1860–62), the text is marked by a number of significant time lapses. Between chapters 6 and 7 there is a twenty-one-year gap, and another gap of twenty-seven years abruptly separates chapters 7 and 8. On an initial organizational level, therefore, *Il Gattopardo* displays an episodic framework, its chapters being loosely related in a frame of temporal succession but also relatively independent from one another. In other words, in light of Aristotle's notion of plot, one could argue that each part is not inevitably tied to the preceding one.[24] The connection of the events within the parts is also, to a certain degree, episodic in nature. The narration proceeds through a set of discrete episodes or scenes, according to the traditional scheme of an epic narrative:

> Rosario e presentazione del Principe - Il giardino e il soldato morto - Le udienze reali - La cena - In vettura per Palermo - Andando da Mariannina - Il ritorno a S. Lorenzo - Conversazione con Tancredi - In Amministrazione: i feudi, e i ragionamenti politici - In osservatorio con padre Pirrone - Distensione al pranzo - Don Fabrizio e i contadini - Don Fabrizio e il figlio Paolo - La notizia dello sbarco e di nuovo il Rosario. (15; see appendix 24)

This technique is based on a minimal narrative reorganization of actual events. In the epic mode, a number of events are merely juxtaposed in an orderly yet not essential way. The episodic dimension of a story draws "narrative time in the direction of the linear representation of time" and exemplifies the closest rendition of the irreversible order "common to physical and human events" (Ricoeur, *Time* 1: 67). On this level, therefore, Piccioni's claim of the horizontal dimension of *Il Gattopardo* seems legitimate.

Upon a closer analysis, however, the novel's narrative framework reveals, from page to page, "a literary craftsmanship nothing less than architectonic" (Cowart 124). The overt narrator claims immediate responsibility for two interrelated levels of meaning: the level of the novel's narrative content and the level of this content's formal arrangement. Through personal comments,[25] ironic asides, proleptic and extradiegetic information,[26] the narrator's voice emerges with clear reference to the present time of his writing. This strategy, reminiscent of the narrator of Manzoni's *I promessi sposi,* establishes a close link between the events of the past and the present acts of organization and interpretation of these events. *Il Gattopardo* points out what contemporary historians like Marrou, Aron, White, and de Certeau emphasize in the field of historiography, namely, the strong ideological implication of historians in their work and, consequently, history's ties to the present. In this way, Lampedusa also exposes the subjective and ultimately constructed (as opposed to merely reflected) nature of the narrator's representation of the past. This recalls what Ricoeur terms the "configurational" dimension of time. This dimension challenges the simple juxtaposition of episodes as it transforms the succession of events into one meaningful whole. The configurational arrangement becomes the mediative moment between the linear, successive experience of the story's episodes and the synthetic grasp of the plot as a significant unity.[27] The creation of this sense of unity is the narrator's responsibility, as are the selections, the omissions, and the specific methods of emplotment through which a silent past is given a voice. It is from this perspective, therefore, that the claim of the ideological import of formal organization is most justified.

Throughout the text, Lampedusa draws attention to the configurational dimension by emphasizing the act of configuration itself. The overt narrator embodies an "ideal" historian who is endowed with absolute omniscience over the facts narrated, and who is quite selective and determined to manipulate, however subtly, the time of mimetic experience. The episodic narrative sequence and the explicit time references that mark the narration underscore, by contrast, all that is left out—the gaps, silences, and empty spaces that are also, by default, inscribed in the text. Far from aiming at providing a total representation and a complete historical account, *Il Gattopardo* reveals that the historical picture it provides is both fragmentary and provisional. If the end of a story constitutes the "point of view from which the story can be perceived as forming a whole" (Ricoeur, *Time* 1: 67), *Il Gattopardo* immediately relativizes this concept by providing two endings, a "logical," or linear, one and a configurational one. Several critics have commented on the accessory nature of the novel's last chapter, considering Don Fabrizio's death, in chapter 7, the real closing episode of the text. If the repetition of a story governed by its ending constitutes an alternative to the representation of time as flowing from past to future, *Il Gattopardo*'s multiple endings force us to readjust the focal point of the narrator's and our own reconfiguration of past events. Once again, this strategy draws the reader's attention to the provisional character of all reconstructions, including historical and partially historical ones, and thus highlights their susceptibility to multiple revisions from different points of view.

It seems no longer far-fetched, at this point, to reverse traditional interpretations of *Il Gattopardo* and consider the novel as a modernist text insofar as it lays bare its artifice and speaks about its own construction. If narrative "orders" experience and fiction's formal artifice rivals reality, is fiction, as a result, an exorcism of chaos, in Ricoeur's words a "consoling lie," an aesthetic fraud appealing to our "nostalgia for order"? (*Time* 1: 72). The answer that *Il Gattopardo* provides fills the gap left between neorealism and the neo-avantgarde. Unlike neorealist fiction, *Il Gattopardo* does not present its form as "natural" but reveals its constructive and organizing principles. Unlike the neo-avantgarde, it places the "burden of emplotment" upon itself, defending its structural order, an order, however, whose subjective origin, contingent value, and ideological coloring are continually emphasized.

Discussing the similarity between the writing of history and the writing of fiction, White, like Veyne, argues that they both aim at creating plots. In historical accounts, as in fictional stories, facts are replaced by their verbal textualizations. The same structural act of emplotment is, therefore, at the heart of both historical and fictional narratives. Ricoeur makes a similar point:

> The modes of emplotment . . . are the products of a tradition of writing which has given them the configuration that the historian uses. This aspect of traditionality is in the end the most important thing. A historian, as a writer, addresses a public likely to recognize the traditional forms of the art of narration. . . . Such meaning effects consist essentially of making the unfamiliar familiar. (*Time* 1: 168)

The "reality" of the historical past, to use one of Ricoeur's favorite definitions, is kept alive by using formal structures that allow us to make sense of and recognize both personal and communal pasts. The sharing of traditional forms parallels the sharing of their contents, so that their "reality effect" is not questioned and the claim to truthfulness of historiographic writing is maintained.

Both White's and Ricoeur's arguments run the risk of being oversimplified. White's emphasis on the fictional, or constructed, nature of all historical accounts tends to erase any differentiation between history and fiction. Ricoeur's humanistic bias pushes him to see "form," and therefore the possibility of its recognition, as a universal and atemporal structure, beyond cultural differentiation and historical change. The drastic reversal of the ideology of form that took place in Italy in the late 1950s, with the move from neorealism to neo-avantgarde experimentalism, speaks for the opposite. Formal recognition cannot be defined, as Ricoeur would like, in absolutely universal terms. One should argue instead that such recognition takes place when a certain form becomes part of a specific cultural and conceptual framework—part of a shared pattern of cognitive processes that make it familiar, and therefore acceptable and consequently "true." It is thus clear that the claims to truth of historical writing should not be referred exclusively to the content level of narrated facts, but to their formal organization as well. In spite of the "antinarrativist" trends of twentieth-century historiography, the traditional form of historical emplotment takes shape around a causal chain that knits discrete events into a meaningful unity. The epistemological value of narrative forms lies in the creation of "an ensemble of interrelationships of many different kinds as a single whole" (Mink, "Narrative Form" 144). The coherence of these complex forms in fictional narratives affords aesthetic pleasure, while in historical narratives it entails a claim to truth. Sharing in the claims to truth of historical narratives means, therefore, sharing in the cognitive processes at the basis of their formal configuration. This formal encoding is meant to familiarize the unfamiliar: this is "the way of historiography, whose 'data' are always immediately strange, not to say exotic, simply by virtue of their distance from us in time and their origination in a way of life different from our own" (H. White, "The Historical Text" 49).

On the other hand, according to the Russian formalists, and Šklovskij in particular, the value of a literary work lies exactly in the opposite claim, in the uncanny ability, that is, of making the familiar strange. Unlike historical narrations, the main goal of art is to neutralize the mechanisms of habituation promoted by conventional modes of perception. In other words, art defamiliarizes what is too familiar and creatively deforms the usual and the normal. Disrupting stock responses, the artist reconstructs our ordinary perception of reality in order to make us really "see" the world instead of "numbly recognizing it" (Hawkes 62). The work of art, therefore, makes the audience aware that the cognitive and interpretative schemes with which we make sense of reality are not natural or eternal, but culturally and historically determined and, consequently, capable of modification and change.

By combining history and fiction in *Il Gattopardo,* Lampedusa contrasts the modes of addressing historical and fictional narratives, one aiming at satisfying the readers' expectations to recognize the familiar codes of historical representation, the other provoking instead surprise and a sense of estrangement. The repetitive and analogical patterns that characterize *Il Gattopardo* define a secondary mode of historical emplotment that, while subverting the causal and progressive chains of historical narrations, spins a reassuring web of recurrence and continuity over the incessant flow of history. In this way, *Il Gattopardo* features criteria of formal arrangement that are not strictly based on the demand of logic and causality, and promotes the analogical schemes of memory and desire as alternative, yet legitimate, methods of organizing and making sense of the past. In this light, *Il Gattopardo* redirects E. M. Forster's claim that a plot is a "narrative of events, the emphasis falling on causality" (58). The novel's formal construction demonstrates, in fact, that these "secondary" narrative modes, based on patterns of analogy, similarity, and repetition between past and present, are as effective in ordering the past as are the "primary" ones based on the establishment of close causal connections between discrete historical events. While providing the aesthetic pleasure of establishing surprising and uncanny relationships between past and present, the analogical modes of historical encoding also afford the comfort, however illusory, of recognizing the old in the new. At this point, two questions must be answered: To what degree does the "truth" that *Il Gattopardo* provides, based on the cohabitation of logical and analogical cognitive schemes, claim to mirror the objective past? And to what degree does that truth claim to be faithful, rather, to the subjective, creative projections of one's memories, hopes, and desires?

* * *

Historical understanding is generally regarded as the retrospective intelligibility that organizes congeries of circumstantial happenings into connected sequences of events (Mink, "The

Autonomy" 191). The historical configuration emerging from this process is an a posteriori intellectual construction that no interpreter "could have put together when the events were occurring, since this backward way of proceeding would be unavailable to any contemporary witness" (Ricoeur, *Time* 1: 157). The historian's temporal distance from the historical facts allows a comprehensive view of the historical scene, and the emplotment of past events is founded on "the absence of chance and on conformity to the requirements of necessity or probability governing succession" (Ricoeur, *Time* 1: 39). The kind of universality that a plot calls for corresponds to its logical inner ordering, its ability, that is, to surpass the mere enumeration of facts in a serial order by extracting a "configuration" from a "succession":

> To the extent that in the ordering of events the causal connection (one thing as a cause of another) prevails over pure succession (one thing after another), a universal emerges that is, as we have interpreted it, the ordering itself erected as a type. (Ricoeur, *Time* 1: 69)

The kind of configuration that a historical or literary work offers responds, in Ricoeur's vision, to a nostalgia for order, to a conviction that "order is our homeland *despite everything*" (Ricoeur, *Time* 1: 72).

What kind of order, then, does the historical and fictional narrative of *Il Gattopardo* provide? One of the common objections to the novel regards the relevance, in terms of Ricoeur's configurational scheme, of some chapters in the text, namely, those regarding Father Pirrone's visit to his home village of San Cono and Concetta's existence after the Prince's death. Direct causal connections between the bulk of the novel and these tangential sets of events seem to be blatantly missing. Rather than disclosing a fundamental structural flaw, the lack of such connections directs us toward other structuring criteria. *Il Gattopardo* provides a combination of the episodic mode (mere chronology and juxtaposition of disparate facts) with the configurational mode (logical causation and strict necessity) and the analogical mode (based on similarity and repetition). While logical causation remains the primary cognitive instrument in order to make the flux of experience comprehensible, *Il Gattopardo* shows how metaphorical and analogical processes constitute significant rivals to causal logic in the process of historical reconfiguration. The analogical mode does not entirely substitute for the closure and the inner connections of the causal pattern, but it establishes vertical relations that further complicate linear sequences and progressive narrative schemes. *Il Gattopardo* provides, therefore, neither a progressive nor a cyclical vision of history, but a combination of both. Cyclical repetitions in the form of a close-knit web of recurring images and analogical structures disrupt the narrative progression, temporarily halting the forward movement of history. These structures work on a double level, as they direct both the narrator's configurational act and the protagonist's intellectual and emotional approaches to historical reality.

The superimposition of images of recurrence over the scene of historical change identifies a particular type of repetition at work in *Il Gattopardo:* a "Nietzschean" rather than "Platonic" repetition, to borrow Gilles Deleuze's terminology (256–66). While the Platonic repetition is based on identity, as it establishes an archetype that the following replicas duplicate without ever disrupting its status as the original model, the Nietzschean repetition is based on difference: everything is unique and unrepeatable, inherently different from all other things. Similarity, therefore, emerges against this background of basic differences. As J. Hillis Miller observes, "[t]hese are ungrounded doublings which arise from differential interrelations among elements which are all on the same plane" (6). Miller compares this second repetitive form to Marcel Proust's involuntary memory. This memory in fact creates an imaginary life, "a vast intricate network of lies, the memory of a world that never was" (7). If the tapestry of memory is woven on the basis of the experience of recurrence, the two forms of recurrence differ. "Daylight, willed memory works logically, by way of similarities which are seen as identities" (Miller 8). The second involuntary memory is associated with the world of dreams. Here one thing is experienced as repeating something that is different from it but at the same time is similar. The similarities are therefore paradoxically based on the difference between two things: "They create in the gap of that difference a third thing, what Benjamin calls the image [*das Bild*]" (Miller 9). The image corresponds to the meaning generated by the echoing of two dissimilar things in the second form of repetition. The image is neither the first nor the second thing, but emerges in the empty space between the two, which is the opaque area that the uncanny similarity crosses: this is the world of *simulacra* rather than of *copies* (Deleuze 256). As he longs for and attempts to construct a stable universe of copies, Don Fabrizio discovers that all he can conjure up is the disturbing realm of simulacra, a realm torn by the incessant battle between the opposite principles of difference and identity, repetition and change.

As Don Fabrizio is the main focus of the novel, we are given direct access to his thoughts and emotions. His cognitive processes are tied to associative paradigms that establish patterns of similarity between the recollected past and the present. The Prince's attempts to make sense of the historical world are triggered by desire—specifically one for order. The order that Don Fabrizio seeks expresses itself in his quest to recognize figures of sameness upon a scheme inevitably marked by change and progression. Thus, on the sweltering carriage trip to Donnafugata, he is refreshed by the recognition of familiar places: the Dragonara ravine, the Misilbesi crossroads, and the Shrine of Our Lady of All Graces appear to repeat and confirm the familiar landmarks of his mental maps in the world of reality. The sense of peace and permanence evoked by the Prince's memories and the feeling of "everlasting childhood" that Donnafugata bestows upon its feudal lord distance, in both time and space, the anxiety of impending doom caused by the turmoil of Palermo. Upon arriving at Donnafugata, Don Fabrizio's constant preoccupation is to trace likes in unlikes and recognize the old in the new: "Grazie a Dio, mi sembra che tutto sia come al solito" ("Thanks be to God, everything seems as usual") (76; 65), the Prince exclaims alighting from his carriage, and soon after he reassures himself: "Non c'è da dire; tutto è rimasto come prima, meglio di prima, anzi" ("Yes indeed; everything is the same as before, better, in fact, than before") (77–78; 66). The usual encounter with the townsfolk and municipal authorities, the Te Deum in the Duomo, and the visit to the Convent of the Holy Spirit acquire symbolic resonance as they represent the victory of a past of privilege and tradition over a present marked by uncertainty and oblivion.[28]

In a similar manner, the various sets of rituals by which Don Fabrizio organizes his life—the daily Rosary, lunch and dinner, the autumnal evening reading of modern novels, the early morning hunting expeditions, and the night stargazing are ways of exorcising the paradigm of change upon which history is built, and of replacing it with one of reassuring repetition. The two revolutionary events mentioned in the first chapter of the novel, the outbreaks of the fourth of April and Garibaldi's landing in Marsala, are framed, and frozen so to speak, within the circle of the Rosary that, day after day, marks the liturgical routine of the Salina household. Even mundane repetitions such as the Prince's morning shaving and dressing become absorbing rites as they temporarily and wishfully cast aside the thought of rapid and unwanted historical transformations. The world-weary Prince is aware that he can overcome the tyranny of time and the specter of change only through the hypnotic recurrence of rituals, the affected idealizations of art, and the crystalline abstractions of mathematics. He also knows that those are only *palliativi,* ephemeral escapes and man-made constructions, like the frescos that transfigure the Conca d'Oro and its aristocratic inhabitants into a mythical landscape populated by Tritons and Dryads and untouched by the vagaries of time.

In Don Fabrizio's mind, the complex set of gestures that precede and accompany his hunting expedition into the heart of Sicily is elevated to the level of a sacred ceremonial that has been repeated, without change or variation, since those remote times in which "per la caccia s'invocava Artemide" ("Artemis was invoked for the chase") (125; 108). The evocative description of Don Fabrizio's sequential repetition of minute actions—shaving in a room still dark, crossing dormant drawing rooms, passing through the motionless garden in the dim twilight, escaping through the ivy-hung wicket gate—constitutes one of the novel's strongest assertions of the desire for sameness and stability that manages to place history in parentheses.[29] Sicily becomes a mythical space untouched by progress and change, a blocked landscape and a triumph of unchanging permanence:

> si svoltava su per un pendio e ci si trovava nell'immemoriale silenzio della Sicilia pastorale. Si era subito lontani da tutto, nello spazio e ancora di piú nel tempo. Donnafugata con il suo palazzo e i suoi nuovi ricchi era appena a due miglia, ma sembrava sbiadita nel ricordo come quei paesaggi che talvolta si intravedono allo sbocco lontano di una gal-

> leria ferroviaria; le sue pene e il suo lusso apparivano ancor piú insignificanti che se fossero appartenuti al passato, perché, rispetto alla immutabilità di questa contrada fuor di mano, sembravano far parte del futuro. (114–15; see appendix 25)

The Sicilian scene halts the movement of history. The merciless rigor of the chronological succession of past, present, and future, as well as the existential drama of being caught in the current of linear time, are momentarily exorcised by Don Fabrizio's immersion in the unchangeable dimension of an atemporal nature:

> Quando i cacciatori giunsero in cima al monte, di fra i tamerici e i sugheri radi riapparve l'aspetto della vera Sicilia, quello nei cui riguardi città barocche ed aranceti non sono che fronzoli trascurabili: l'aspetto di una aridità ondulante all'infinito, in groppe sopra groppe, sconfortate e irrazionali, delle quali la mente non poteva afferrare le linee principali, concepite in un momento delirante della creazione: un mare che si fosse ad un tratto pietrificato nell'attimo in cui un cambiamento di vento avesse reso dementi le onde. (126; see appendix 26)

If the time of geography appears motionless, it is not blocked in an ideal moment of supreme natural harmony; objective reality is by no means objective, but rather witnesses the delirious and absurd triumph of chaos that in Don Fabrizio's mind represents the true, timeless essence of Sicily: a primeval natural scene caught in a grimace of pain, disorder, and irrationality. The incoherent aspect of the Sicilian scene contrasts with the harmony of the heavens—"[la] sublime normalità dei cieli" ("the sublime routine of the skies") (56; 48). For Don Fabrizio, order, in its sublimest form, is represented by the trajectories of the stars:

> Sostenuti, guidati, sembrava, dai numeri, invisibili in quell'ora ma presenti, gli astri rigavano l'etere con le loro traiettorie esatte. Fedeli agli appuntamenti le comete si erano abituate a presentarsi puntuali sino al minuto secondo dinanzi a chi le osservasse. Ed esse non erano messaggere di catastrofi come Stella credeva: la loro apparizione prevista era anzi il trionfo della ragione umana che si proiettava e prendeva parte alla sublime normalità dei cieli. (56; see appendix 27)

The Prince's infatuation with the abstract precision of mathematical calculations is a "flight toward abstraction" (Saccone 175), as it reflects the desire to escape into a dimension that exists outside of history and linear time, into the "atarassiche regioni dominate dall'astronomia" ("the starry regions of astronomy") (45; 38).

If he is successful at mapping out the skies, Don Fabrizio remains unable to give satisfactory shape to his historical present. In the crisis of subjectivity and of the historical world, the burden of organization falls entirely upon the subject. However, the analogical and repetitive paradigms that Don Fabrizio exploits are unable to perform this ordering feat. He is forced to live with the awareness that pure repetition as the exact reproduction of the same (the Platonic repetition in Deleuze's terminology) cannot exist in the world of history. Thus, as he looks at himself and Tancredi reflected in the mirror, Don Fabrizio recognizes himself in his young nephew[30] only to discover that their separate placement in the arrow of time underscores their fundamental difference: the Prince is able to understand, but not to keep up with, history's momentous changes, while Tancredi can foresee, adapt himself to, and profit from the historical events that are rapidly succeeding one another (as he shifts, with the utmost *sprezzatura,* from being part of the Bourbon nobility, to becoming a revolutionary *garibaldino,* and eventually a regular soldier of Victor Emmanuel II, first king of the United Kingdom of Italy).

While Don Fabrizio attempts to contain the flood of change within the imaginary boundaries of repetition, he is also aware that repetition itself is no solution for his existential and historical tragedy. The private world of his solitary musings is constructed upon circular and regressive patterns that draw meaningful connections between past and present: "Per il Principe . . . il giardino profumato fu causa di cupe associazioni di idee" ("the heavy scents of the garden brought on a gloomy train of thought for the Prince") (23; 18). The smell of the rotting roses in the palace's garden repeats, in his mind, the putrid odor of a soldier's body that was found a month before in a corner of the garden. These images, whose *trait d'union* is the idea of death and decay, reemerge throughout the text, establishing indirect forms of repetition. The six slain baby lambs (a gift from Don Fabrizio's farmers), the rabbit that the Prince wounds and kills during the hunting expedition, and the wagon of dead bulls coming from the slaughterhouse create a subterranean analogical chain that carries a meaning beyond the purely literal. They become symbols, or images, of an existential condition trapped in the flux of time and haunted by the feeling of mortality and by the apocalyptic sense of the ending of all things. For the Prince, repetition is, paradoxically, both a way to resist historical change and a reminder of his own inescapable finitude: his being doomed to exist within time's forward motion.

Even when repetition succeeds in achieving the longed-for immobility, Don Fabrizio is forced to recognize its gloomy and desperate side. The narrator's descriptions of the crude Sicilian sun that conquers every will and maintains everything in a state of servile immobility is echoed by Don Fabrizio's "ideological inferno" as expressed to the Piedmontese *Cavaliere,* Aimone Chevalley, who visits Donnafugata in order to invite the Prince to become a senator of the kingdom. Chevalley's lively and naive idealism regarding the future of Sicily after the union (annexation) to the Kingdom of Italy contrasts with the Prince's skeptical and sophistic rationalism, which insists on the distinction between his "support," which he offers, and his "participation," which he must deny. In this conversation, Chevalley emerges as Don Fabrizio's absolute Other, as Sicily appears to be the absolute Other of the new Italy envisioned by the Piedmontese diplomat. A colony for 2,500 years, Sicily, Don Fabrizio explains, has been fated to the unredeemed repetition of one conquest after another, of one civilization on top of another, all from the outside, all obeyed, none of them understood. By now unresponsive to change, Sicily cannot be channeled into the flow of Universal History, or, less abstractly, into the life of the newly created Italian state:

> Il sonno, caro Chevalley, il sonno è ciò che i Siciliani vogliono, ed essi odieranno sempre chi li vorrà svegliare, sia pure per portar loro i piú bei regali; e, sia detto fra noi, ho i miei forti dubbi che il nuovo regno abbia molti regali per noi nel bagaglio. Tutte le manifestazioni siciliane sono manifestazioni oniriche, anche le piú violente: la nostra sensualità è desiderio di oblio, le schioppettate e le coltellate nostre, desiderio di morte; . . . le novità ci attraggono soltanto quando

> sono defunte, incapaci di dar luogo a correnti vitali; da ciò l'incredibile fenomeno della formazione attuale di miti che sarebbero venerabili se fossero antichi sul serio, ma che non sono altro che sinistri tentativi di rituffarsi in un passato che ci attrae soltanto perché è morto. (210–11; see appendix 28)

A member of the old ruling class, inevitably compromised by association with the Bourbon regime, Don Fabrizio knows that he belongs to that unfortunate generation "swung between the old world and the new," and ill at ease in both. As he exits from the cynical portrayal of unrelieved stagnation and historical circularity, he experiences no liberating epiphany: change is only a change for the worse. As the Prince interprets it, Tancredi's proverbial assertion of sameness[31] conceals the signs of inexorable social and political transformations: "Noi fummo i Gattopardi, i Leoni: chi ci sostituirà saranno gli sciacalletti, le iene" ("We were the Leopards, the Lions; those who'll take our place will be little jackals, hyenas") (219; 191). Clinging to one's name, one's memories, and the family's past, living in the world of repetition as Don Fabrizio does, means becoming a scapegoat in the order of change, the symbolic "ornate catafalque" at the center of a grotesque *danse macabre* celebrating the end of the Sicilian ancien régime. It is with a mixture of resigned pessimism and worldly humor that Don Fabrizio finally approaches the inevitable change, as witnessed by the narrator's description filtered through the Prince's point of view, of Don Calogero's ludicrous grand entrance at the first dinner at Donnafugata, the tails of his poorly tailored coat pointing "verso il cielo in muta supplica" ("straight to heaven in mute supplication") (95; 82).

To cherish recurrence while understanding the necessity of change means for Don Fabrizio leading a vicarious life, repeating in his imagination what "his nephew accomplishes in deed" (Lucente, "Figure and Temporality" 201). Tancredi therefore does not merely repeat or double his uncle: change is inherent in repetition, and Tancredi stands for what Don Fabrizio cannot be. There is, however, a moment of identity between the two men, and it occurs during the ball at Palazzo Ponteleone. Only within the stylized and choreographed scene of the ball can Don Fabrizio, by dancing the evening's first waltz with Angelica and replacing Tancredi on the dance floor, act out the bittersweet compromise of repeating the past while embracing the future: "ad ogni giro un anno gli cadeva giú dalle spalle: presto si ritrovò come a venti anni, quando in quella stessa sala ballava con Stella, quando ignorava ancora cosa fossero le delusioni, il tedio, il resto" ("at every twirl a year fell from his shoulders; soon he felt back at the age of twenty, when in that very same ballroom he had danced with Stella before he knew disappointment, boredom, and the rest") (271; 236). Like Angelica's affected social graces, however, this is, after all, only a spectacle. The only real and ultimately inescapable way to overcome the tearing dichotomy of sameness and change is to be found not in illusory constructions but in the leap into timelessness: the absolute of death. Cloaked in different images, death represents the most pervasive form of recurrence in the novel. In a perfectly circular manner, *Il Gattopardo* opens and closes under the sign of death: the "*Nunc et in hora mortis nostrae*" of the first chapter, and the "end of everything" of the concluding one. As a skillfully orchestrated *mise en abyme,* the ball scene is preceded, permeated, and completed by images of death: a priest bearing a ciborium with the Blessed Sacrament, Don Fabrizio musing over a copy of Greuze's *Death of the Just Man,* and a wagon stacked with bulls killed shortly before at the slaughterhouse. It is death that provides the absolute signified, the ultimate truth separating reality from fantasy, the inevitable from the accessory, time from eternity. It is death that allows for the Prince's final discovery: his symbolic lifting of Venus's veil on the final hour of his life.

* * *

The same associative patterns that guide Don Fabrizio's historical understanding (as well as his historical misinterpretations)[32] also define the narrator's dimension. Father Pirrone's visit to his home village of San Cono (chapter 5)—like the ensuing narration of how he managed to straighten out a family quarrel and arrange the wedding of his pregnant niece, Angelina, to his cousin Santino—has often been criticized as an accessory and unnecessary episode (Blasucci 119–20). Exactly like the novel's final chapter, in which a secondary character, Concetta, suddenly becomes the main focus of the story, Father Pirrone's section was considered irrelevant to the central narrative. This section finds its own *raison d'être* if its links to the preceding chapters are sought not in a logical or chronological framework but, rather, in an analogical one, in a pattern, that is, that highlights the underlying similarities between two separate events. The chapter works, in other words, in the same way as the subplot did in the tradition of Tudor and Jacobean dramas. Furnishing a comic counterpoint to the main plot, it sheds new light, through analogy and contrast, on the main plot, its characters and situations.

Father Pirrone "enters S. Cono just as triumphantly as Don Fabrizio had earlier returned to Donnafugata" (Lucente, "Figure and Temporality" 198) and the commemorative Mass for Pirrone's father parallels the Te Deum crowning the Prince's appearance in his feudal estate. Like Don Fabrizio's arrival at Donnafugata, Father Pirrone's arrival at his hometown is disturbed by the signs of the new (the patriotic pictures of a flame-colored Garibaldi arm in arm with an aquamarine Santa Rosalia) and consoled by those of the old (the remembrances of his father that he shares with the carter during the five-hour trip). Don Fabrizio's memories of things past are paralleled by Father Pirrone's more humble recollections, which, like those of the Prince, are triggered by the joy of discovering the return of the same:

> Appena entrato in casa fu assalito, come sempre, dalla dolcissima furia dei ricordi giovanili: tutto era immutato, il pavimento di coccio rosso come il parco mobilio; l'identica luce entrava dai finestrozzi esigui; il cane Romeo, che latrava breve in un cantone, era il trisnipote rassomigliantissimo di un altro cerviero compagno suo nei violenti giochi. (225; see appendix 29)

The dialogue between Father Pirrone and Don Pietrino, the herbalist, mirrors that between the Prince and Chevalley, as in both cases the impassioned speakers address an uncomprehending audience and the discourses turn into inspired, albeit ineffective, monologues. The marriage between Tancredi and Angelica finds its equivalent in minor key in the match between Angelina and Santino, just as Father Pirrone replaces Don Fabrizio in negotiating the financial details of the wedding. In Father Pirrone's subplot, the matchmaking process reduces itself to the rapacious financial exchange that the sensual aura, the aesthetic appeal, and the play of manners and strict behavior of the palace had somehow managed to conceal.[33]

* * *

The novel's last chapter, set at a twenty-seven-year remove from the preceding one dedicated to the Prince's death, centers on Don Fabrizio's daughter Concetta. Imposing and authoritative like her father,[34] Concetta represents the excess of an emotional involvement in the reconstruction of the past. In the course of a conversation with the also elderly Angelica, the name of Tassoni, one of Tancredi's comrades in the assault on the Origlione monastery, is brought up. With it reemerges the memory of the famous dinner at Donnafugata fifty years earlier when Concetta witnessed the beginning of Angelica's and Tancredi's love story. On that occasion, Tancredi had narrated an audacious anecdote about his and Tassoni's assault on a cloistered monastery of nuns that had amused Angelica and scandalized Concetta. One of the climactic moments in the book, this scene shows the two girls passing "each other like meteors, one rising, the other sharply descending" (Meyers 52). On the basis of Tancredi's anecdote, Concetta constructed a coherent image to which she remained faithful throughout her life: "Era stata la svolta della sua vita, quella; la strada imboccata allora la aveva condotta fin qui" ("It had been the turning point of her life, that; the road she'd taken then had led her here") (316; 276). Tassoni's visit to Angelica and Concetta fifty years after the telling of the anecdote brings a new revelation: the old man narrates that Tancredi had confided to him that the whole story had, in fact, been just a whimsical joke. On the fiftieth anniversary of Concetta's broken heart, a new disclosure reveals to her that she has built her life on a story, a construction—in the end, a lie:

> Fino ad oggi, quando essa, raramente, ripensava a quanto era avvenuto a Donnafugata in quella estate lontana, si sentiva sostenuta da un senso di martirio subíto, di torto patito. . . . Ora, invece, questi sentimenti derivati che avevano costituito lo scheletro di tutto il suo modo di pensare si disfacevano anch'essi. Non vi erano stati nemici, ma una sola avversaria, essa stessa; il suo avvenire era stato ucciso dalla propria imprudenza, dall'impeto rabbioso dei Salina; e le

> veniva meno adesso, proprio nel momento in cui dopo decenni i ricordi ritornavano a farsi vivi, la consolazione di poter attribuire ad altri la propria infelicità, consolazione che è l'ultimo ingannevole filtro dei disperati. (320; see appendix 30)

The major traumatic event of Concetta's life has delivered up its meaning over time, in a fifty-year span, allowing her to write and rewrite her life around it. A single event, endowed with too much emotional meaning because of its traumatic impact, has "stayed" with her, dictating her future choices and courses of action. Concetta's behavior introduces a further temporal dimension in the text, that of a paradoxical past that does not pass:

> This apparent anomaly can be explained if we admit that all events which are dense in meaning (whether it be traumatic or joyous) do not deliver up their meaning all at once or only once, but continue to release it gradually over a long period, often in interminable processes. (Bodei 7)

Concetta's life, in other words, is built according to a plot of unconscious responses to the reenactment of that epiphanic moment at the dinner at Donnafugata. Her private memories are idiosyncratically and compulsively arranged or displaced according to a preestablished pattern. Cast in a role like Luigi Pirandello's characters in *Sei personaggi in cerca d'autore* (*Six Characters in Search of an Author,* 1921), Concetta seems able to act out only one part, the one that repeats and adapts itself to that crucial moment fifty years earlier. Like a neurotic patient, she has overemplotted that event, "has charged [it] with a meaning so intense that, whether real or merely imagined, [it] continue[s] to shape both [her] perceptions and [her] responses to the world long after [it] should have become 'past history'" (H. White, "The Historical Text" 50). In a sense, Tassoni assumes the role of the psychotherapist. He forces Concetta to reemplot her entire life by altering the meaning and import of that traumatizing memory. All of a sudden, therefore, the security of Concetta's past collapses, and she finds herself forced to reexamine her own mental and sentimental maps.

Concetta's quest for the truth, however, proves arduous, and her past as it really was remains forever unattainable. The "true facts" are elusive ghosts; she can grasp only constructions, molded in the crucible of love and desire; subjective transfigurations resulting from interpretative patterns that are emotionally overcharged:

> Ma era poi la verità questa? In nessun luogo quanto in Sicilia la verità ha vita breve: il fatto è avvenuto da cinque minuti e di già il suo nocciolo genuino è scomparso, camuffato, abbellito, sfigurato, oppresso, annientato dalla fantasia e dagl'interessi: il pudore, la paura, la generosità, il malanimo, l'opportunismo, la carità, tutte le passioni, le buone quanto le cattive, si precipitano sul fatto e lo fanno a brani; in breve è scomparso. (321; see appendix 31)

Like her sisters, who see the "Madonna of the Letter" in a painting of a girl that, for the Cardinal of Palermo, represents only a sensuous country girl, Concetta lets her own desire impose meanings upon external reality.[35] As in a perfect fictional plot, each event is not independently meaningful, but finds its sense through the web of relationships that it establishes with all the other events.

Anniversaries, in this context, play a significant role in *Il Gattopardo.* Events, persons, and things are not seen in their uniqueness, but as signs pointing back to earlier events, persons, or things, "standing for them" (Miller 13). The fiftieth anniversary of Concetta's romantic disappointment is also the fiftieth anniversary of the landing of the *Mille* in Sicily. Young Fabrizio, the nephew and namesake of the old Prince (another figure of repetition), is invited to participate in the celebrations and in a commemorative procession. As Angelica comments, young Fabrizio's participation represents a way to show the alliance of the old aristocracy with the new political order: "Un Salina renderà omaggio a Garibaldi. Sarà una fusione della vecchia e della nuova Sicilia" ("A Salina rendering homage to Garibaldi! A fusion of old and new Sicily!") (314; 275). But *Il Gattopardo* shows that even this alliance is an illusion, a product of wishful thinking and a strong emotional involvement that the course of events and the progress of history have shown to be fatally flawed. As Don Fabrizio had anticipated, Tancredi's cryptic statement that things will have to change in order for things to remain the same does not proclaim continuity but implies instead the bitter end of a family and of a social order.

From this perspective, the temporal coincidence of two anniversaries is by no means casual. The shock of a specific event (Concetta's romantic disappointment or the *Mille*'s landing in Sicily) produces, on quite different scales, similar effects. On the grand plane of a whole social class—the Sicilian aristocracy as represented by Don Fabrizio and Concetta—the traumatic historic and communal event of Italy's unification has stayed with its members, dictating behaviors, soliciting responses, and suggesting improbable solutions, like the long-cherished illusion of the alliance between old and new. The subjective ways to cope with a personal or communal crisis appear to follow from the same psychological responses. *Il Gattopardo* chronicles both a historical and a personal crisis: when a dialectical and positive relationship between the individual and external reality fails, strong subjective trends emerge that tend to shape and mold reality and the past according to unconscious and emotional patterns that prevail over logical and rational schemes.

The power of the past as repository of emotionally overcharged images is made clear in the description of that "inferno of mummified memories," Concetta's bedroom. The inlaid furniture, with figures of dogs, huntsmen, and game, the padlocked wooden cases with Concetta's fifty-year-old trousseau, the portraits of dead family members, and the embalmed Bendicò, all in meticulous order, are there to signify the stubborn resistance of times past in the idiosyncratic archives of Concetta's mind. Don Fabrizio's favorite dog—one of the symbolic figures of repetition in the text—appears once again at the close of the novel to witness Concetta's rejection of that past, together with the true and the constructed memories associated with it. When Concetta finally decides to get rid of it, Bendicò metamorphoses, for a fleeting instant, into that charged symbol, the imperious Salina Leopard. Then everything finds its peace in a "little heap of livid dust":

> Mentre la carcassa veniva trascinata via, gli occhi di vetro la fissarono con l'umile rimprovero delle cose che si scartano, che si vogliono annullare. Pochi minuti dopo, quel che rimaneva di Bendicò venne buttato in un angolo del cortile che l'immondezzaio visitava ogni giorno. Durante il volo giú dalla finestra la sua forma si ricompose un istante: si

> sarebbe potuto vedere danzare nell'aria un quadrupede dai lunghi baffi, e l'anteriore destro alzato sembrava imprecare. Poi tutto trovò pace in un mucchietto di polvere livida. (326–27; see appendix 32)

Unlike previous mnemonic reconstructions based on similarities that see things in their metaphor—as "standing for" other things—the end of the novel marks a path that moves from the symbolic ("un quadrupede dai lunghi baffi") to the literal ("un mucchietto di polvere livida"). No longer a metaphor and an emblem, Bendicò is described, through Concetta's new perspective and the narrator's voice, finally in his unique, literal meaning. No longer even a repudiated symbol of bygone times, Bendicò does not bear the displaced meaning of a whole past. His existence is exclusively tied to its literal present: a pathetic lump of moth-eaten fur. With him a whole past, and all the emotional maps that it had traced, are therefore consigned to oblivion.

At this point, the last question that remains to be addressed regards the ideological implications of this complex relationship with the past. This relationship involves the pairings of remembrance and forgetfulness, discovery and creation, logical constructions and associative patterns, cognition and desire. Upon a linear scheme based on progress and change, we have seen powerful structures of similarity and repetition being created. Are these structures to be ascribed to a reactionary view, history as "un'apologia del 'sempre eguale' a partire dal sempre diverso" ("an apology for the 'perpetually identical' originating from the perpetually different"), to cite Fortini (245)? Moreover, what are the claims to truth of this historical picture that emphasizes the subjective and artificial nature of its formal emplotment and flaunts its emotional rather that rational origin? At key points in the novel, the narrator intervenes with a number of references to his modern perspective that find their *trait d'union* in revolutionary discoveries such as modern jet travel (121), psychoanalysis (134), medicine (140), and the cinema (167).[36] The narrator's incremental self-assertion throughout the novel demystifies his own reading of history based on analogical patterns of recurrence by suggestively bringing up some of the major fundamental changes in modern society.

The two modes of making sense of the past, one logical and the other analogical, do coexist, if paradoxically, within the same structure. It would be simplistic, however, to argue that the former refers to a progressive and the latter to a cyclical notion of history. The novel's recurrences have a creative force that distinguishes them from the regressive and reactionary associations with which critics have imbued them. As Remo Bodei points out, "in the face of sudden and unexpected changes, in the face of collapsing regimes or vanishing ways of life, we are often amazed by the great number of men and women who forget a substantial part of their history and modify the meaning of their past" (1). Interestingly, Don Fabrizio considers himself the "last of the Salinas" even though, technically, as he has seven children, this is not the case. However, even if he is not the last scion of the family, he is the only one in touch with the family's memories:

> Era inutile sforzarsi a credere il contrario, l'ultimo Salina era lui, il gigante sparuto che adesso agonizzava sul balcone di un albergo. Perché il significato di un casato nobile è tutto nelle tradizioni, cioè nei ricordi vitali; e lui era l'ultimo a possedere dei ricordi inconsueti, distinti da quelli delle altre famiglie. . . . Lui stesso aveva detto che i Salina sarebbero sempre rimasti i Salina. Aveva avuto torto. L'ultimo era lui. Quel Garibaldi, quel barbuto Vulcano aveva dopo tutto vinto. (291–92; see appendix 33)

Don Fabrizio stands on the edge of a radical societal change and is aware that, once the leap forward is taken, oblivion and disintegration of a whole patrimony of memories will slowly but inevitably take place. Forgetfulness is in fact dramatically tied to "the collapse of those energies which (actively) mold and promote, and (passively) maintain and preserve historical memory" (Bodei 5).[37] In the face of this awareness, it appears clear to Don Fabrizio as well as to the story's narrator that the past, which is in danger of being obscured and then abandoned because of inevitable historical transformations, can be reintegrated into the present through a pattern of "elective affinities"—in figures, that is, "that resemble (or that are believed to resemble) the lost images" (Bodei 9). Repetition, therefore, acquires a surprisingly positive feature by simultaneously preserving the past of individuals and keeping communities alive.

The analogical and repetitive schemes that characterize *Il Gattopardo* do not claim direct correspondence to the world of historical becoming. As Miller points out, and as *Il Gattopardo*'s narrator makes clear, "the 'unconscious' human state of illusion is the cause of repetition" (13). However, the novel proves that even illusions do not have a merely consolatory value, but serve a practical and ethical function. *Il Gattopardo*'s cyclical patterns of memory and desire, in fact, counteract historical progress and inevitable change so as to help creatively maintain and preserve the voices of all those who are silenced by all external and internal forces of oblivion.

Chapter Three

Fiction and Women's History

Elsa Morante's *La Storia*

> *Egli è l'Adamo che mette il nome a tutto ciò che vede e sente. Egli scopre nelle cose le somiglianze e le relazioni più ingegnose. . . . Egli è quello . . . che ha paura al buio, perchè al buio vede o crede di vedere; quello che alla luce sembra sognare, ricordando cose non vedute mai; quello che parla alle bestie, agli alberi, ai sassi, alle nuvole, alle stelle: che popola l'ombra di fantasmi e il cielo di dei.*
>
> Giovanni Pascoli
> "Il fanciullino"
> See appendix 34

Elsa Morante's 1974 best-selling novel *La Storia* weaves together the fates of Ida Ramundo, her children Nino and Useppe, and the pageant of their acquaintances from 1941 to 1947, the years that saw the horrors of Fascism, Nazism, and World War II. *La Storia* is based upon a binary opposition between the report of historical events and the narration of fictional adventures. While the invented characters do not appear in the brief accounts of political occurrences that precede every chapter, the fictional plot relates how these characters face, resist, and finally succumb to history's destructive force. In this way *La Storia* complicates its formal binary configuration on the level of its narrative contents. History, in fact, constantly intervenes in the fictional world by shaping, directing, and finally destroying the characters' lives, while fiction has no visible and immediate impact upon history. The novel's characters, and the fiction they inhabit, however, have a potentially subversive power, as they question and withstand the laws of authority, violence, and prevarication represented by the order of history.

Structurally, *La Storia* seems to follow the classic Aristotelian juxtaposition between "poetry" and "history." While the historical sections provide a mere chronicle of political happenings organized around the paratactic scheme of contiguity and succession, the fictional parts present a complex and ordered formal emplotment that is unified, intelligible, and based on the subordination of the parts to the whole (Gossman 9). According to Aristotle, history reports what has happened; poetry (he refers, of course, to the tragic plot) addresses what is likely to happen according to the rules of probability and necessity. Consequently, the truth of history remains tied to the merely contingent and the particular, while poetic truth, instead, is more universal and, therefore, more philosophical (32–33). Although Aristotle does not concern himself with the metaphysical dimensions of human life, the universalistic approaches to poetic discourse underscore this very dimension, and literature has often purported to afford a superior, intuitive knowledge of the ideal as opposed to the exclusively practical relevance of historical knowledge.[1]

In *La Storia,* Morante questions the Aristotelian juxtaposition of history and poetry by reshaping the boundaries of the two disciplines and redefining the notion of historical and fictional truths. Morante challenges the validity of historical truth by denouncing the omissions and the silences that plague canonic historical texts. As the accuracy of feminist historiography cannot be founded exclusively on the authority of the archives of patriarchal history, the truth of which is condemned as partial and biased, fiction becomes one of the most effective tools to recount the stories of women. Morante also revises the transhistorical and universalistic definitions of fictional truth. Fiction is not the exclusive and fetishized sphere of the ideal, utterly detached from the degraded realm of history; it is instead part of a revisionary historiography that is no longer oblivious to women's experiences in history. Not only does fiction alter and integrate the existing record by recounting the alternative deeds of marginal figures, it also experiments with forms of representation that question the primacy of historical chronology as a linear succession of discrete, meaningful episodes. *La Storia* also broaches the issue of subjectivity by presenting a narrator who reverses the claims of impersonality and objectivity of orthodox historical writing and passionately asserts the feminine voice of her revisionary historical and fictional discourse. This voice's prophetic thrust challenges historical determinism by evoking a utopian future that is unconstrained by the causal laws of patriarchal history.

Revising the Canon: *La Storia*, Feminist Historiography, and the Boundaries between History and Fiction

In a conversation with Miss Tilney concerning their preferences in fiction and the then popular gothic novels, Catherine Morland, the young protagonist of Jane Austen's *Northanger Abbey* (1818), distinguishes fiction from history as she explains to her friend:

> I read [history] a little as a duty, but it tells me nothing that does not either vex or weary me. The quarrels of popes and kings, with wars or pestilences, in every page; the men all so good for nothing, and hardly any women at all—it is very tiresome: and yet I often think it odd that it should be so dull, for a great deal of it must be invention. The speeches that are put into the heroes' mouths, their thoughts and designs—the chief of all this must be invention, and invention is what delights me in other books. (123)

Here Catherine pinpoints the source of a traditional division of labor: history is purported to provide factual, documented, and therefore true reports of past events. It belongs to men. Historians paint a world in the masculine where women have little or no impact at all.[2] Fiction instead, Catherine argues, with its inventive charm and imaginative flights, escapes from the realm of mere factuality and better suits women by allowing for female authors as well as female protagonists. Catherine's words express her dissatisfaction with a historiographic method that reports only sudden and disruptive events like battles and wars and that favors narratives of statesmanship, diplomatic missions, and political achievements featuring single historical protagonists. However, Catherine also subscribes to a rigid separation of research fields and sexual identities: history and men on one side, fiction and women on the other.

Manzoni's essay *Del romanzo storico* makes a similar claim, although not in a gender-specific context. By rejecting the historical novel as an impure combination of two disciplines that have contrasting methods and goals, Manzoni erects a boundary between the two neighboring discourses. He views history as being devoted exclusively to truth, and fiction to invention. Morante certainly had Manzoni in mind when she wrote *La Storia.* Like Manzoni, she polemically contrasts official historical records with the otherwise silent account of humble characters and everyday situations. Like Manzoni's, Morante's antiheroes are passive recipients of history rather than active advocates of change. Morante's novel presents a distinct opposition between the history of the power structures and decision-making processes during and immediately after World War II and the obscure but tragic story of a lower-middle-class family in one of the poorest neighborhoods of Rome. Unlike Manzoni, however, Morante is aware that the opposition between history and fiction is also an opposition between sexual identities, and she reinscribes women into history by reinterpreting the meaning of fictional invention as opposed to historical truth.

A half-fictional and half-historical work written, narrated, and partly interpreted by women, *La Storia* focuses attention on a significant and disturbing gap. The novel highlights, in fact, the omission of women from most historical reconstructions of the past. Moreover, *La Storia* asks whether this silence reproduces an objective datum (there are no women in history) or refers to a process of selection, preservation, and field definition that reveals the ideological biases on the part of the societies and the historians that produce those abridged texts.[3] De Certeau identifies the germ of the historiographic act in an admission of otherness and a restitution of temporal distance, even a fascination with difference, which reminds us of the "law of the other" (91). If this is indeed the historian's starting point, the following step is that of reshaping the unfamiliar into the familiar, exorcising the foregone strangeness by channeling it through customary interpretative codes and into contemporary visions of the world. Historians therefore become colonizers of the past and, like those invaders who renamed exotic lands with familiar names (Plymouth, New England, Jamestown, and New York), they build a bridge that transfers their epistemological geography into the alien regions of the past. The result is that the topography of the past is captured and colonized, mostly in the name of the father.[4] Invisible to the selective gaze of the historian, the feminine continent is erased from the map, as women are systematically exiled from the official chronicle. Not only does the historical account of human societies have a male scribe, but the masculine signature is soon universalized, so that the "identification of men with 'humanity' [results] for the most part in the disappearance of women from the record of the past" (J. Scott, "The Problem" 5).

By juxtaposing fiction and history, *La Storia* provides a running commentary on this situation.[5] The novel's fictional side gives a voice to women while decrying the crushing force of the dominating order in a significant moment of crisis, and by opposing itself to history, also questions what usually makes its way into the historical record. *La Storia* challenges the current historiographic model—what Braudel calls *histoire événementielle*—that favors the report of sudden, nervous changes and political and social upheavals. This model, dating back to Leopold von Ranke's influential historiographic paradigm, exclusively narrates the story of the power structures, economic as well as ideological, that support historical research, influence the historian's production, and thus direct the process of what is preserved and what is silenced in the act of historical writing. With *La Storia* Morante argues that women are indeed absent from history, but from a history that is erudite and empirical, exclusively interested in the actions, accomplishments, and failures of chiefs of state, military leaders, ministers, and diplomats. *La Storia,* therefore, reflects one of the major concerns in feminist discussions of history: that what is traditionally considered interesting in history is what causes and provokes rapid and visible transformations. All that seems to be stable, cyclical, or subject to gradual change appears only in the background, as a series of very slow and almost imperceptible modifications occurring in the natural world rather than within the man-made realm of history (Pomata, "La storia" 1434).

In her innovative historical research, Gianna Pomata inserts into Braudel's historiographic methodology the sexual dimension that he ignored, envisioning a new form of historiography that provides a subtler definition of historical time and accounts for the plurality of social times and human experiences. Such historiography would give not only a voice, but also a written word, a place in a new historical archive, to women's otherwise silent experiences.[6] By establishing Ida as the protagonist of her novel, Morante argues, along similar lines, that the pressing issue is not so much to start writing histories about women as heads of governments, political leaders, and military chiefs, but to question the methods and aims of mainstream historiography. Only by breaking down its own boundaries can historiography finally allow for the expression of women's history; and disciplines as different as sociology and biology, anthropology and demography, psychoanalysis, philosophy, and linguistics have from different perspectives much to contribute to the definition of feminine historiography. With *La Storia* Morante demonstrates that in terms of interdisciplinarity, methodology, theory of observation, and narrative strategies, the contribution of fiction is equally important for the resurfacing of women's voices from the depths of historical oblivion.[7] In this sense the title of Morante's novel is significant. A title inevitably establishes some interpretative coordinates for the text it names. It opens possible avenues of reading and thus directs the readers' responses to the text (Barthes, "Textual Analysis" 87). By entitling her novel *La Storia: romanzo* (*History: A Novel*), Morante claims not only that official history—with its silences and biases—is ultimately a fiction, but also that her fiction—with its account of silenced voices and untold stories—is history. In this way, she attributes to herself the dual role of feminist historian and novelist, correcting on both ethical and ideological grounds Manzoni's proscription of the "amphibious genre."

It was in the 1970s that pioneering women historians, just like Morante the novelist, had to invent how to write women's history. This endeavor was all the more difficult because orthodox historiography had very little to contribute to this often frustrating research. Feminist historians had to devise a different way of looking at historical records, a way that would also allow discovery of traces of women's stories in the canonic texts.[8] Looking at official records from a new perspective, finding the reasons and biases behind the silence of women, and discovering and exploring documents such as diaries, memoirs, private correspondences, and novels are some of the new avenues proposed by feminist historians, who urge the writing of history to become "a source of freedom, releasing the powers of fantasy and imagination" (Perrot, "Making History" 59). It is in its call for intertextuality, its refusal of all forms of genre regimentation, and most of all the defense of the value of imagination in historical narratives that feminist historiography ideally rejects the rigid binary opposition between fiction and history. As Pomata contends:

> Un problema cruciale in proposito mi pare questo: se, come sembra, l'ortodossia storica che abbiamo ereditato si è basata su una distinzione molto rigida tra storia e romanzo, la sfida per noi oggi è ripensare criticamente, ripensare da capo, questa distinzione. Il nostro problema non è solo *che cosa* scrivere (rinnovare il contenuto oggettuale della storia), ma anche e forse soprattutto *come* scrivere: sperimentare nuove forme di narrazione storica più adeguate alle finalità conoscitive della storia delle donne. ("Commento" 119; see appendix 35)

It is precisely from this perspective that Morante's *La Storia* establishes fruitful connections with contemporary feminist historiographic theories. The novel, in fact, implicitly addresses all the theoretical questions that women historians have been asking for the last thirty years. Although *La Storia* polemically separates historical chronicle from fictional plot, when the issue of truth is discussed an interesting reversal occurs. Because of its absurd brutality and its illogical obsession with evil, history becomes the land of untruth, of "*irrealtà.*" Truth is set on the side of the fictional invention that acquires, in this way, an important ethical value. Fictional reality bears the essence of a valuable historical and poetic truth, one that recounts the parallel story of women, children, and other marginal characters as they cope, endure, and in their different ways challenge the dominant order. In a 1959 article on the novel, Morante stated that

> Il valore, anche *storico,* di un romanzo non dipende dai suoi pretesti narrativi, ma dalle sue verità. Tocca all'intelligenza, alla libertà di giudizio e all'attenzione dei contemporanei riconscere le proprie verità—fino a quelle più occulte o inconfessate—nelle rappresentazioni dei loro poeti. ("Sul romanzo" 1511; see appendix 36)

In her view, therefore, historical novels have a fundamental political value. They become in fact the subversive media that recount the true stories that patriarchal historiography has long neglected or refused to recount. By the same token, historical novels acquire an important ethical function. As Croce claims in his 1944 discussion of Proust, "the historical conception of reality is a profoundly religious and moral conception, the only one that is equal to the idea of religion and morality" (145). According to Croce, history, once it has occurred, assumes the form of historical necessity, and yet, the same history, seen in the actuality of its becoming, is "a continuous creation of liberty" (145). Croce is able to relate historical knowledge to ethics because he sees the moral need to know as inextricably tied to the need to act, and in turn the need to act as an expression of spiritual freedom. Therefore, the moral imperative is at the roots of both thought and action. The quest for truth and the knowledge of history become moral categories, as they all contribute to the creation of liberty. Although Croce's philosophical idealism is fraught with naive generalizations (Who creates liberty? Are we all in the same position to translate our moral needs into actions?), the connection it establishes between historical knowledge and moral life remains ideologically compelling. It certainly had a deep influence on Morante's *La Storia.* For Morante, telling the truth of women is both part of a process of historical knowledge and an act of moral commitment. It is, in other words, the necessary starting point for the creation of women's liberty in the historical world.

La Storia's Feminine Voice: The *Narratrice* and the Problem of the Subject

The most explicit criticism of mainstream historiography has often appeared in fictional works. Jane Austen's novels ridicule Hume's and Robertson's enlightened historiography, and George Eliot's *Middlemarch*—not unlike the works of Manzoni and Morante—focuses on the "unhistorical acts" usually deleted from official records. Fiction therefore appears as fertile ground to historians trying to find a voice and a narrative form suitable for expressing women's historical experiences.[9]

In spite of their criticism of historical realism, several twentieth-century historians still depend on its methodology. Undoubtedly, the concept of a universal objective truth has been dismantled from several angles. If the subjective contribution of the historian is by now acknowledged with all its implications, no mainstream historiographer is willing to address it from a gender-defined perspective. By confronting the issue of subjectivity in the reconstruction of the past, *La Storia* emphasizes the feminine voice of its narrator. Morante's novel also reshapes the boundaries between private and public experiences (valuing the former over the latter), comments on the contribution of oral reports to this alternative form of historiography, and directs us toward a significant modification of traditional chronologies. Finally, *La Storia* points to narrative forms—both fictional and historical—that can account for the specificity of women's experiences, while at the same time denouncing the crushing force of patriarchal epistemological codes.

La Storia explicitly employs a female narrator, whose gender, however, has been generally overlooked. *La Storia*'s narrator is clearly sexualized in the feminine, thus defying an interpretation that is bound to a totalizing definition of the narrative voice in a masculine or neutral form. Reviewing *La Storia* in the avant-garde journal *Il Verri,* Barilli argued that Morante exaggerated certain aspects of the naturalist model by creating characters that are socially and intellectually quite inferior to the narrator. The narrator, therefore, exploits an attitude that oscillates between open commiseration and satisfied superiority:

> Questi guai derivanti da personaggi deliberatamente costretti a una inferiorità sociale e psichica si ricollegano ad un altro [patetismo] ancora più grave che consiste nell'adozione del cosiddetto narratore onnisciente: il narratore padreterno che vede e sa tutto delle sue creature, che le domina con sguardo olimpico, nascondendo ipocritamente il dato fondamentale che prima ancora di sapere di loro, egli le fa, le crea. (Rev. of *La Storia* 106; see appendix 37)

Barilli sexualizes *La Storia*'s narrator in the feminine only when he is ready to dismiss her as a pupil of the "Divino Marchese" ("Divine Marquis"), a "subdola portatrice di buone dosi di sadismo" ("a cunning bearer of good doses of sadism")—one that pitilessly destroys all her characters and places the blame on destiny, nature, or history (rev. of *La Storia* 107). In his account, Barilli shifts from a pseudostructuralist definition of the narrator that sees her as an unsexed function rather than a living creature—but that actually emphasizes masculine connotations—to a psychologizing one that accounts for its gender specificity in negative terms.

Barilli's uneasiness about *La Storia*'s female narrator reflects a number of theoretical assumptions on the linguistic subject that only recent feminist approaches have begun to challenge. These assumptions mainly relate to influential linguistic theories such as those by Ferdinand de Saussure, Noam Chomsky, and Emile Benveniste. Since Saussure's seminal *Cours de linguistique générale* (*Course in General Linguistics,* 1913), the distinction between *langue* and *parole* originated a binarism between a privileged sphere (*langue*) as the abstract linguistic repertoire—the conventional system of signs based on the relationship between signifiers and signifieds—and another area (*parole*) that defines the empirical field of personal actualization of the language by the speaking subject that produces it. Structural linguistics exclusively examines the space of *langue* as a system existing independently from the subject's conscious activity, which is the individual appropriation of *langue* through a concrete speech act (Saussure 37).[10] Even if *langue,* as the founding linguistic code, is the necessary presupposition for the existence of *parole,* Saussure agrees that there could be no *langue* without *parole,* language's concrete manifestation into specific speech acts. Only *parole* in fact can modify, enrich, and renew the abstract code. In spite of these concessions, structural linguistics remains exclusively interested in the dimension of *langue.* Developing Freud's definition of the two primary psychic processes of similarity and contiguity, Saussure identifies the unconscious structures regulating the linguistic system in the paradigmatic and syntagmatic relationships between the signs in the realm of *langue.* The dimension of *parole,* with its empirical, concrete, and conscious subject (possibly also a feminine one) is thus excluded from scientific analysis.

The insertion of the distinct subject into the linguistic system occurs with the generative grammar that identifies a Cartesian subject as founder of linguistic constructions. Chomsky argues for an area of general "normalcy" for linguistic productions, that of the logical, linear creation of syntactic structures. In other words, speaking subjects have, according to Chomsky, an innate set of rational structures that allow for the generation of an endless range of sentences starting from the same set of logical tools (20).[11] Privileging the syntagmatic concatenation and the analytical approach, Chomsky overlooks other forms of production of meaning, like those of poetry, dreams, and the *écriture feminine* that polemically reject all forms of causally organized discourse while seeking to articulate other, and more profound, levels of meaning. In fact, Chomsky's definition of the speaking subject implies a strong, unitary subject that organizes consciousness, writing, and speaking along strictly logical and rational patterns.

Even if Benveniste introduces the idea of *énonciation* as the individual act of appropriation and utilization of language, his subject remains a universal and abstract principle. Certainly, Benveniste recognizes that the subject emerges from within the linguistic process, as there is, according to him, no subjectivity outside of language. In other words, the act of foundation of the subject is strictly linguistic in nature: it is an "*ego*" that creates itself in the act of saying "*ego*" (224).[12] However, even if Benveniste pays more attention to the speaking subject, in his theory this subject remains a general function of the linguistic process, unable to articulate the principle of sexual difference. By identifying the subject with a Cartesian Cogito, or what Husserl terms the "Transcendental Ego," Benveniste defines a universal subjective entity and a synthesizing consciousness that excludes the variety as well as specificity of individual subjects.[13] Keeping in mind Barilli's comment on Morante's narrator, it is easy to conclude that the "universal subject" is a misnomer, as it is an implicitly masculine form. Morante's *La Storia* constitutes a valuable *presa di posizione* against linguistic theories such as those of Saussure, Chomsky, and Benveniste. Morante chooses to speak in a feminine voice, a voice that emerges in critical moments throughout the narration, often highlighting its feminine gender, such as when she lovingly speaks about Useppe:

> Che mi si lasci, dunque, restare ancora un poco in compagnia del mio pischelluccio, prima di tornarmene sola al secolo degli altri. (625; see appendix 38)

The overt *narratrice* challenges a number of historiographic demands as well. These demands, however, amount to what

Mink would term "conceptual presuppositions," or generalized assumptions that, because of their being ingrained in our cultural and intellectual frameworks, imply universal assent without critical evaluation ("Narrative Form" 132). One of these demands is that of the historian's impersonality. Even if impersonality itself, a criterion that dates back to the rhetoric of historical realism, has been widely contested, the use of lyrical or confessional writing in historical accounts is still regarded with much suspicion. The profound innovation of texts like Jules Michelet's *La Sorcière* (*The Sorceress,* 1862), for example, is disturbing even for modern historians, and they do not wish to emulate it.

In *La Storia* the narrative voice is not only gender specific, but always emotionally charged. Since she does not directly participate in the narrated events, the narrator could be termed external. By reiterating her personal emotional involvement in these events, she also becomes, in some respects, an internal narrator (Bernabò 46),[14] that "donna del Testaccio, senza volto, senza nome" ("woman from Testaccio, without a face and without a name") disparaged by Giacinto Spagnoletti (12). Two of the major objections that critics raised against Morante's historical novel are the intrusiveness of this unusual narratorial voice and the abuse of terms of endearment and other emotional utterances emerging here and there in the text (Barilli, rev. of *La Storia* 106–07; Asor Rosa 78). It is the cross-reference with the canon of historiographic writing that raises this concern. The historian is universally regarded as one "who attempts coolly to solve problems that are absolutely external to him" (Gossman 28). In opposition to this viewpoint, the narrator of *La Storia* is an integral part of her story, and her ties to it are emotional as well as intellectual. While she conjures up the fictional past of her characters and re-creates the broader picture of world-historical events, she also progressively creates her own self, her feminine narrative persona, inscribing it into the present of her discourse:

> nel momento di fissare la propria *verità* attraverso una sua attenzione del mondo reale, il romanziere moderno, in luogo di invocare le Muse, è indotto a suscitare un *io* recitante (protagonista e interprete) che gli valga da alibi. Quasi per

> significare, a propria difesa: "S'intende che quella da me rappresentata non è *la* realtà; ma una realtà relativa all'io di me stesso, o ad un altro io, diverso in apparenza, da me stesso, che in sostanza, però, m'appartiene, e nel quale io, adesso, m'impersono per intero." Così, mediante la prima persona, la realtà nuovamente inventata si rende in una verità nuova. Questa *prima persona responsabile,* dunque, è una condizione moderna. (Morante, "Sul romanzo" 1505; see appendix 39)

All claims to truth are therefore emptied of universalizing pretensions, as they are subordinated to the narrator's subjective vision and her emotional participation in past events.

The narrator reveals her selective and interpretative presence by separating historical chronicle from fictional narration. The world events narrated in the opening sections of each chapter are structurally quite different from the events of the narration itself. The most evident difference is that the female narrator denies emplotment to official history, which is forced to exist exclusively as a syntagmatic chain of happenings organized in a rigidly chronological order. As we have seen in *Il Gattopardo,* the act of emplotment marks the historian's subjective constructive act; by choosing the basic structuring principle of a chronicle for the historical sections, the *narratrice* of *La Storia* refuses any constructive participation in the past that she examines. The two parts of the narration, however, are also somewhat related, as it is the narrator's emotional involvement that binds the official record and the private account. Although the style in the historical chronicle is generally dry and matter-of-fact, the narrator does occasionally intervene at crucial moments with critical statements such as on the title page, where history is "Uno scandalo che dura da diecimila anni" ("A scandal that has lasted ten thousand years"). Adolf Hitler is presented as "un ossesso sventurato, e invaso dal vizio della morte" ("a poor maniac, viciously obsessed by death") (9; 6), and Benito Mussolini as an "arrivista mediocre, e 'impasto di tutti i detriti' della peggiore Italia" ("a mediocre opportunist, a 'compound of all the flotsam' of the worst Italy") (9; 5). If the two parts of the narration remain structurally separated, the common element is the explicit presence of the narrator and her emotional participation in both history and story.

Against orthodox historical attitudes, *La Storia* features a subjective, all but impersonal narrator who does not always speak in omniscient terms (unlike an all-knowing historian and contrary to Barilli's claim).[15] On the contrary, she repeatedly confesses her doubts and uncertainties: "Non saprei come né dove, aveva scovato certi testi di Proudhon, Bakunin, Malatesta, e altri anarchici" ("[I wouldn't know how or where] he had dug up texts by Proudhon, Bakunin, Malatesta, and other anarchists") (22; 19), the *narratrice* states while discussing Ida's father and his education in anarchism. She continues, "Io non conosco abbastanza la Calabria" ("I don't know Calabria well") (28; 24) and "Non ho potuto controllare l'ubicazione precisa di quell'osteria" ("I have been unable to discover the exact location of that tavern") (40; 34). Commenting on Carlo's work at the factory, she points out that she has no information regarding his precise job there (414), and after she narrates Nino's roaming around in the blacked-out city during the alarms, she admits that what she has provided is only a partial reconstruction of Nino's mysterious wanderings, nor can she give any further information about them (134).

Though she freely admits her uncertainties about factual events and geographical locations, the narrator nonetheless does possess absolute knowledge of her characters' feelings.[16] Her ties to them are emotional rather than logical. One of the most significant and moving examples of this narratorial attitude toward her characters occurs with her maternal "Buona notte, biondino" ("Good night, Giovannino") (387; 329), which concludes the powerful and visionary reconstruction of Giovannino's last moments of life in snow-covered Russia. The "memory" to which the narrator refers at the beginning of this section does not result from either direct participation in the event or other people's oral reports. It is, rather, a sympathetic and creative "narration from within" of Giovannino's last thoughts, fears, sensations, and dreams, which accounts for the narrator's ability to express both graphic vividness and heartfelt pathos. The screen of fictional constructions, therefore, allows for the foregrounding of a notion, that of subjectivity, which is still not frequented by professional historians, other than polemically (Passerini 12). Even unorthodox Marxist historiography would look askance at the narration of phenomena that only concern individuals and their inner lives. The notion of subjectivity made its way into historiography thanks to the insertion of memory as an acceptable historical source.[17] In Morante's text, the temporal distance separating the narrator and her materials is significantly short. One generation separates her from Ida, and her story is mainly built from her memories, direct oral reports,[18] and odd documents like photographs and other family heirlooms.[19] This choice opposes the official history of archival records, addressing another method of making history, a method that unveils forgotten historical treasures—"le poche memorie dei morti" ("the few reminiscences of the dead") (28; 24)—and affectionately conserves the fragile testimonies of unwritten tales.[20]

La Storia's Counterhistory and Its Ideological Significance

May one conclude, at this point, that by destroying the boundary between history and fiction, and by subscribing to a subjective voice, Morante rejects the possibility of even attempting to express a collectively perceived objective reality? *La Storia* redefines the borders between subject and object. While the narrator is ignorant of factual events, she is omniscient regarding her characters' inner lives. Significantly, the narration of their dreams occupies a substantial part of the story. The kind of psychofictional history that Morante sketches in *La Storia* is revolutionary not only because it questions the distinction between fiction and history in the terms that Manzoni established in his essay *Del romanzo storico.* By detailing the impact of history on the external and inner lives of her characters, Morante also dismantles the opposition between public history and private stories and argues for the historicity of human psychic structures. By writing the story of Ida and Useppe, Morante suggests that historical subjects may be created from everyday existence. Consequently, Ida and Useppe are granted what Luisa Passerini calls a double right: to be in history and to have a history. Such history is made of daily events and psychic adventures: reporting them means redefining the opposition between interior and exterior, public and private, subject and object, and history and psychology.

La Storia shows that certain psychological patterns are not universal but can be tied to precise historical and social occurrences. Ida—like her mother, Nora, before her—is paralyzed by the fear of racial persecution. Like Nora, she hides and conceals all traces of her Jewish origin, to the point of keeping it a secret even from her son, Nino. The more she lives her racial identity as a curse and a sin, the more she is unconsciously attracted to the Jewish ghetto (Re 364). If the laws of the fascist regime force her to cast her own identity into oblivion, the laws of the unconscious work in the opposite direction, lulling her into rediscovering a subterranean link with her people: "lei che prima delle leggi razziali non aveva mai incontrato nessun ebreo fuori di Nora, seguendo una sua pista incongrua s'orientò a preferenza nella cerchia del Ghetto romano" ("she who, before the racial laws, had never encountered another Jew except Nora, began to follow an incongruous trail of her own, preferring the confines of the Roman Ghetto") (58; 49–50). Coming to terms with this side of history counteracts the official forces of racial cancellation. In the ghetto Ida is no longer estranged from her origins but a participant in a form of "collective identity," to borrow Maurice Halbwachs's definition (21):

> Si sentiva attirata là da un richiamo di dolcezza, quasi come l'odore di una stalla per un vitello, o quello di un suk per un'araba; e insieme da un impulso di necessità ossessiva, come di un pianeta gravitante intorno a una stella. (93; see appendix 40)

In the ghetto, Ida is in touch with a set of mental representations that surpass the time and space frames of single individuals; thus she unconsciously and emotionally profits from the experiences and knowledge accumulated by entire generations.

In one of the most powerful and tragic scenes of the novel, when Ida and little Useppe are at the train station and see the trains carrying the Jewish people away to the German concentration camps, Ida hears the voices coming from inside the cars:

> E Ida riconosceva questo coro confuso. . . . tutto questo misero vocio dei carri la adescava con una dolcezza struggente, per una memoria continua che non le tornava dai tempi, ma da un altro canale: di là stesso dove la ninnavano le canzoncine calabresi di suo padre, o la poesia anonima della notte avanti, o i bacetti che le bisbigliavano carina carina. Era un punto di riposo che la tirava in basso, nella tana promiscua di un'unica famiglia sterminata. (245; see appendix 41)

The positive value of this memory has a very dangerous counterpart. By sharing the collective memory of her people, Ida establishes a parallel history that is in deadly conflict with that of her times and that cannot possibly exist in conjunction with it. While savoring these unconscious memories, she forces herself into a practical condition of marginality. From a psycho linguistic perspective, one could argue with Julia Kristeva that Ida estranges herself from the Symbolic order, the order of the law, of the father, finally of history. As Lucia Re points out, "Ida's dreams, hallucinations, and visions in the novel represent a series of ruptures, absences, and breaks in the symbolic; they appear as her unconscious attempts to reject it. . . . This disruption or negativity—Morante suggests—can indeed turn into a death wish, the most radical of all the drives of the imaginary in its opposition to the symbolic" (364–65). This is particularly evident in all the images of regression that inform Ida's desires and shape her fantasies and dreams. The atmosphere of the Jewish ghetto, in particular, enthralls Ida like a "nenia bassa e sonnolenta" ("low and somnolent dirge"), marked by those irresistible rhythms known by all those who are "subject to death" (337; 288).[21] In search of a lost earthly paradise, Ida is able to transform reality, as the ghostly apartments, vacated after the Nazis' raids, become for her the "stalla materna, calda di respiri animali" ("maternal stable, warm with animals' breath") (238; 203) where she and Useppe can fall asleep and, finally, rest.

In this perspective, little Useppe's adventure repeats, from another perspective, his mother's. While Ida, a prisoner of the crushing force of the Symbolic order, can relate to the Imaginary in a confrontational way, as it is for her both salvation and destruction, Useppe is cast within the Imaginary, which maintains for him all its positive traits. The description of his acquisition of language and sexuality, for instance, is a daring rejection of both Jacques Lacan's psycholinguistic theories and Freud's psychoanalytic ones. In Morante's own words, Useppe appears as "una vivente smentita (ovvero forse eccezione?) alla scienza del Professor Freud" ("a living refutation of the science of Professor Freud [or perhaps the exception to it]") (405; 345). Useppe exists in a space that precedes the definition of sexual identities and sexual roles:

> Per essere maschietto, difatti, lo era senz'altro, né gli mancava nulla; ma per ora (e si può credere alla mia testimonianza giurata) del proprio organo virile non se ne interessava affatto, né piú né meno che dei propri orecchi o del proprio naso. (405; see appendix 42)

He embodies Morante's conviction that gender, rather than being naturally inscribed in a genetic code, is a matter of cultural and social regimentation.[22] It is a "social category imposed on a sexed body," and a way of referring to the "exclusively social origins of subjective identities of men and women" (J. Scott, "Gender" 1056).

A similar interpretation guides Morante's description of Useppe's coming to terms with the order of language. According to Lacan, the self is created within a division, as it "can only conceptualise itself when it is mirrored back to itself from the position of another's desire" (Mitchell 5). A child's acquisition of language and selfhood is not a totalizing adventure. On the contrary, it is marked by scission and division. It is in the "stade du miroir" ("mirror phase") that the child acquires a sense of the self through an experience of negativity. Identity is paradoxically grasped in alterity: the "self" as "other" from itself. It is an individual psychical process (recalling Freud's *Ichspaltung*) that has its collective counterpart in language itself (Lacan 93–110). As Saussure argues, the linguistic sign, divided as it is between signified and signifier, maintains an arbitrary relationship with the referent (the concrete object or abstract idea to which the sign refers) (100). If nature becomes culture through the process of nomination, language becomes the intermediary between people and nature. But, just as obviously, language can only function by naming an object in its absence. "Words," therefore, "stand for objects, because they only have to be spoken at the moment when the first object is lost" (Rose 31). From these presuppositions, Lacan sees the acquisition of language as the moment of a separation from an ideal state of oneness and totality. This situation of undivided pleasure in the fusion with nature is immediately lost with "the introduction of an articulated network of differences," which henceforth exclusively refers to objects as separated from a subject (Kristeva, "Women's Time" 198). For Lacan, therefore, the necessary precondition to the acquisition of language is separation; the "subject is . . . constituted in language *as* this division or splitting"

(Rose 31). Introduction to the order of language (the Symbolic) is dramatically marked by a break or rupture. Unity (what Lacan terms the Imaginary and Kristeva the Semiotic) becomes a utopia, a longing for a moment of wholeness that is ontologically as well as epistemologically unattainable. As Jacqueline Rose remarks, "identity is constructed in language, but only at a cost. Identity shifts, and language speaks the loss which lay behind that first moment of symbolisation" (32).

Contrasted to Lacan's theorization, Useppe's acquisition of language is marked by an attitude of immeasurable joy and wonder. He favors analogies and associations rather than differences. By focusing on the identities between different objects, Useppe is able to conceptualize the world in paradigmatic, rather than syntagmatic, terms. As Lucente comments, Useppe is a natural poet, "in cognitive as well as imaginative terms, [his] procedure is also . . . that of the creation of metaphor" ("History" 251):

> Non s'era mai vista una creatura piú allegra di lui. Tutto ciò che vedeva intorno lo interessava e lo animava gioiosamente. Mirava esilarato i fili della pioggia fuori della finestra, come fossero coriandoli e stelle filanti multicolori. . . . lui non vedeva le cose ristrette dentro i loro aspetti usuali; ma quali immagini multiple di altre cose varianti all'infinito. (120; see appendix 43)

For little Useppe, similarity, not difference, is the root of linguistic discovery:

> Una delle prime parole che imparò fu *ttelle* (stelle). Però chiamava ttelle anche le lampadine di casa, i derelitti fiori che Ida portava da scuola, i mazzi di cipolle appesi, perfino le maniglie delle porte, e in séguito anche le rondini. Poi quando imparò la parola *dóndini* (rondini) chiamava dóndini pure i suoi calzerottini stesi a asciugare su uno spago. . . . I mobili e le masserizie erano case, treni. Gli asciugamani, gli stracci e anche le nubi erano *dandèle* (bandiere). Le luci delle stelle erano erba, e le stelle medesime erano formiche intorno a una mollichella (la luna). (120, 131; see appendix 44)

If, according to current psycholinguistics, the acquisition of language is based on a progressive appropriation of a system of differences, poetic discourse and the language of dreams are subversive, as they instead highlight similarities and identities. Useppe, a natural poet and innocent revolutionary, prefers to follow analogical and metaphorical patterns, setting into crisis the basis of communicative, purpose-oriented speech. The result is an attitude of childlike wonder (Lucente, "History" 251) and untainted pleasure. Like Giovanni Pascoli's *fanciullo divino,* Useppe frolics in the undivided joy of naming things for the first time, highlighting creativity and closeness rather than separation from the outside world, engaging in a universal dialogue with the entire cosmos. Useppe is the antihistorian *par excellence:*[23] thinking, for him, is not a rational procedure, but corresponds to the ability to fantasize and invent oral poems that, by activating the register of the Imaginary over that of the Symbolic, express a unique and nonregimented relationship between the subject and reality:

> Il sole è come un albero grande
> che dentro tiene i nidi.
> E suona come una cicala maschio e come il mare
> e con l'ombra ci scherza come una gatta piccola.
> (632; see appendix 45)

As he conceptualizes the world by means of similarities and recurrences, Useppe expresses a utopically different way of coming into the sociosymbolic contract, one that implies a radical difference in the relationship to power, language, and history. This difference is articulated through a unique experience of temporality. Useppe appears happy when he manages to live in a wholly subjective dimension in which the current time frames are modified in a utopically eternal present:

> è un fatto che, mentre lui stava cosí a pensare, il tempo comune degli altri per lui si riduceva quasi a zero. Esiste nell'Asia un piccolo essere detto *panda minore,* di un aspetto fra lo scoiattolo e l'orsacchiotto, il quale vive sugli alberi in boschi di montagna irraggiungibili; e ogni tanto scende in terra in cerca di germogli da mangiare. Di uno di questi panda minori si diceva che trascorresse dei millennii a pensare sul proprio albero: dal quale scendeva in terra ogni 300 anni. Ma in realtà, il calcolo di tali durate era relativo: difatti, nel mentre che in terra erano passati 300 anni, sull'albero

> di quel panda minore erano passati appena dieci minuti. (282; see appendix 46)

In Maurice Blanchot's terms, Useppe is a figure of prophecy. In his existence Useppe lives, in fact, what Blanchot calls prophetic time, "un temps d'interruption, cet *autre* temps qui est toujours présent en tout temps" ("a time of interruption, this *other* time which is always present in all times") (101), a time that belongs to the people who are deprived of every form of power (significantly Blanchot speaks of the widow and the orphan). The quintessential expression of these subjective temporal experiences occurs in one of Useppe's wanderings out of town, when with his dog, Bella, he arrives in "un luogo maraviglioso" ("a wondrous place") (507; 430): a round clearing in the woods:

> In fondo ai prati, il terreno si avvallava, e incominciava una piccola zona boscosa. Fu lí che Useppe e Bella a un certo punto rallentarono i passi, e smisero di chiacchierare.
>
> Erano entrati in una radura circolare, chiusa da un giro di alberi che in alto mischiavano i rami, cosí da trasformarla in una specie di stanza col tetto di foglie. Il pavimento era un cerchio d'erba appena nata con le piogge, forse ancora non calpestata da nessuno, e fiorita solo di un'unica specie di margherite minuscole, le quali avevano l'aria d'essersi aperte tutte quante insieme in quel momento. . . . Pareva proprio di trovarsi in una tenda esotica, lontanissima da Roma e da ogni altra città: chi sa dove, arrivati dopo un grande viaggio; e che fuori all'intorno si stendesse un enorme spazio, senz'altro rumore che il movimento quieto dell'acqua e dell'aria. (508–09; see appendix 47)

In this symbolic place, Useppe experiences a sudden convergence of all space and time into one single moment. Here he exists in a dimension akin to Kristeva's semiotic *chora,* the maternal womb and nourishing receptacle, the pre-Oedipal space not yet organized into a structured system of differences (*Revolution* 25–26). Here he also exists beyond the linear time of history in a monumental temporality that recalls Kristeva's definition of women's time. According to Kristeva, there is a basic difference between the time of history and women's time. History is exclusively conceptualized in terms of linear time, "time as project, teleology, departure, progression and arrival" (Moi 187). Kristeva relates linear time (what she calls "cursive time," borrowing Nietzsche's definition) to the time of language in its ordered, syntagmatic sequence of words. Female subjectivity, instead, retains the cyclical time of repetition and the monumental dimension of eternity from among the various modalities of time experienced through the history of civilizations:

> On the one hand, there are cycles, gestation, the eternal recurrence of a biological rhythm which conforms to that of nature and imposes a temporality whose stereotyping may shock, but whose regularity and unison with what is experienced as extra-subjective time, cosmic time, occasion vertiginous visions and unnameable *jouissance.* On the other hand, and perhaps as a consequence, there is the massive presence of a monumental temporality, without cleavage or escape, which has so little to do with linear time (which passes) that the very word "temporality" hardly fits [as it is] all-encompassing and infinite like imaginary space. ("Women's Time" 191)

Expressing these notions of time means accessing the archaic or mythical memories and the intrasubjective and corporeal experiences "left mute by culture in the past" (Kristeva, "Women's Time" 194). In this sense, the notion of "women's time" is less a matter of gender than a method—accessible to both women and men—of relating to what is traditionally suppressed from common conceptualization and, consequently, historical representation.

While verbalizing these temporal dimensions, *La Storia* also chronicles the progressive alienation from this ideal temporality, as Useppe becomes progressively immersed into history through a series of traumatizing events. His access to historical time is marked in fact by a number of epiphanies of horror. The most striking ones are his visit to the Tiburtina Station, where he sees the cattle trains carrying the Jewish prisoners to the German concentration camps, and his discovery of pictures of horrifying Nazi crimes in a magazine. Participation in historical time is devastating for Useppe. If historical awareness appears destructive in *La Storia,* his ability to relate to this other time—which the narrator attributes to his epileptic pathology—has the paradoxical nature of being both healing and annihilating.

Useppe lives in a visionary state, an absolute present in drastic contrast to the linear time of history, conjuring up a collective, monumental dimension that parallels Ida's discovery of her racial roots in the ghetto. In these moments, Useppe is totally happy, as he is able to experience "la festa totale del mondo" ("the total festivity of the world") (121; 104). Euphoria emerges in the novel only when the usual time and space frames are overcome and Useppe becomes part of the undifferentiated dimension of the Semiotic. Unfortunately, this dimension is also one of marginalization, dangerously close to absolute isolation[24] and self-destruction.[25]

* * *

The result of a rape perpetrated by a German soldier against a woman of partly Semitic descent, Useppe bears, inscribed on his body and handed down through his heritage, the ominous signs of the scapegoat. According to René Girard, there are general and recurring criteria for the identification of victims, and these criteria are based on cultural, ethnic, and religious presuppositions: it is a fact of transcultural evidence, in fact, that racial and religious minorities, as well as socially and economically marginal groups and individuals, tend to polarize the majority against them. In addition to the cultural and religious parameters guiding the selection of victims, there are also significant physical and psychological traits according to which victims are identified. "Sickness, madness, genetic deformities, accidental injuries, and even disabilities in general tend to polarize persecutors" (Girard 18). All that is perceived as abnormal, in other words, acts as the potential trigger for the victimization/persecution mechanism. If, in a specific social system, the normal corresponds to the average and the integrated, all that inhabits the regions that are more removed from the center of normalcy constitutes, by opposition, the heterogeneous cauldron in which dangerous difference brews. The more a system is closed and structured along fixed boundaries and stable directives, the more active it will be in eliminating all that is perceived as a threat to its own norm, all those extremes that actively or passively defy integration within the its controlled structures, and all that is a reminder of the system's tendency toward entropy; that is, toward progressive disorder and final inertness.

In *La Storia,* Useppe is a conglomerate of victims' signs: fatherless in a patrilinear society, he is legally granted family ties only to his mother and therefore is branded as the most scorned outcast, a "*bastardo di padre ignoto*" ("*bastard of unknown father*") (286; 244), as Ida in one of her fear-induced fixations thinks to herself. Because of her Jewish roots, Ida herself is a potential victim of racial persecution and a social pariah as a single mother. Her son embodies all those extremes that accompany the selection of victims: "sottosviluppato, malnutrito, povero campione senza valore" ("underdeveloped, undernourished, poor valueless remnant") (287; 244), little Useppe is uncommonly beautiful, in some ways excessively precocious and in others surprisingly slow. Too small for his age, he is also abnormally weak, as he suffers from epilepsy, a disease that he probably inherited from his mother. Traditionally associated with deviant figures such as prophets, visionaries, and mad people, the grand mal is perceived as a scandal to be hidden from the world, the unmentionable mark of a fatal transgression, and the obscure stigma identifying the scapegoat and activating the scapegoat mechanism: "una prova immane e senza colpa, la scelta inconsapevole d'una creatura isolata che raccogliesse la tragedia collettiva" ("an immense and guiltless trial, the unconscious selection of an isolated creature who would sum up the collective tragedy") (30; 25). With its sudden losses of identity and temporary abolition of consciousness of time and space, epilepsy represents the complete obliteration of all differences and, with them, of all hierarchies. For a society that has radicalized the concept of difference, distorting it into the rhetoric of racial superiority and ethnic cleansing, Useppe represents the subversive abolition of all criteria of differentiation. These criteria are those upon which the patriarchal order has traditionally thrived, criteria that establish codes of inclusion and exclusion, superiority and inferiority, based on a hierarchically thwarted concept of difference.

Difference also appears eliminated in the dark shelter in Pietralata where Ida and Useppe move after their house is bombed and destroyed. Pietralata is a sterile country zone in the furthest outskirts of Rome where the fascist regime has created a "villaggio di esclusi" ("village for pariahs") (179; 153), populated by families driven by the authorities from their own residences in the center of the city. It is a "zona franca e fuori legge" ("no-man's-land, beyond the law") (179; 153), a giant area of confinement, a dismal colony where the poor, the unemployed, the insane, the homeless, and the sick are left to fend for themselves, although under command of the regime's silent authority, the "forte militare, torreggiante in vetta a un monte" ("military fort, standing high on a hill") (179; 154), symbol of the pervasive and controlling power that purges itself of the undesirable Other by marginalizing and excluding it in that sociogeographical wasteland, Pietralata.

Within the refugee shelter, the ideological reasons that trigger the process of exclusion and confinement become clear: difference is perceived as dangerous because it embodies a dark disorder and a moving chaos; it breeds uncontrollable forms of agitation and disturbance, evoking the fear of the ultimate contagion, that of an all-encompassing principle of indetermination in the collapse of all codes, hierarchies, and laws. Significantly, the numerous family nicknamed *I Mille* (The Thousand) appears to Ida as a chaotic and promiscuous amalgam of heterogeneous human beings, emblematic of all that the regime sought to erase and conceal. For Useppe instead, existing as he does in a situation that precedes the internalization of the concept of difference, *I Mille* are like "a single body and a single soul" (Re 368), for he is oblivious of all distinctions:

> per lui non esistevano differenze né di età, né di bello e brutto, né di sesso, né sociali. Tole e Mémeco, erano, veramente, due giovanotti stortarelli e rincagnati, di professione incerta (borsari neri, oppure ladri, secondo i casi), ma per lui erano tali e quali a due fusti di Hollywood o a due patrizi d'alto rango. La sora Mercedes puzzava; ma lui, quando giocava a nascondarella, sceglieva a preferenza, come nascondiglio, la coperta che lei teneva sui ginocchi. (185–86; see appendix 48)[26]

The question to be asked at this point regards the ideological import of the code of indeterminacy that Useppe embodies. Is the realm of the undifferentiated characterized by wholly positive connotations in the text? Is it attainable on practical grounds? What would its effects be? The lack of differentiation as experienced by Useppe—a dweller in the realm of the

Imaginary—is entirely positive: "lui, se avesse dovuto inventare un cielo, avrebbe fabbricato un locale sul tipo 'stanzone dei Mille'" ("asked to invent a heaven, he would have built a place along the lines of the 'big room of The Thousand'") (557; 472). For Ida, instead, the Imaginary with its code of indetermination bears positive connotations only when approached through nonrational channels—those depending upon the secret and labyrinthine workings of desire and the unconscious. When conceptualized through the regimented logic of the Symbolic order, the lack of difference appears to Ida as frightening and dangerous.

The code of the undifferentiated carries contrasting implications for the narrator herself. While sharing Ida's desire to reach that "regno orientale dove tutti sono bambini, senza coscienza né memoria" ("Oriental realm where all are children, without consciousness or memory") (239; 204), the narrator is aware that within the system of history, the code of the undifferentiated is at the basis of great social crises, as it becomes a synonym of chaos and utter confusion. Wars, plagues, and famine are often represented by their destructive effects on the social, legal, and moral organization of a certain group (Girard 30), and Giovanni Boccaccio's depiction of the plague in the Florentine society of the fourteenth century is a case in point. Morante's description of the effects of the war on the numerous inhabitants of the shelter in Pietralata, and the physical as well as moral degeneration of the family of *I Mille*—unseen by Useppe but very much perceived by Ida's less innocent eyes—parallels Manzoni's narration of the effects of the Milanese plague, culminating in the scene of the *lazzeretto* at the end of *I promessi sposi.* In both Morante and Manzoni the ultimate sign of the undifferentiated is by no means idyllic, as it is offered through the frightful images of numberless dead bodies, the "cadaveri . . . ignudi . . . ammonticchiati, intrecciati insieme, come un gruppo di serpi" ("naked [corpses] . . . piled up and interwoven together . . . like a cluster of snakes") (*Opere* 2.1: 590; *The Betrothed* 633) in Manzoni's description of the *monatti*'s carts, and the "corpi senza numero, talora accumulati a decine e a centinaia, cosí come erano stati massacrati in comune uno sull'altro" ("numberless bodies . . . sometimes heaped up by the tens and the hundreds, as they had been collectively massacred, one on top of the other") (326; 278) in Morante's picture of Nazi mass murders. Both portray humanity in its bare essentials, a humanity deprived of all the structures and codes that cultural and social orders have imposed, positively and negatively, upon people.

Epilepsy, the fatal mark that identifies Useppe as sacrificial victim, bears the same contradictory connotations. It represents both his potential salvation and his final destruction. In this sense, Useppe is essentially a tragic figure: he stands for the impossible coexistence of two orders that are dramatically juxtaposed and therefore mutually exclusive. Within the order of the Symbolic—representing a contract that, sooner or later, everyone has to sign—the emergence of the undifferentiated order of the Imaginary constitutes both a challenge and a curse. As the quintessential scapegoat, Useppe personifies all that is marginalized, silenced, and repressed, the diseased body that risks contaminating and disrupting (symbolically, of course) the entire social fabric. Inscribed in his maternal genes are the reasons for his culpability and his transgression (his illness or what his illness stands for, and his being, as Ida puts it, "senza razza" ["without race"] [287; 244]). Neither entirely Jewish nor truly Gentile, Useppe's double heritage represents a mark of impurity and contamination; the crime of the oblivion of differences, the specter of confusion that haunts the rational structures of the patriarchal order. In this way, Useppe shifts from historical to mythical grounds. As Girard reminds us:

> In historical persecutions the "guilty" remain sufficiently distinct from their "crimes" for there to be no mistake about the nature of the process. The same cannot be said of myth. The guilty person is so much a part of his offense that one is indistinguishable from the other. His offense seems to be a fantastic essence or ontological attribute. (36)

By existing on both historical and mythical levels, Useppe justifies two different temporal dimensions. He embodies the radicalization of a conflict in a historically specific moment, that of the Fascist dictatorship in Italy. By shifting into mythical territories he also speaks for the monumentality of such conflict. In varying degrees and changing forms, this conflict, which is identifiable in the opposition of the Imaginary against the

Symbolic, has marked all of patriarchal history. But *La Storia*'s ideological implications do not stop here. By attributing to the Imaginary contradictory connotations, the novel implicitly recognizes the Imaginary's subversive potential while arguing that it is not to become a permanent dwelling site. It is not the loss of an earthly paradise that we should mourn. The realm of the Imaginary defines, rather, a mental disposition that must be cherished as representing the wish for a new starting point, a potential *tabula rasa* from which to build a new epistemological code—one in which diversity, rather than hierarchical differentiation, would play a key role. Not surprisingly, it is the narrator who becomes the spokesperson for this outlook in *La Storia.*

The novel's characters appear either subjugated to the repressive order of history, or estranged into the antagonistic, antihistorical space that merges into the Imaginary. In varying degrees, they all fall prey to the deadly logic of binary oppositions: you are *either* in the order of history and language *or* outside of it; you are either in culture or in nature. The *narratrice* inhabits an ontological space that does not belong to either order, while sharing in both. What is most significant about the narrator in *La Storia* is the marriage of a distinctly feminine subjectivity with an ability to oscillate between multiple identities, take up different personas, and speak in different voices. On the one hand, she mimics the language of famous anarchists and politicians, of historical characters and literary figures. On the other, she imitates the colorful jargon of Roman *borgate* and sings popular songs and traditional lullabies. With one voice she reproduces—in order to mock it—the style of official historical records; with another she lovingly emulates a mother's talk to her infant, thus filling the gaps created by male-oriented linguistic patterns. It is a polyphonic, non-unitary voice that *La Storia* conjures up, a voice

> that probes, questions, remembers what was forgotten, raises doubts, shifts the focus of the master discourse, multiplies and diversifies its perspectives without, however, pretending to provide answers, definitions, positive assessments, totalizations, systematic interpretations. (Re 371)

La Storia is not solely committed to faithfully portraying the oppression of women, particularly during the Fascist era and generally under the patriarchal order; the novel also succeeds in what Hélène Cixous terms bringing "women to writing" (245) by expressing experiential areas that are traditionally bound to oblivion and by presenting a feminine narrative persona that manages to maintain her sexual specificity even as she disrupts the patriarchal notion of the unitary subject. By giving a voice to the *umili* in her novel, Morante not only takes up Manzoni's hallowed legacy; she also addresses linguistic issues similar to those confronted by the author of *I promessi sposi.* Manzoni had to literally invent a narrative language for Italian prose that would be accessible to a wide audience and would overcome regional linguistic barriers. Morante emulates Manzoni's endeavor by writing a text that experiments with a new narrative language of the feminine and childhood. This language is accountable for describing the world, both historical and fictional, that women and children often tragically and silently inhabit.

One of the most discussed areas of feminist criticism concerns the existence and the features of a specifically feminine discourse.[27] According to Xavière Gauthier, women are forced to find "their" place within the linear linguistic system:

> As long as women remain silent, they will be outside the historical process. But, if they begin to speak and write *as men do,* they will enter history subdued and alienated; it is a history that, logically speaking, their speech should disrupt. If, however, "replete" words (*mots pleins*) belong to men, how can women speak "otherwise," unless, perhaps, we can *make audible* that which agitates within us, suffers silently in the *holes of discourse,* in the unsaid, or in the non-sense. (162–63)

By underscoring their estrangement from the arena of male-dominated linguistic patterns and by endorsing the counter-discourse emerging from the gaps of the master code, women succeed in expressing traditionally neglected areas of human experiences. According to Kristeva, in "women's writing, language seems to be seen from a foreign land. . . . Estranged from language, women are visionaries, dancers who suffer as they speak" ("Oscillation" 166). Important as it is, however, this position must not be absolutized. The pressing issue is that of reintroducing women into history in order to modify it, instead of relegating them to an experience of marginality. In order to achieve this, their participation in history must not be limited to a mere repetition of patriarchal epistemological codes. By shifting from one voice to another, from public to private histories, and by moving between different temporal organizations, *La Storia*'s narrator avoids being chained to either a repetitive masquerade[28] of male scripts or a self-marginalizing affirmation of the woman's world as one in absolute disengagement from the existing order.

Finally, through the fluidity and "multivoicedness" of her narrator's persona, Morante rejects one of the *loci communes* of Western thought and one of its supposedly founding categories, the dichotomy between nature and culture (with the former subordinated to the latter and, consequently, the body subordinated to the mind). According to Sherry Ortner, women universally occupy a subordinate position because they are associated with what culture devaluates as inferior to itself, nature (7). Even historians who paid attention to untraditional time structures, such as the so-called ethnographic present of extra-European cultures, have associated these structures with "primitive" elements present in Western societies: women, isolated communities, farmers, children (Cohn 242–43). Much like Kristeva, Bernard Cohn argues that these groups develop a different relationship to time, one that is expressive, magical, and finally nonhistorical. The time of history, that of progress and conscious human action, development and change, is widely juxtaposed to a natural, feminine, and primitive time marked by repetition, circularity, and permanence. However, feminine time is also negatively defined as illogical, emotional, and tied to a human condition (a supposedly unchanging feminine nature) crushed by unconquerable forces: the biological drives and needs of the body (Pomata, "La storia" 1435).

Morante's portrayal of Ida's total estrangement from her body[29] and unconscious repression of sexuality[30] denounces the cruelty of a system that debases and represses women while exploiting them. But *La Storia* also shows that in the unwelcoming and leveling landscape of history and the written word, women express and leave traces of themselves that remain outside the conventions of the dominant discourse. As Pomata points out, from the dominant point of view, women are ambiguously set between the world of history and that of nature, between the world of culture and that of myth. The characters of *La Storia* show that, since they are forgotten immigrants in the land of history, their belonging to a different order simultaneously and paradoxically is their curse and salvation. It is exactly this fluctuating and multiple ontological status that the narrator of *La Storia* embodies with a vengeance. She calls for rethinking the validity of binary oppositions set in a hierarchical framework. Significantly, the *narratrice* cherishes the values of nature in the narration of history, as she adopts an emotional and intrasubjective posture defending femininity and the body. In this way she, and Morante through her persona, succeed in emplotting women's experiences by means of a historical voice that asserts her right to feminine subjectivity without falling prey to the authoritative and omniscient bias of traditional historiography and the centralizing logic of male-autographed discourses.

La Storia's Prophetic Thrust

At first reading, the plot of *La Storia* appears hopelessly tragic: history is frozen into the unrelieved repetition of the "noto principio immobile della dinamica storica: *agli uni il potere, e agli altri la servitú*" ("well-known, immobile principle of historical dynamics: *power to some, servitude to the others*") (7; 13). "Real" history tyrannically shapes the lives of the humblest, the latter having no power to manipulate events to their advantage, let alone understand them. While for Manzoni there is a possibility for redemption (that *meraviglioso cristiano* of providential interventions, the *coup de théâtre* that sets justice on the side of the poor), for Morante no salvation is possible. A somber beginning only foreshadows an even sadder ending. A positive history can, however, exist. It emerges in the text as the projection of the narrator's desires in a proleptic form. It lies outside the text's chronological framework and calls forth a utopian dimension that ideally reverses the grim determinism of the plot and counterbalances the cynical assumption that "la Storia [è] una maledizione" ("History [is] a curse") (18; 15).

In this way, *La Storia* corrects the deterministic framework of conventional historical accounts. The value of a historical text lies in the coherence of its construction—the way, that is, in which historians organize and select the facts from the past so that they lead, logically and coherently, toward the present. Thus, the historical construction justifies the present's social and political order and reveals its subjugation to the politics of any age (J. Scott, "The Problem" 6). Collingwood aptly noted that the difference between nature and history resides in the fact that in nature instants die and are replaced by others—"the past, in a natural process, is a past superseded and dead"—while in history the same event, known historically, "survives in the present" (225). What survives, however, is what is finally meaningful for the current sociopolitical order, allowing this order to stretch toward the uncharted regions of the future. In this sense, historiography proves to be a highly deterministic enterprise. The first link of the ideal chain of events that forms a historical narrative does not originate in a set moment of the past. It emerges, instead, from the present, and the chain is retroactively built with the aim of justifying the current order. The present assumes an aura of inevitability, as it becomes the logical, and therefore unquestionable, end result of a process leaving little space for future modifications. The future is seen at most as an extension of the present. Conceived in these terms, history is an altar to the current status quo; radical change is exorcised a priori. If our age seeks in the past the reasons for confidence in the future, then the historical record becomes less a narration of past events than a "repository of society's values and of its understanding of the world" (Gossman 35). Anna Davin points out along the same lines that:

> The dominant version of history in any society will be one which bolsters an existing situation. Thus in a class society history has meant the history of rulers, in an imperialist society the history of empire, in a male-dominated society the history of men. Such history will also reflect the general assumptions and concerns of the dominant group. It will embody belief in their superiority—over women, the young, those of other race, religion or nationality, the poor, the landless, the illiterate. It will focus on the powerful and their doings—political leaders, the military, royalty, the great men of industry, finance, and landed property. Of course there are other histories, other assumptions, other concerns, but to let them be heard is not always easy. (60)

In trying to universalize the present and extend it toward the future, historiography becomes the exact opposite of prophecy.

This is so not only in the obvious sense that prophecy is proleptic and history analeptic, but also in a deeper epistemological sense. Contrary to historiography, prophecy implies a fundamental reversal of current situations. Prophecy in this sense is the inner revolutionary force dormant in *La Storia*.[31] The prophetic voice is subjected to the deterministic discourse of history within both the time frame of the novel and, by explicit narratorial intervention, the wider terms encompassing all of the past. But its very presence acts as a utopian counterdiscourse that, unlike historiography, shapes the third dimension of the future as one of potentially radical opposition to past and present.

La Storia starts in January of 1941, but the chronological sequence of events is soon interrupted by a long analeptic sequence presenting Ida's family. The flashback that opens this wide narrative parenthesis onto the extradiegetical past bears ideological implications that sharply contrast with the proleptic forces of utopia in the novel. The analeptic mode reveals that past and present are inextricably linked by a pattern of repetition. With her obsessive fears of revealing the "fault" of her Jewishness, her childish attitudes, mediocre intelligence, and final descent into madness, Ida "repeats" her mother, Nora; Carlo Vivaldi with his naive anarchic faith repeats Ida's father, Giuseppe Ramundo, who, in turn, in many ways anticipates Ida's husband, Alfio Mancuso. Finally, Useppe's epilepsy repeats, carrying it to a deadly extreme, the same pathology that characterized his mother and grandmother before him. Repetition causes historical stagnation and sharply denies progress.[32] When variation occurs within a story marked by grim repetition, it indicates a definite change for the worse. Describing Useppe's first trip to the Stazione Tiburtina with Nino, the narrator lingers on Useppe's gaze of sadness and suspicion toward a lonely calf, tied to an iron bar and looking down from the open platform of a car (125). Useppe's gaze anticipates, here, the indescribable vision of horror as, in his subsequent visit to the Tiburtina Station with Ida, the solitary calf is replaced by hundreds of Roman Jews imprisoned in the windowless cattle-cars.

* * *

The discourse of prophecy counterbalances, in *La Storia,* that of irreversible determinism and hopeless recurrence. *La Storia* presents two kinds of prophetic voices: one can be more precisely termed an intuitive foresight, while the other is truly prophetic. Vilma, one of the most intense characters in the novel, appears, in Ida's eyes, as a sort of mad prophetess, the bearer of a forbidden and ominous clairvoyance, a bizarre and illogical foresight that nobody is willing to take seriously:

> Da qualche tempo Vilma, attraverso i suoi giri quotidiani di faticante, riportava nel Ghetto delle informazioni strane e inaudite, che le altre donne rifiutavano come fantasie del suo cervello. E difatti, la fantasia lavorava sempre, come una forzata, nella mente di Vilma; però, in seguito, certe sue *fantasie* dovevano dimostrarsi molto al di sotto della verità. (60; see appendix 49)

Vilma prophesies a new holocaust, worse than that of Herod, and begs all the members of the Jewish ghetto to at least save their children. As history unfolds, Vilma's words prove to be truly anticipatory of future events. In this sense, Vilma's status is not truly prophetic. At most, she refers to another type of knowledge, based not upon logic, with its inductive and deductive schemes, but on intuition and premonition.[33] As Blanchot points out, prophecy is not simply a proleptic statement announcing the logical or inevitable succession of a current set of events. On the contrary, the prophetic word emerges when "tout est impossible, . . . alors la parole prophétique qui dit l'avenir impossible, dit aussi le 'pourtant' qui brise l'impossible et restaure le temps" ("everything is impossible, . . . then the prophetic word that expresses the impossible future also expresses that 'and yet' that breaks the impossible and restores time") (100). It is the ideal presence of this *pourtant* that makes *La Storia* a prophetic text, a text that uncovers the subterranean discourse that shatters the old discursive frames and foresees a new course for history.

This prophetic voice is also cast within Davide Segre's drunken and unconnected speech, an ideological cauldron mixing anarchic, Marxist, and loosely evangelical inspirations, climaxing in his Franciscan view of the messiah who silently exists within every leper, beggar-woman, or idiot child and waits to be recognized and listened to (591). Davide's illogical discourse represents the spirit of Blanchot's *pourtant:*

the century-old resistance, within the folds and crannies of the patriarchal code, of all those alternative voices who carry on, often in spite of self-destruction, the promise of a yet unrealized attitude toward power, human relationships, and history. In spite of Davide's death, the prophetic voice is not silenced in *La Storia,* as it reemerges in the novel's closing statement: "Tutti i semi sono falliti eccettuato uno, che non so cosa sia, ma che probabilmente è un fiore e non un'erbaccia" ("All the seeds failed, except one. I don't know what it is, but it is probably a flower and not a weed") (657; 557). This final cryptic quotation from Gramsci's *Lettere dal carcere* (*Prison Letters,* 1947) (it is left anonymous in the novel) embodies the *espoir prophétique* that Blanchot sees as the revolutionary interruption, the sudden break in the monotonous course of history and the victory of change over hopeless cyclicity. This final opening toward a potential turning point sketches the utopian dimension of a positive future already inscribed (albeit repressed) within a present and a past that remain tragically dystopian.

In *La Storia,* the narrator's act of emplotment reveals a profound pessimism stretching backward into the dawn of history and forward into her narrative present. Only the future remains free of this entropic drive: it represents the still unexploited potential for a radical redefinition of current historical geographies. This utopian and prophetic spirit, in Cixous's eloquent words, frees the future from being determined by the past:

> I do not deny that the effects of the past are still with us. But I refuse to strengthen them by repeating them, to confer upon them an irremovability the equivalent of destiny. . . . Anticipation is imperative. (245)

In this spirit, the future becomes the free, uncharted, and unrepresented space that will allow women to invent creatively their stories while, lovingly and often painfully, inscribing the records of their history.

Chapter Four

Transhistorical Narratives

The Apocalypse and the Carnival in Umberto Eco's *Il nome della rosa*

> *In the midst of the street of [the city], and on either side of the river,* was there *the tree of life, which bare twelve* manner of *fruits,* and *yielded her fruit every month. . . .*
>
> Revelation 22.2

Discussing the protean nature of modern fiction, Bakhtin argues that the almost endless variety of its forms can be only partially accounted for and explored. Being the sole genre that currently continues to develop, the novel has no unique canon of its own, yet it can include and transform other genres in a multifocal and plurivocal process that exploits its own tendencies toward hybridization (*Dialogic* 4–5). In a similar vein, but focusing on the interpretative act, Roland Barthes rejects all monological approaches and single hermeneutical pretensions by defining textual analysis as an attempt to follow the plurality of the text—to explore the text's multiple avenues of meaning and the ways in which it "bursts forth and is dispersed" ("Textual Analysis" 84). Bakhtin's and Barthes's statements seem particularly appropriate for a novel like Umberto Eco's *Il nome della rosa.* A truly encyclopedic work combining detective and historical fictions, thriving in the wonders of unlimited semiosis, reflecting itself into metafictional mirrors, and playing ironic hermeneutical games that question all foundational certainties, *Il nome della rosa* appears as the quintessential text disclosing its inexhaustible possibilities.

It may seem both a simple and somewhat arbitrary exegetical task to address Eco's novel as a pure example of historical fiction. However, such an approach can provide a valuable key to unlocking Eco's labyrinthine textual space by furnishing a vantage point that is bound to throw into relief the other narrative systems at work in the novel. Indeed, because of its multifarious nature, *Il nome della rosa* as historical fiction addresses issues that surpass a narrow definition of genre. As historical fiction, *Il nome della rosa* involves an analysis of the values and limits of narrativity as a way of articulating our knowledge of the world. It also delves into the complex exchanges between textual and factual realities, and finally explores the possibilities of defining truth within the framework of current linguistic systems and mnemonic or documentary reconstructions of the past.

Ideologies of Representation: The Return of the Plot

In "Postille a *Il nome della rosa,*" Eco states that one of postmodernism's main characteristics is the rediscovery of plot:

> Dal 1965 a oggi si sono definitivamente chiarite due idee. Che si poteva ritrovare l'intreccio anche sotto forma di citazione di altri intrecci, e che la citazione avrebbe potuto essere meno consolatoria dell'intreccio citato. (528; see appendix 50)

Eco maintains, implicitly, that the notion of plot is almost inevitably related to that of a certain consoling, not to say escapist, emotional value. Although he does not linger on this point as he proceeds to discuss the relationship between postmodern writers and their use of the past (528–29), Eco's point is worth further analysis: if the traditional plot is consoling, why does one of its most recent rejections, that of the neo-avantgarde, have to be reconsidered? And how must plot be revived and modified in order to avoid the danger of becoming again a mere platform for a politics of consolation?

The answer to these problems goes back to the discussions involving Italian neo-avantgarde intellectuals that occurred roughly between 1956 and 1969.[1] In spite of often contradictory ideological and aesthetic positions, the Italian neo-avantgarde repudiates conventional language by organizing a systematic attack on the mystifying constructions of logical discourses and prefabricated rational systems. The rejection of all representations of reality as a single and coherent totality is the starting point for an engaged art aimed at denouncing the disintegration of the subject in an alienating environment. Neo-avantgarde art is meant to provoke resistance, rather than emotional assent or participation, by disrupting the cognitive and linguistic structures and the usual modes of perception and representation. Art is an act of rebellion, a source of shock, in perennial battle with the reality of conventional language and reactionary institutions. At its best, the literary work must provide a critical mimesis not of an order, but of a universal schizophrenia, a reflection of an alienated and fragmented individual and social state. In other words, art must faithfully reflect the anthropological crisis and the social disintegration characterizing modern times and defy all those practices that seek to provide a mystified account of the relationship between life and literature, in which the latter records the order that the former presents. Art, if anything, must provoke resistance and Brechtian estrangement and explosively attack the forms of bourgeois mimetic realism.

One of the major reservations against this aesthetic agenda is that it provides only a new paradoxical mimesis, one in which formal disintegration simply mirrors the predicament of modern society. Speaking, generally, of the modernist dismantling of the plot, Ricoeur complains that

> Today it is said that only a novel without a plot or characters or any discernible temporal organization is more genuinely faithful to experience, which is itself fragmented and inconsistent, than was the traditional novel of the nineteenth century. But this plea for a fragmented, inconsistent fiction is not justified any differently than was the plea for naturalistic literature. The argument for verisimilitude has merely been displaced. (*Time* 2: 13–14)

If once it was the supposed inner order of reality that was reflected by the structural wholeness and narrative coherence of the great realist masterpieces, now it is reality's fragmentation that is similarly reproduced. By duplicating the chaos of reality with that of fiction, modern literature returns mimesis to its weakest function, that of merely photographically reproducing the outside world (Ricoeur, *Time* 2: 14). In polemical opposition to similar arguments, Italian neo-avantgarde intellectuals reject even the possibility of a mere reflectionist approach in modern literature: Guglielmi, for example, argues that since all connections between language and reality have been severed, language cannot represent, in a mirrorlike fashion, the objective world. Language can only act from *within* the chaos of the contemporary world in order to simply monitor, like a tape recorder, the world's most irrational features. Another option is for language to denounce the current situation by sheer exaggeration, by carrying disintegration itself to its most extreme consequences, making it hyperreal, in order to achieve a new hallucinatory and apocalyptic revelation ("Avanguardia" 19).

Eco's response to these debates involves a meditation that he carried on in several of his critical works. In his contribution to the first meeting of the Gruppo 63 in Palermo (1963), Eco juxtaposes the opposing forces of the avant-garde and what he terms the *conservazione.* Eco maintains that the avant-garde has exhausted its revolutionary potential. *Conservazione,* in fact, has become so "duttile e smaliziata da far suo ogni elemento di disturbo, da fagocitare ogni proposta di eversione e neutralizzarla immettendola in un circolo dell'accettazione e del consumo" ("supple and cunning that it has appropriated all elements of disturbance, swallowed up all subversive proposals, and neutralized them by inserting them into the cycle of acceptance and consumption") ("La generazione" 412). If subversion is immediately exorcised and is forced into the orders of the museum, the library, and official literary prizes, Eco asks, how should intellectuals organize effective denunciations of the current status quo? In 1964 Eco's proposal is strikingly generic, even if it foreshadows a new, critical relationship with the past as a way of understanding the present: "al gesto rivoluzionario si deve sostituire la lenta ricerca, alla rivolta la filologia . . . grazie a questo lavoro si sta configurando un nuovo modo di vedere le cose, di parlare delle cose, di individuare le cose per agirvi" ("the revolutionary act must be replaced by slow research, rebellion by philology . . . thanks to this work a new way of seeing things, speaking about things, and identifying things in order to act upon them is being configured") ("La generazione" 413).

In *Opera aperta* (*The Open Work,* 1962, 1967, 1971), Eco addresses this problem in detail. Together with his neo-avantgarde colleagues, he attacks the uncritical automatic responses forced upon their public by conventionally "closed" representations of reality. Ambiguity and open-endedness become in Eco's view a positive response to totalizing interpretative systems. Unlike traditional art, he argues, which is unambiguous and unidirectional, modern art leaves the reader with the possibility of inferring some of the possible orders envisioned by the text. Whether it is the structural construction that is left open or its semantic content, the text does not provide an apodictic truth but flaunts fragmentation, indeterminacy, and plurality. Neither Eco nor the neo-avantgarde, however, advocate formal anarchism or absolute semantic randomness. Significantly, Corti defines the neo-avantgarde's project as an exquisitely rational one (*Il viaggio* 111). In his preface to *I Novissimi,* Alfredo Giuliani argues that chaos becomes appealing only as far as it entails structuring problems (6). Like the surrealist advocates of "objective chance," the Italian neo-avantgarde believes in the paradoxical existence of the contradictory principles of randomness and hidden order within the same textual space.

It is precisely the nature of this paradox that Eco finds intriguing. In an article entitled "Del modo di formare come impegno sulla realtà" ("Formal Strategies as Social Commitment"), published in 1961 for Vittorini's *Il Menabò* and included in the 1967 edition of *Opera aperta,* Eco claims that the neo-avantgarde's destruction of traditional language "si vota all'incomunicazione, e quindi a una sorta di ritiro aristocratico" ("is condemned to noncommunication, to some sort of aristocratic withdrawal") (261). However, Eco continues, opting for a wider audience would necessarily entail a compromising acceptance of worn-out expressive forms.[2] The *impasse* gives way to the apocalyptic belief of living in a universe in full crisis:

> È in crisi perché all'ordine delle parole non corrisponde piú un ordine delle cose (le parole si articolano ancora secondo l'ordine tradizionale mentre la scienza ci incita a vedere le cose disposte secondo altri ordini oppure addirittura secondo disordine e discontinuità); . . . adottando una nuova grammatica fatta non tanto di moduli d'ordine quanto di un progetto permanente di disordine, [l'intellettuale] ha accettato proprio il mondo in cui vive nei termini di crisi in cui esso si trova. Quindi di nuovo egli si è *compromesso,* col mondo in cui vive, parlando un linguaggio che egli artista crede di

> avere inventato ma che invece gli è suggerito dalla situazione in cui si trova; e tuttavia questa era la sola scelta che gli rimaneva. ("Del modo" 263; see appendix 51)

In 1961, Eco fully embraces a philosophy of crisis, as no positive solution seems available. The options, in fact, are either to deny the crisis and enter the theater of mystification or embrace it and succumb to one's inevitable alienation.

The pressing question, at this point, concerns the definition of a constructive ideological and aesthetic agenda. Is the aesthetic rendition of the unformed and the fragmented a constructive way of "seeing the world"? Like the Calvino of "Il mare dell'oggettività" ("The Sea of Objectivity," 1960), Eco is aware of the dangers of a passive adhesion to the uninterrupted flux of reality. Yet, starting from the paradoxical assumption that the only structural order achievable is that of organized randomness, Eco concludes that this very disorder allows for a *presa di coscienza* of the situation. The salvation lies for him in the self-conscious ability to estrange oneself from the chaos of factual reality by transposing it into the narrative structure ("Del modo" 276). Awareness, however, although a necessary starting point, can hardly be conceived as a satisfying solution. Eco's suggestion offers a way out from a serious double bind, yet the work of art assumes a merely therapeutic function rather than a cognitive one. Moreover, by subscribing to an aesthetic of chaos, two consequences become unavoidable. On the aesthetic side, the distinction between good and bad art merely becomes a question of subjective response (Robey 66). Ideologically, all charges of absolute relativism, irrationalism, and, finally, nihilism cannot be substantially withstood.

It is the aesthetic notion of "organized disorder" that Eco strives to redefine, and to which he subscribes with a number of partially developed reservations. Like his colleagues, Eco believes that neo-avantgarde productions are "un progetto permanente di disordine" ("a permanent project of disorder") ("Del modo" 263). At the same time, he significantly speaks of "organic" works able to express themselves through the cohesion of their structure, and the logic of their formal connections ("Del modo" 287). While defending the neo-avantgarde systematic project of chaos, Eco is interested in discovering the formative intention that, according to him, is inherent in every work of art. Eco's exploitation of the notion of organic form is particularly significant, and in some way paradoxical, in the avant-garde context in which he works. Historically, the concept of organic form defines exactly the opposite aesthetics from that of the avant-garde. In its romantic framework, the organic form refers to a totalizing aesthetic unity that is achieved, often partially unconsciously, thanks to an innate set of organizing creative tools. It denies, therefore, the neo-avantgarde tendency toward fragmentation and decentralization, as well as its technical, wholly rational creative agenda. Eco's 1961 article does not acknowledge the contradiction, appearing at times inconclusive and paradoxical. It shows, albeit *in nuce,* Eco's dissatisfaction with a negative philosophy and speaks for the constructive side of his aesthetic project. It also foreshadows Eco's revival of a notion of order whose inherent connotations must be entirely redefined: it is a provisional, multifaceted, and yet structured order that

> can contribute significantly to this process of understanding and transforming the world, because its function is essentially cognitive. . . . Art represents the world—or more exactly our experience of the world—through the way it organizes its constituents . . . rather than through what the constituents themselves represent. This representation is a form of knowledge by virtue of the element of organic form. (Robey 68)

According to Eco, art represents the artist's experience of the world through its form: "Dove si realizza una forma si ha una operazione consapevole su un materiale amorfo ridotto a dominio umano" ("Where a form is realized there is a conscious operation on an amorphous material brought under human control") ("Del modo" 287). Therefore, modern art must not stop at the cynical denunciation of an apocalyptic situation. As Eco states in his first preface to *Opera aperta,* the modern open work not only makes us aware of the contemporary crisis, but seeks to find a solution by offering "delle immagini del mondo che valgono quali *metafore epistemologiche:* e costituiscono un nuovo modo di vedere, di sentire, di capire e accettare un universo in cui i rapporti tradizionali sono andati in frantumi e in cui si stanno faticosamente delineando nuove possibilità di rapporto" ("images of the world that function as *epistemological metaphors* and constitute a new way of seeing, feeling, understanding, and accepting a universe in which traditional relationships have been shattered and new possibilities of relationships are being arduously delineated") (*Opera* 3). Technically, therefore, the open work implies not only a redefinition of the forms of language, but of its narrative structures as well.

Eco's discussion already foreshadows most of the aesthetic and ideological concerns of *Il nome della rosa.* The sense of living in an age of crisis accompanies Eco's hope for change and his belief in the function of art in bringing about such change by exploring the potential and denouncing the limitation of our epistemological and aesthetic constructions. Eco's 1961 article closes with a statement that sums up the tension between the nostalgia for order and the awareness of its mystifications; this tension constitutes the cluster of his then unresolved ideological *impasse:*

> In ogni caso, comunque, l'operazione dell'arte che tenta di conferire una forma a ciò che può apparire disordine, informe, dissociazione, mancanza di ogni rapporto, è ancora l'esercizio di una ragione che tenta di ridurre a chiarezza discorsiva le cose; e quando il suo discorso pare oscuro è perché le cose stesse, e il nostro rapporto con esse, è ancora molto oscuro. ("Del modo" 289–90; see appendix 52)

* * *

Eco's attempt to shape a constructive aesthetic ideology represents a strong resistance to current views of mass culture. Unlike Eco, the neo-avantgarde (and in particular Sanguineti) share, to a certain degree, Theodor Adorno's pessimism on this matter. As early as 1938, Adorno attacked the culture industry that treats art as a commodity to sell to vast audiences who quickly digest it, only to crave more of the same standardized, simplified, and ordinary materials ("On the Fetish-Character" 271). Sanguineti, in turn, maintained that to avoid commodification and the law of the marketplace and to thwart the mystification of the capitalist order, the artist must play on the nonmarketability of his production, the inaccessibility of which becomes a potential threat to the market by defying its rules of mass consumption and profit. This notion runs the risk of promoting, as it indirectly did, a hermetic elitist art, utterly separated from the substructure of economic reality, one finally causing a divorce between culture and politics. By accepting its inability to act upon a wide social reality, this art raises some questions concerning the practical validity and possibility of dissemination of the new forms of knowledge it nevertheless provides. If art manages to avoid the order of the marketplace, it then ends up in the artificial and enclosed space of the museum, where it becomes a mere expression of what "no money can buy" (Sanguineti 66). In this perspective, Sanguineti agrees with the positions of the Frankfurt School. In particular, he shares Adorno's and Max Horkheimer's indictment of the culture industry, which dispenses pseudosatisfaction to pacified audiences eager to evade their own anxieties. Mass culture, therefore, becomes only the degraded realm of extreme commodification, the visible sign of consciousness's capitulation "before the superior power of the advertised stuff" (Adorno, "On the Fetish-Character" 287).

Eco's *Apocalittici e integrati* (*The Apocalyptic and the Integrated,* 1964) explores two different attitudes toward mass media and mass culture. Apocalyptic intellectuals reject mass culture and adopt a nihilistic stance verging on silence. For them "la cultura è un fatto aristocratico, la gelosa coltivazione, assidua e solitaria, di una interiorità che si affina e si oppone alla volgarità della folla" ("culture is an aristocratic matter, the jealous, assiduous, and solitary cultivation of an interior Self that perfects and opposes itself to the vulgarity of the masses") (*Apocalittici* 3). For the apocalyptic intellectual, Eco explains, mass culture is the anticulture. The integrated intellectual instead accepts mass culture *in toto:* "l'integrazione è la realtà concreta di coloro che *non dissentono*" ("integration is the concrete reality of those who *do not dissent*") (*Apocalittici* 4). Eco provides a third position that, while accepting mass culture as promoting a wider access to information, recognizes its shortcomings. In particular, Eco criticizes the consolatory works that reaffirm the public's confidence in the status quo and convey "a standardized, oversimplified, static and complacent vision that masks the real complexity of things and implicitly denies the possibility of change" (Robey 71). The solution for Eco is to work with the mass media to provide a more honest rendition of our complex historical world. By welcoming reflection and a critical attitude, constructive mass entertainment can in fact generate "a sense of independence and choice instead of conformism and passivity" (Robey 71).

* * *

Eco's growing preoccupation with the connections between art's epistemological function, its ideological implications, and its appeal to a wider audience is again addressed in the 1971 issue of the *Almanacco Bompiani,* significantly entitled "Cent'anni dopo: il ritorno dell'intreccio" ("One Hundred Years After: The Return of the Plot"). Witnessing the revival of detective stories, gothic romances, and traditional novels such as those by Emilio Salgari, Dumas, and Octave Feuillet, the editors of the *Almanacco,* Cesare Sughi and Eco himself, declare that in the second half of the 1960s we saw the return of the "gusto per l'intreccio a ruota libera, il trionfo della narrativa, la trama *über alles*" ("the enjoyment of an unbridled story, the triumph of narrative, the plot above all") ("Questo Almanacco" 3).[3] Eco and Sughi do not analyze this return from a sociohistorical perspective, but refer to the assumption, developed by Claude Lévi-Strauss's cultural anthropology, that "il gusto della narrativa è un'esigenza costante che non può essere ignorata" ("the pleasure of narrative is a constant need that cannot be ignored") (4). As Barthes puts it, narrative "is international, transhistorical, transcultural: it is simply there, like life itself" ("Introduction" 79). While narratives are raised into the realm of universal necessity as "panglobal facts of culture" (H. White, *The Content* 1),[4] Eco and Sughi express concern with some of the possible ideological implications of this narrative revival. In particular, they discuss the dissolution of the denunciatory spirit of avant-garde art:

> la grande stagione dell'intreccio ottocentesco è stata anche la grande stagione della consolazione a puntate. Ogni ritorno alla narratività pura contiene in sé qualcosa di equivoco, rappresenta una fuga dal problematico. ("Questo Almanacco" 4; see appendix 53)

Eco develops this concern in an article entitled "L'industria aristotelica" ("The Aristotelian Craft"), in which he argues that

Aristotle's theorization of plot, and specifically his comments on catharsis, may be interpreted in two different ways. In the "problematic" novel, while catharsis unravels narrative knots, it does not reconcile or pacify the audience: "La trama, e con essa l'eroe, sono problematici: finito il libro, il lettore rimane confrontato con una serie di interrogativi senza risposta" ("The plot, and the hero with it, are problematic: once the book is over, the reader is left to face a series of unanswered questions") (6). In popular fiction, instead, everything follows a causal pattern, as all the events unfold exactly as the audience wishes. The narrative organization, as well as the social and psychological orders, remains unaltered. As Eco comments:

> una costante resterà a distinguere il romanzo popolare dal romanzo problematico: ed è che sempre si dipanerà nel primo una lotta del bene contro il male che si risolverà sempre o comunque, sia lo scioglimento intriso di felicità o di dolore, in favore del bene, il bene rimanendo definito nei termini della moralità, dei valori, dell'ideologia corrente. Il romanzo problematico propone invece finali ambigui proprio perché sia la felicità di Rastignac che la disperazione di Emma Bovary mettono esattamente e ferocemente in questione la nozione acquisita di "Bene" (e di "Male"). ("L'industria" 9; see appendix 54)

Although it exploits some of the devices of popular fiction, *Il nome della rosa* is essentially a "problematic" novel. As Eco states in his postscript to the novel, one way of rediscovering the plot is by means of citations of other plots, and these citations may become less consoling than the plots they cite (528). In assuming the framework of historical fiction, *Il nome della rosa* explores the validity of our narrative understanding of the past. The novel exploits the linear organization of a simple plot line while questioning its epistemological value. Causal connections and the chronological scheme, the power of language to write the historical past and capture the objective world, the possibilities of rational knowledge and ethical judgment, and, finally, the tension between referential reality and the narrative order, between mimesis and semiosis, are all at issue in Eco's postmodern metahistorical project. Therefore, *Il nome della rosa* is as much a historical novel as a discussion of the methods of historical fiction. As Eco observes in an interview for the *Nouvel Observateur:*

> On ne peut plus "raconter" de façon innocente; on n'a jamais pu le faire, pas plus à l'époque de Sterne qu'aujourd'hui. Depuis *Tristram Shandy* jusqu'à *Si par une nuit d'hiver un voyageur* de Calvino . . . on a voulu faire le roman du roman; on a théorisé sur le récit par le récit. Dans *Le nom de la rose,* l'histoire s'entrecroise avec l'Histoire un peu comme s'il s'agissait de réconcilier Alexandre Dumas avec l'Ecole des Annales. ("Le Tueur" 53; see appendix 55)

In this way, Eco transcends the double bind that had frustrated the neo-avantgarde. *Il nome della rosa*'s narrative structure responds to the necessity of organizing and giving formal coherence to the chaos of events. However, Eco does not pose this order as given, transparent, and neutral. He exploits the popular scheme of a detective novel and manipulates the literary framework of historical fiction in order to test and question the epistemological power and the ideological implications of narrative itself as a "central form of human comprehension" (Hutcheon 121).

In *The Sense of an Ending* (1966), Frank Kermode assumes, much like Eco and Sughi, that narrative is a basic method of organizing the raw flux of experience into a coherent form, in which the aesthetic value of the work of art resides:

> our scepticism, our changed principles of reality, force us to discard the fictions that are too fully explanatory, too consoling. . . . We probably have to accept . . . an historical transition . . . from a literature which assumed that it was imitating an order to a literature which assumes that it has to create an order, unique and self-dependent, and possibly attainable only after a critical process that might be called "decreation." (161, 167)

Kermode, like Ricoeur, believes that plots organize time by giving it form: "Time cannot be faced as coarse and actual, as a repository of the contingent; one humanizes it by fictions of orderly succession and end" (Kermode 160). Therefore, as narrative understanding is a universal human need, Kermode continues, finding orderly patterns in historical time is a purely anthropological activity. Both fiction and historiography organize time so that from mere succession it becomes, in Giovanni Gentile's words, an "inter-connexion of parts all mutually implied and conditioned in the whole" (cited in Kermode 57). By embracing a staunchly humanistic perspective, Kermode accepts the notion of art's constructive function, and in the face of chaos he appeals to the consolation of the aesthetic order:

> the novelist, though he may aspire—in the language of Tillich—to live in conditions of reality unprotected by myth, has to allow room for different versions of reality, including what some call mythical and some call absolute. Also we find that there is an irreducible minimum of geometry—of humanly needed shape or structure—which finally limits our ability to accept the mimesis of pure contingency. (132)

Even if Eco, like Kermode and Ricoeur, proclaims himself a great admirer of Aristotle's poetics,[5] he questions both the value of narrative understanding and its final emotional appeal. To what extent, Eco asks, is plot contingent upon consolation, and when and how is it not? The answer that Eco proposes concerning the postmodern relationship to the past can be easily applied to his ideas on plot as expressed in "Postille a *Il nome della rosa*": "visto che non può essere distrutto, perché la sua distruzione porta al silenzio, deve essere rivisitato: con ironia, in modo non innocente" ("since it cannot really be destroyed, because its destruction leads to silence, [it] must be revisited: but with irony, not innocently") (529; 67). Through the formal unity of its plot, *Il nome della rosa* proposes a critical revisitation of the past and an assessment of the cognitive instruments presiding over its organization.

In the Aristotelian narrative paradigm, the principle of aesthetic composition is based upon the notion of mimesis. Mimesis creates an artificial narrative order that depends upon the two universal categories of probability and necessity. In other words, "To the extent that in the ordering of events the causal connection (one thing as a cause of another) prevails over pure succession (one thing after another), a universal emerges that is . . . the ordering itself erected as a type" (Ricoeur, *Time* 1: 69). Eco's critical reassessment of the Aristotelian model implies accepting that the act of giving form to the unformed hides the trap of a "consoling treachery":

> At best, it furnishes the "as if" proper to any fiction we know to be just fiction, a literary artifice. This is how it consoles us in the face of death. But as soon as we no longer fool

> ourselves by having recourse to the consolation offered by the paradigms, we become aware of the violence and the lie. We are then at the point of succumbing to the fascination of the absolutely unformed and to the plea for that radical intellectual honesty Nietzsche called *Redlichkeit*. . . . [T]he narrative consonance imposed on temporal dissonance remains the work of what it is convenient to call a violence of interpretation. The narrative solution to the paradox is just the outgrowth of this violence. (Ricoeur, *Time* 1: 72)

Il nome della rosa examines, on both structural and thematic levels, the functional advantages and intellectual pitfalls of its own formal emplotment as a means of organizing the flux of history and cognitively coming to terms with the real. Specifically, Eco tests the narrative paradigms of the Apocalypse and the Carnival both in terms of their transhistorical persistence and of their specific usage as paradigms among others, with no claim of universality and no ambition to fully and finally exhaust the dynamics of narrative.

The Apocalypse as Structuring Narrative Principle

Kermode's original contribution to the debate over narrative order lies in his definition of the apocalyptic model as one of the archetypes for narrative organization. The Bible is, structurally, the perfect model for concordance, where the "end is in harmony with the beginning, the middle with beginning and end" (6). Moreover, the Bible's concluding book, the Apocalypse of John the Apostle, is traditionally held to resume the whole structure of the sacred book. As the quintessential master narrative, therefore, the Apocalypse provides us with a sense of unity and concordance. Caught as we are "in the middle," we make sense of our existence by referring to what we perceive as a similar, although wider, temporal frame marked by a fixed beginning and an end justifying and accounting for all that takes place in the middle. According to Kermode the apocalyptic sequence speaks for the desire to establish coherent patterns "which, by the provision of an end, make possible a satisfying consonance with the origin and with the middle" (17). Apocalyptic narrative structures, from the biblical archetype onward, represent perfect examples of the persistence of fictional structures in their essential qualities as end-oriented and concordant.

It appears ironically appropriate that Eco chose the Bible as the master narrative behind the intertextual patchwork characterizing *Il nome della rosa.* The Bible, and particularly the Apocalypse, are both thematic presences and structural principles in Eco's novel.[6] Like the Apocalypse, *Il nome della rosa* features a prologue and an epilogue that frame a text organized according to the linear chronology of seven successive revelations. Thematically, the novel conveys the sense of living in a moment of transition that anticipates a radical turning point in history. The struggle between Papacy and Empire has reached a climactic point, and each of these systems is facing severe inner fragmentation. The clashes between the Conventuals and the Spirituals within the Franciscan order, concerning the poverty of Christ and, by extension, the Church's involvement in secular matters, are the most evident examples of a wider pattern of fragmentation involving multiple heretical groups and chiliastic sects. A world on the verge of new social and economic organizations is also reassessing the ways that have dictated the configuration of knowledge. In Foucault's words, we witness the dissolution of a universe on the threshold of an epistemic break, a moment in which the rules "of formation of discursive rationality" (Best and Kellner 40), as well as sociopolitical organization, are being submitted to fundamental historical change.

Several characters in the novel relate to change in an apocalyptic manner.[7] Adso, the young Benedectine novice and narrator of the story, perceives a world where everything is on the wrong path as he gives shape to a scheme of progressive decadence:

> Gli uomini di una volta erano belli e grandi (ora sono dei bambini e dei nani), ma questo fatto è solo uno dei tanti che testimoni la sventura di un mondo che incanutisce. La gioventù non vuole apprendere più nulla, la scienza è in decadenza, il mondo intero cammina sulla testa, dei ciechi conducono altri ciechi e li fan precipitare negli abissi, gli uccelli si lanciano prima di aver preso il volo, l'asino suona la lira, i buoi danzano, Maria non ama più la vita contemplativa e Marta non ama più la vita attiva, Lea è sterile, Rachele ha l'occhio carnale, Catone frequenta i lupanari, Lucrezio diventa femmina. Tutto è sviato dal proprio cammino. (23; see appendix 56)

Adso reads the carved stones on the portal of the monastery's church as narrating the apocalyptic saga of "una umanità terrestre giunta alla fine della sua vicenda" ("a terrestrial humankind that had reached the end of its story") (49; 40). While observing these stones, Adso has a vision that repeats John's vision in the Apocalypse. Like John, Adso believes he is divinely summoned to write down what he has seen, which he interprets as the symbolic prefiguration of the tragic events that are about to happen in the abbey. Sharing Adso's pessimism, Abo, the monastery's abbot, faces up to the decline of the monastic system amidst the rising secular and economic powers in cities. "[I]l mondo sta sospeso sul ciglio dell'abisso" ("the world is teetering on the brink of the abyss") (44; 34), he sullenly comments as he warns Adso and William that "la fine del mondo si approssima" ("the end of the world is approaching") (45; 35). The oldest monk of the abbey, Alinard of Grottaferrata, claims that the mysterious murders that have disturbed the life of the abbey follow the pattern of the seven trumpets of the Apocalypse.[8] With an increasing sense of urgency, Jorge of Burgos repeatedly predicts the imminent advent of the Antichrist, while the destructive fire that razes the library and the abbey's edifice marks the narrative climax of Adso's apocalyptic narration.

The Bible is one of the most familiar models for our narrative understanding, as it creates the illusion of a completed and unified symmetry between factual and textual realities (Kermode 6). In the Bible, in fact, a perfect consonance is created so that the beginning of the world coincides with the beginning of the book. Similarly, the end of the world and the end of the text also coincide. The Bible is "the grandiose plot of the history of the world, and each literary plot is a sort of miniature version of the great plot that joins Apocalypse and Genesis" (Ricoeur, *Time* 2: 23). Eco exploits the apocalyptic model, and yet he questions the coincidence the model establishes between the text and the world, between the form of history and the form of its narrative understanding, thus forcing us to reconsider the ingrained view that historical actuality has narrative form. Mink relates the idea that past reality is an untold story to the notion of Universal History, which he dates back to Augustine's *City of God,* and follows its progress through Immanuel Kant's and

Friedrich von Schiller's beliefs that "the plotline of history is the hidden intention of nature" (Mink, "Narrative Form" 136). According to these views, in the variety of historical occurrences it is possible to discern a single theme, so that what appears as confused and disorganized to the single individual may be seen from the point of view of the whole human race to be a consistent and gradual evolution. The concept of Universal History, therefore, "explains the whole contemporary world by discerning those chains of events that have led up to the present, and displaying them as a single coherent whole" (136).

Clearly, the idea of Universal History predates the work of Augustine, Kant, and Schiller. Universal History reproduces, homologically, "le discours que Dieu lui-même tient aux hommes, sous forme précisément de l'Histoire qu'il leur donne: . . . l'Histoire des hommes est l'Ecriture de Dieu" ("the discourse that God himself delivers upon humanity, in precisely the form of the History he accords that humanity: . . . human history is God's writing") (Barthes, "Le Discours" 68). History and the Word of God coincide, as God coincides with the Word: "In the beginning was the Word and the Word was with God, and the Word was God." The beginning of the Gospel according to Saint John that Eco borrows for Adso's prologue constitutes what Barthes would call an "ouverture performative" ("performative opening"), one of the inaugural forms of historical narration where "la parole y est véritablement un acte solennel de fondation" ("the word is indeed a solemn act of foundation") ("Le Discours" 67). Language founds the plot of Universal History, where history is already teleologically framed and written out for us. The opening sentence of the Gospel according to Saint John establishes the illusion of an absolute transitivity verging on identification, the temptation of perfect referentiality, the idea that somehow and somewhere the history of the world has already been planned out, that there is indeed a preestablished plot behind the course of history.

With *Il nome della rosa,* Eco questions the presupposition of Universal History represented by the apocalyptic scheme upon which he ironically founds the novel, both structurally and thematically. *Il nome della rosa* relativizes the foundational value of the opening quotation from the Gospel according to

Saint John by using it as merely one of the three possible provisional beginnings of the novel (De Lauretis, *Umberto Eco* 82).[9] The absolute validity of the apocalyptic model as transposed from the realm of factuality to that of textuality is also dismantled by Eco's choosing Adso's subjective voice as the internal narrator of *Il nome della rosa.* Theoretically, Adso should function like Danto's "Ideal Chronicler" or Barthes's paradoxical "personne objective" ("objective persona") ("Le Discours" 69). One does not need to be Eco's "model reader" to be skeptical of Adso's naive propositions:

> mi accingo a lasciare su questo vello testimonianza degli eventi mirabili e tremendi a cui in gioventù mi accadde di assistere, ripetendo verbatim quanto vidi e udii, senza azzardarmi a trarne un disegno. . . .
>
> Il Signore mi conceda la grazia di essere testimone trasparente degli accadimenti che ebbero luogo all'abbazia di cui è bene e pio si taccia ormai anche il nome, al finire dell'anno del Signore 1327. (19; see appendix 57)

While in traditional historical narration and realist fiction the illusion of absolute referentiality occurs through the obliteration of all marks of the narrator's discourse, Adso chooses to assert his objective persona instead.

By initially vowing unconditional objectivity, Adso promises not a narrative, but a mere chronicle, imposing no design upon past events other than that found in the events themselves: "[non] ti ho promesso un disegno compiuto, bensì un elenco di fatti (questi sì) mirabili e terribili" (". . . I [don't] promise you an accomplished design, but, rather, a tale of events [those, yes] wondrous and awful") (26; 12). His narration, therefore, claims faithfulness to a strictly chronological pattern, marked by the succession of days and divided into the various phases of the abbey's canonical hours. The apocalyptic scheme emerging from Adso's narration appears consequently as a projection of an order found in—and not built from—the historical occurrences of which he was a witness. At times, Adso seems aware of the possible discrepancies between the factual past and its textual transposition, as when he confesses that he might have attributed to Salvatore actions and transgressions that were committed by others.[10] However, when he finally juxtaposes his vow to faithfully record the truth of past events against the constructive and selective power of his recollections, he dismisses memory's creative force and promises a totally objective report:

> mi sono ripromesso di raccontare, su quei fatti lontani, tutta la verità, e la verità è indivisa, brilla della sua stessa perspicuità, e non consente di essere dimidiata dai nostri interessi e dalla nostra vergogna. Il problema è piuttosto di dire cosa avvenne non come ora lo vedo e lo ricordo . . . ma come lo vidi e lo sentii allora. E posso farlo, con fedeltà di cronista, perché se chiudo gli occhi posso ripetere tutto quanto non solo feci ma pensai in quegli istanti, come se copiassi una pergamena scritta allora. (246; see appendix 58)

When Adso's faith in universals finally fails, he finds himself despairing of any possible order, natural or artificial, in the course of the historical events: "più recito a me stesso la storia che ne è sortita, meno riesco a capire se in essa vi sia una trama che vada al di là della sequenza naturale degli eventi e dei tempi che li connettono" ("the more I repeat to myself the story that has emerged from them, the less I manage to understand whether in it there is a design that goes beyond the natural sequence of the events and the times that connect them") (503; 610).

If modern readers are quite at ease with the concept of the unreliable narrator, they are far less at ease with that of an unreliable historian. Fiction, Manzoni reminds us, appeals to a sense of aesthetic wholeness; history, to the necessity for factual truth. By revealing himself throughout the story as a naive and unreliable narrator, Adso forces us to question the value not only of what he is narrating, but of the model upon which he has based his narration. In other words, it is the quality of the apocalyptic model as founder of a specific narrative order that asks to be tested. As it is projected through Adso's point of view, the apocalyptic model does not exist independently of its narrator, but becomes a subjective choice fraught with cultural and ideological implications. As the apocalyptic model loses its absolute value, it becomes in fact only one of the many possible orderings of the same sets of events. Moreover, the reference to the several textual reconstructions of Adso's story more decidedly deconstructs the notion of an immediate transitivity between the order of the world and that of the text. If, as Kermode reminds us, the apocalyptic model is a model for the plot, and if the textual organization of a plot speaks for the way in which we organize our experiences and make sense of them, it is the set of cognitive tools that make the order of the plot possible that must be investigated.

* * *

On a basic level of narrative organization, *Il nome della rosa* exploits the linear, successive scheme of the traditional detective novel. The detective novel is structurally ideal for Eco's narrative agenda, as it rests upon a notion of order founded on certain philosophical and ethical categories, the values of which, however, are challenged in the novel. As Eco points out, the detective story is based upon "un ordine stabilito, una serie di rapporti etici paradigmatici, una potenza, la Legge, che li amministra secondo ragione" ("an established order, a series of paradigmatic ethical relationships rationally administered by the power of the Law") ("Del modo" 273). The Benedectine abbey to which William and Adso are summoned to participate in the historical meeting between the legates of the Pope and the Emperor represents the objective correlative of this notion of order. Its octagonal shape, Adso explains, is a perfect form, one that expresses "la saldezza e l'imprendibilità della Città di Dio" ("the sturdiness and impregnability of the city of God") (29; 15). Surrounded by powerful walls and perched on top of a mountain, the abbey's isolation underscores the social autarchy exercised by the abbot. The monastery is a perfectly closed system, with its moral economy, its idiolect (clerical Latin), and its specific temporal organization founded upon the perfect balance between the succession and recurrence of rituals and work. The monks are defined by the functions they perform, and subjects are therefore constituted within power relations depending on rank and age. In strictly functional terms, the abbey is the perfect counterpart of other closed spaces, such as the Sadian's libertine castle of Silling (Barthes, "L'albero del crimine" 38). The Law (both God's and the abbot's) is based upon a fundamental interdiction. In the abbey the interdiction is to enter the library and taste the apple of potentially subversive knowledge. While the Law is supposedly governed by reason, it is in fact administered through fear of punishment, appeal to superstition, and recourse to the ordering force of the past. Since the foundation of the abbey, only the librarians are allowed access to the secrets of the library:

> La biblioteca è nata secondo un disegno che è rimasto oscuro a tutti nei secoli e che nessuno dei monaci è chiamato a conoscere. Solo il bibliotecario ne ha ricevuto il segreto dal bibliotecario che lo precedette, e lo comunica, ancora in vita, all'aiuto bibliotecario. . . . E le labbra di entrambi sono suggellate dal segreto. (45; see appendix 59)

The order, however, is challenged. Following the basic pattern of the detective story, "interviene un fatto che turba quest'ordine, il delitto" ("there intervenes a fact, the crime, that upsets this order") (Eco, "Del modo" 273). The sequence of horrible murders is the most evident attack on a commonly shared ethical code. Each one of the murders, however, is only a window that is flung open upon a number of other subversive acts: homosexual and heterosexual eroticism challenges the order of the monks' chastity, and the rise of vernaculars questions the monolingual domination of Latin. The growing cosmopolitan and temporal orders of the university, the economic powers of new national monarchies, and the social heterogeneity of the new urban civilization (*Comuni*) shake the political universalism of the Empire. Even more dangerously, the expanding fragmentation of millenarian and heretical sects challenges the order of the *respublica christiana,* the orthodoxy of religious dogma with its absolute monopolization of both secular and religious knowledge.[11] The English Franciscan monk and ex-inquisitor William of Baskerville is asked to investigate the murders. William, however, questions and in part deconstructs the classic definition of the "whodunit" scheme:

> scatta la molla dell'indagine che è condotta da una mente, il detective, non compromessa col disordine dal quale è nato il delitto, ma ispirata dall'ordine paradigmatico; il detective discerne tra i comportamenti degli indiziati quelli ispirati al paradigma da quelli che se ne allontanano; scevera gli allontanamenti apparenti da quelli reali, e cioè liquida i falsi indizi, . . . individua le cause reali, che, secondo le leggi

> dell'ordine . . . hanno provocato l'atto delittuoso; individua chi caratteriologicamente e situazionalmente era sottoposto alla azione di tali cause: e scopre il colpevole, che viene punito. Regna di nuovo l'ordine. (Eco, "Del modo" 273–74; see appendix 60)

William's quest is as much a search for the murderer as a study of the validity of the hermeneutical tools employed in this process and a scientific exploration of the methods of rational knowledge. A careful observer of details and clues, William is keen on inductive and deductive reasoning, yet he shuns the excesses of deterministic thought:

> ragionare sulle cause e sugli effetti è cosa assai difficile, di cui credo che l'unico giudice possa essere Dio. Noi già fatichiamo molto a porre un rapporto tra un effetto così evidente come un albero bruciato e la folgore che lo ha incendiato, che il risalire catene talora lunghissime di cause ed effetti mi pare altrettanto folle che cercare di costruire una torre che arrivi sino al cielo. (38; see appendix 61)

In this case, William is not so much arguing about the value of causal thought, as its universal pretensions. A careful empiricist and a follower of Francis Bacon's rationalism, William systematically doubts and tests his rational constructions, refusing to make them become absolute foundations of the world. Therefore, William opposes all metaphysical pretensions to truth and argues instead for what Gianni Vattimo would call the "practical" character of rational procedures, leading to the discovery of reason not as foundational certainty but simply as "strategy" (*Le avventure* 20). As Adso observes:

> Avevo sempre creduto che la logica fosse un'arma universale, e mi accorgevo ora di come la sua validità dipendesse dal modo in cui la si usava. D'altra parte, frequentando il mio maestro mi ero reso conto . . . che la logica poteva servire a molto a condizione di entrarci dentro e poi di uscirne. (266; see appendix 62)

Does William accept or reject the belief that we have unmediated access to reality? In other words, does he believe that the mind is a mirror of nature and the subject an observer of the world? Although he trusts the power of empirical observation, William realizes that the mind is constructive rather than reflective of the world. As he explains to Adso: "Perché vi sia specchio del mondo occorre che il mondo abbia una forma" ("In order for there to be a mirror of the world, it is necessary that the world have a form") (127; 136). Causality has no foundation upon a universal scheme, has no necessary value, and does not reflect a factual established order. Order (that of the abbey, the library, and by extension the universe) is a product of the human mind, a purely intellectual construct, like the plot that Adso narrates several years later.

While Adso believes in the importance of essences and universals, William prefers to base his philosophy upon empiricism and the experience of the singular. William's philosophy attests to a decisive fracture within an apparently monolithic culture as it marks the passage "from symbols to signs, from essences to functions, from hermeneutics to semiotics" (Schiavoni 576). The development of William of Occam's critical nominalism destroyed the vertical dimension of symbolic discourse that was thus deprived of its transcendental foundation. Contrary to classical theology and Aristotelian thought, Occam's nominalism rejected the real existence of universals and accepted the horizontal multiplicity of the particulars, the nonhierarchical plurality of the empirical world (Kristeva, *Le Texte* 149).[12] By embracing Bacon's empiricism and Occam's critical nominalism, William faces the variety of the world with a diverse supply of interpretative options, unencumbered by a priori ideas.[13] By adhering to linguistic nominalism[14] he also considers the possibility of an idealism that denies the world any external reality outside of discourse.

William's questioning and deconstruction of the rational scheme results in a number of consequences that are of great modern urgency. If truth, and therefore consensus or opposition, are impossible and unattainable, if right and wrong have no stable meaning, but shifting Janus-like shapes, then political thought becomes utterly preposterous, and finally ethically impossible. What are then the advantages and the disadvantages of William's "radical philosophy of contingency"? (Schiavoni 577). The rejection of universals and founding certainties, when carried to an extreme, leads to the opposite chasm of absolute relativism, where questions, doubts, and caution become paralyzing hindrances rather than checkpoints in a constructive epistemological project. At times, William complains of being unable to distinguish the real from the unreal, truth from falsity,[15] saints from demons, heaven from hell. "Quando parlo con Ubertino," William states, "ho l'impressione che l'inferno sia il paradiso guardato dall'altra parte" ("When I talk with Ubertino I have the impression that hell is heaven seen from the other side") (73; 71). In this sense, the dogmatic Jorge of Burgos is William's perfect foil. "Il riso è fomite di dubbio. . . . Quando si dubita occorre rivolgersi a un'autorità, alle parole di un padre o di un dottore, e cessa ogni ragione di dubbio" ("Laughter foments doubt. . . . When you are in doubt, you must turn to an authority, to the words of a father or of a doctor; then all reason for doubt ceases") (139; 151), Jorge states in one of his stubborn tirades against laughter in defense of the books of orthodox authorities.

The significance of William's philosophy is, of course, extraordinarily modern. In their extreme applications, William's assumptions approach Jean-François Lyotard's and Jean Baudrillard's notions that the implosion of all distinctions between political spheres makes choice preposterous. If normative epistemologies have come to an end, systemic relations are abolished, and if ethical thought has no grasp upon reality, then two options seem solely possible: mystical thought such as Ubertino of Casale's, which states the truth as sudden illumination and prophetic intuition that does not need to be rationally demonstrated, or the a priori refusal of all involvement, renunciation of hope for political and social change, and antiutopianism. Is *Il nome della rosa* finally submitting to Baudrillard's "melancholy" as an acceptable response to the disappearance of previous systemic rational constructions (39)? Adso's last question to William, "Intendete dire . . . che non ci sarebbe più sapere possibile e comunicabile, se mancasse il criterio stesso della verità, oppure che non potreste più comunicare quello che sapete perché gli altri non ve lo consentirebbero?" ("Do you mean . . . that there would be no possible and communicable learning any more if the very criterion of truth were lacking, or do you mean you could no longer communicate what you know because others would not allow you to?") (496; 600), is left significantly unanswered. Adso's question is whether any epistemological quest is even approachable without foundational anchors and, at the same time, whether these very anchors might not become hindrances to the free transmission of knowledge.

Overall, *Il nome della rosa* does not leave these questions unresolved. As Eco points out, "Il vero *contenuto* dell'opera diventa il suo *modo di vedere il mondo* e di giudicarlo, risolto in *modo di formare,* e a questo livello andrà condotto il discorso sui rapporti tra l'arte e il proprio mondo" ("The real *content* of a work is its *vision of the world,* and its judgment of it, expressed in its *way of structuring* it. Any analysis of the relationship between art and the world will have to take place at this level") ("Del modo" 270). Can the ideology of the novel be summed up by the apocalyptic scheme upon which it *ironically* depends? Is history, in Adorno's sense, an apocalyptic continuation of disaster "leading from the slingshot to the megaton bomb" (*Negative* 320)? *Mundus senescit,* Abo complains. Eco's constructive message lies in the fact that, for him, rational systems and structural models are not to be absolutely dismissed, but can and actually must be rediscovered in their practical, contingent values, as tools, and not essences, to be used, exploited, and eventually disposed of. This is particularly relevant to Eco's theoretical discussions, especially in *Trattato di semiotica generale* (*A Theory of Semiotics,* 1975). Eco rejects a definition of semiotics as the abstract theory interested in defining the linguistic competence of an idealized producer. According to Eco, semiotics is the empirical analysis of social phenomena that are constantly subject to change and revision. Communication, Eco argues, is a social function, and in order to elaborate a theory of communication it is imperative to avoid considering its discourse as neutral, objective, and immune to ideology (*Trattato* 44–45). Eco, therefore, reiterates the argument that Kristeva develops in her essay significantly entitled "Semiotics: A Critical Science and/or a Critique of Science" (1969). Semiotics is a mode of thought in which science sees itself as a theory:

> semiotics is at once a re-evaluation of its object and/or of its models, a critique both of these models (and therefore of the sciences from which they are borrowed) and of itself

> (as a system of stable truths). As the meeting-point of the sciences and an endless theoretical process, semiotics cannot harden into *a* science let alone into *the* science, for it is an open form of research, a constant critique that turns back on itself and offers its own auto-critique. (77)

In this way semiotics constitutes the kind of thought that can be systematic without rising to the level of an abstract and absolute system and can produce models while self-consciously discussing the ideological coordinates of its own model-making.

Il nome della rosa is an evaluation of the specific structuring models that allow us to emplot and thus make sense of the world in which we live. In Foucault's broader terms:

> the central issue of philosophy and critical thought since the eighteenth century has always been, still is, and will, I hope, remain the question: *What* is this Reason that we use? What are its historical effects? What are its limits and what are its dangers? ("Space" 249)

Like Horkheimer, Adorno, and Foucault, Eco warns against rationality's coercive force, its tendency toward universalization and dogmatization, its compulsion to classify and organize all forms of experience into systematic constructions and, at the same time, to exclude, marginalize, and silence all that cannot be assimilated.[16] After all, it is with masterful rhetoric and subtle psychological manipulation that Bernard Gui extorts a delirious confession from Remigio of Varagine. Upon this avowal, Bernard builds a logically tight relational system in order to defeat the Imperial delegation by demonstrating that Remigio shared the ideas of the Emperor's theologians:

> E dopo aver mostrato la connessione tra quelle idee, che erano anche quelle del capitolo di Perugia, e quelle dei fraticelli e dei dolciniani, e aver mostrato che un solo uomo, in quell'abbazia, partecipava di tutte quelle eresie, ed era stato l'autore di molti delitti, in quel modo egli avrebbe recato un colpo invero mortale ai propri avversari. (385; see appendix 63)

Il nome della rosa does not proclaim an absolute indictment of rationality, however. Even if the apocalyptic grand scheme did not correspond to the course of actual events,[17] logical thought may still be pragmatically useful, and even a source of intellectual pleasure. As William enthusiastically exclaims:

> trovo il diletto più gaudioso nel dipanare una bella e intricata matassa. E sarà ancora perché in un momento in cui, come filosofo, dubito che il mondo abbia un ordine, mi consola scoprire, se non un ordine, almeno una serie di connessioni in piccole porzioni degli affari del mondo. (397; see appendix 64)

In *Il nome della rosa,* the search for truth becomes a highly self-conscious affair that is both nurtured and frustrated by the doubt that truth is never what it appears to be; that causal thought is a powerful but not infallible cognitive tool, and, finally, that entertaining contradictory propositions, as well as questioning the very criteria of distinction that make choice and judgment possible, are signs of intellectual honesty rather than rational defeatism.

The subtle complexity and the final ironic significance of *Il nome della rosa* emerge from the problematic engagement between its structural framework and its thematic contents. Thematically, the apocalyptic *Weltanschauung* shared by some of the characters in the novel expresses their inability to adjust to progress and change, and their stubborn dependence upon absolute value systems. On the level of the story, however, the apocalyptic logic that supposedly framed the sequence of murders is defeated. Finally, on the level of Adso's discourse, the apocalyptic scheme does provide an organic framework for the entire novel. Thus, *Il nome della rosa* displays how a perfectly shaped aesthetic form may avoid the trap of becoming a consoling artifice by critically turning upon itself and revealing the full spectrum of its epistemological potentials as well as its shortcomings and possible aberrations.

Intertextuality and the Discourse of Carnival versus that of the Apocalypse

Il nome della rosa is what Gérard Genette would term a perfectly transtextual novel. Genette defines "transtextuality" as all that implicitly or explicitly relates a text to other texts

(*Palimpsestes* 7). Within the broader framework of transtextuality, Genette identifies various types of textual relations. The relationship between the Bible and *Il nome della rosa* is of the hypertextual kind, *Il nome della rosa* being the "hypertext" that founds itself upon and at the same time questions the validity of the Apocalypse as its structuring "hypotext." This is not the only kind of textual relation utilized in *Il nome della rosa.* The most relevant form of transtextuality at work in Eco's novel is that of intertextuality, which Genette defines as a relationship of a co-presence of two or more texts, and more often the presence of one text within another. The most explicit form of intertextuality is that of the *citation,* the less explicit that of the *allusion* (*Palimpsestes* 8). From Manzoni to Charles Schultz, and from Dante to Arthur Conan Doyle, *Il nome della rosa* is a mosaic of citations, a book made up of other books. Although many of the tassels in Eco's citational mosaic have been identified, little attention has been paid to the formal and ideological implications behind Eco's intertextual choices. In other words, it is important to examine the bulk of intertextual references in *Il nome della rosa* in their function as "ideologemes." In Kristeva's definition:

> The ideologeme is the intersection of a given textual arrangement (a semiotic practice) with the utterances (sequences) that it either assimilates into its own space or to which it refers in the space of exterior texts (semiotic practices). The ideologeme is that intertextual function read as "materialized" at the different structural levels of each text, and which stretches along the entire length of its trajectory, giving it its historical and social coordinates. ("The Bounded Text" 36)

The citational edifice of *Il nome della rosa* complicates the linear and progressive order of the plot. The arrangement emerging from the citational framework is neither simply historical nor ahistorical, but rather transhistorical. Eco, in fact, uses history in a cumulative rather than additive manner. The historical past exists by force of the sheer citational accumulation that compresses different chronological periods into a single narrative space. The process of historical sedimentation within the textual world challenges the flow of linear chronology: time is no longer seen as a sequence in which one instant is replaced by the following one, but as a dynamic and multivocal space where various temporal dimensions exist all at once.

The transhistorical dimension of *Il nome della rosa* acquires ideological significance both on the macroscale of the narrative order and on the microscale of the narrative voice. As far as narrative order is concerned, the novel's transhistorical scope justifies the persistence of the apocalyptic model. The Apocalypse is a transhistorical model in that it expresses recurrent collective feelings and beliefs, such as the sense of negativity regarding the present, the dysphoric expectation of impending catastrophe, the hope for radical change, and the awareness that this change will engender severe social conflicts (Eco, "Palinsesto" 78). Moreover, even if apocalyptic thought is consistent with progressive rather than cyclical notions of time and history (as it provides a way of organizing the historical flow in a rectilinear manner around the key moments of the Creation, the Original Sin, Christ's Incarnation and Redemption, Christ's Second Coming, the Universal Judgment and the End of Time), it is also endowed with a virtually inexhaustible power of repetition. The apocalyptic model in fact thrives upon its own frustration: the date of the end is calculated and then dismantled, a new date is established, and the cycle repeats itself:

> The great majority of interpretations of Apocalypse assume that the End is pretty near. Consequently the historical allegory is always having to be revised; time discredits it. . . . Apocalypse can be disconfirmed without being discredited. (Kermode 8)

The apocalyptic model accounting for the course of historical events is, more than others, a provisionary one: it can be modified at will without having to be discounted. The dreaded day approaches and finally comes, and the End is once again exorcised. New end-oriented fictions (plots) are created and new calculations made. Reminded that the prophecy contained in the *Libellus de Antichristo* by Adso of Montier-en-Der did not fulfill itself, Jorge of Burgos retorts that it was the prophecy's interpretation, and not the initial calculation, that was mistaken. This notion of ending is akin to the modern idea of crisis. Once imminent, the end becomes immanent:

> it is not merely the remnant of time that has eschatological import; the whole of history, and the progress of the individual life, have it also, as a benefaction from the End, now immanent. History and eschatology, as Collingwood observed, are then the same thing. (Kermode 25)

Remembering Salvatore's words, Adso writes that, in those times, the preachers were always proclaiming the end of the world, but Salvatore's parents and grandparents also remembered the same story in the past, so they reached the conclusion that the world was always about to end (190). The idea of the end is present at every moment, even while it loses its sense of finality. It becomes a provisionary frame, ready to be reshaped and revised in different forms and historical contexts. If, structurally, the Apocalypse is a "closed" work (it emplots history by endowing it with a beginning, a development, and an end), with respect to content it is an "open" work that both inspires and frustrates definitive and univocal readings because of the extraordinary breadth of its symbolic ramifications (Eco, "Palinsesto" 23). The history of biblical exegesis is the history of a sequence of provisionally absolute acts of interpretative closure performed upon the sacred book, each successive interpretation paying tribute to the *auctoritates* that preceded it, while replacing them with its own divinely inspired authoritative reading and its own "exact" calculation of the end of time.

On the microscale of the narrative voice, the apocalyptic model becomes significant if related to Eco's notion of a "mask." Obviously with Manzoni's Anonimo in mind, Eco defines his use of the mask in "Postille a *Il nome della rosa*":

> Mi sono messo a leggere o a rileggere i cronisti medievali, per acquistarne il ritmo, e il candore. Essi avrebbero parlato per me, e io ero libero da sospetti. Libero da sospetti, ma non dagli echi dell'intertestualità. Ho riscoperto così ciò che gli scrittori hanno sempre saputo (e che tante volte ci hanno detto): i libri parlano sempre di altri libri e ogni storia racconta una storia già raccontata. . . . Per cui la mia storia non poteva che iniziare col manoscritto ritrovato, e anche questa sarebbe stata una citazione (naturalmente). Così scrissi subito l'introduzione, ponendo la mia narrazione a un quarto livello di incassamento, dentro a altre tre narrazioni: io dico che Vallet diceva che Mabillon ha detto che Adso disse . . . (512–13; see appendix 65)

Not only does the mask assure the *couleur locale,* as, through Adso's medieval perspective, Eco can better re-create the cosmogony of that world; it also provides the transhistorical quality of *Il nome della rosa,* as each successive narrator identifies a different historical period, a different ontological position from the vantage point of which events are retold and reinterpreted. In this sense, the mask ironically distorts the discourse of truth as provided by the sacred text. In the Bible, there are no semantic and interpretative shifts between the Word of God and its appropriation by its different mouthpieces who act as transparent reporters of a single, indisputable truth. *Il nome della rosa,* on the other hand, explores the ideological import of its own dialogical intersection of narrative voices, thus dismantling the notions of univocal truths and single textual authorities.

Kristeva relates the function of the mask to the discourse of Carnival. Since carnivalesque discourse applied to the order of narrative cannot ultimately destroy the symbolic truth (the Transcendental Signified, that is) upon which it depends, it destroys its singularity of meaning through the function of the "double." The discourse of Carnival disrupts the classic trajectory of communication. Sender, message, and receiver occupy shifting positions, as in a Carnival scene everybody can be the subject of utterance, the subject of enunciation, and the addressee at the same time:

> A carnival participant is both actor and spectator; he loses his sense of individuality, passes through a zero point of carnivalesque activity and splits into a subject of the spectacle and an object of the game. Within the carnival, the subject is reduced to nothingness, while the structure of *the author* emerges as anonymity that creates and sees itself created as self and other, as man and mask. ("Word" 49)

The mask, "marque d'alterité, . . . refus de l'identité" ("mark of alterity, . . . refusal of identity") (Kristeva, *Le Texte* 165), allows for a perpetual and transitive passage between *Auteur* (Eco, in our case) and *Acteur* (Adso) as the subject of the utterance shifts into the subject of the enunciation. In the combination between the two functions, the mask allows the speaker to participate in his or her own language, which becomes a signifying practice in itself, with no relationship with anything external to it. In this manner, the two levels of enunciation and utterance become perfectly synchronized. There is no temporal linearity in the Carnival scene, as all chronology appears condensed in one single point. By destroying the Logos, time, and all distinctions between enunciation and utterance, the mask shatters all discursive possibilities, and the final liberation of the signified corresponds to its death: meaning becomes impossible (*Le Texte* 165–66).

By wearing the masks of his medieval characters, and Adso in particular, Eco revives the destabilizing function of the mask. Ironic and ambiguous, relativizing and dialogical, the mask hides a shifting subjectivity that, by assuming different personas, avoids all monological pitfalls and all essentialist notions of truth. The mask conceals and displaces what Kristeva names the Transcendental Subject, but unlike the Carnival scene, the historic arena of the novel assures narrative temporality and the construction of meaning. While the novel accepts the displacing and multiple discourses of the Carnival within its narrative structure, it also anchors these discourses to the linearity of syntax and the progressive logic of the story line, thus endowing them with finality and meaning. The Carnival, in other words, works *within* the novel's narrative framework: a plot requires a development and a finality and it is exactly this "surplus téléologique" ("teleological surplus") that eventually regulates the ambivalence and plurality of the carnivalesque discourse by addressing it to a specific narrative goal (Kristeva, *Le Texte* 175).

While this process is characteristic of all novels, Eco highlights it by means of accumulation. Not only does Eco reveal his strategic use of Adso as a mask, but he also creates a fictional framework in which Adso (as the original narrator), Maubillon, Vallet, and finally Eco (as the following translators), share the paternity of the narrative discourse and its ensuing transcriptions. By referring to the different time frames of the various rewritings, Eco inserts the plurivocal combinations of the Carnival scene into the linear chronology of the four successive scripts. Together with chronology, he also retrieves expressivity by means of the closed framework of the plot. As Kristeva reminds us, the carnivalesque discourse requires opening up the discursive space to a voluntary suspension of all programmed signification (*Le Texte* 168). There are in *Il nome della rosa* expressions of carnivalesque discourse, such as sudden exits from linear signification in a mad succession of signifiers that are tied together only by their phonic similarities and are not subordinated to the necessities of grammar, syntax, and semantics. Adso's oneiric version of the *Coena Cypriani* stages linguistic games that speak for the absolute liberation of the signifier:

> E tutti a bere, Gesù del passito, Giona del marsico, Faraone del sorrento (perché?), Mosè del gaditano, Isacco del cretese, Aronne dell'adriano, Zaccheo dell'arbustino, Tecla dell'arsino, Giovanni dell'albano, Abele del campano, Maria del signino, Rachele del fiorentino. (433)[18]

Taken to its extreme, the exhilaration before language's infinite possibilities forces the message into absolute intransitivity, stressing its code rather than the construction of meaning. The discourse of the signifier opposes itself to the Transcendental Signified of symbolic discourse and thus establishes itself as a foreign and ultimately incomprehensible word (Kristeva, *Le Texte* 173). Eco avoids radicalizing the dispersion inherent in all carnivalesque discourses by framing it in a way that is so closely constructed as to respect the Aristotelian unities of time, place, and action (Corti, "È un'opera" 108). Coincidentally, however, he complicates chronology and the multilayered relationship between the spaces of enunciation and utterance by ironically mingling different textual and chronological areas. The most famous example is the citation that William credits to a German mystic, and which belongs instead to Ludwig Wittgenstein, "L'ordine che la nostra mente immagina è come una rete, o una scala, che si costruisce per raggiungere qualcosa. Ma dopo si deve gettare la scala, perché si scopre che, se pure serviva, era priva di senso" ("The order that our mind imagines is like a net, or like a ladder, built to attain something. But afterward you must throw the ladder away, because you discover that, even if it was useful, it was meaningless") (495; 599–600).

While exploiting the liberating discourse of the Carnival, Eco is keen to identify its shortcomings and even its dangers. Salvatore represents the insertion of the discourse of the Carnival within the hyperdetermined and hierarchical space of the abbey. He stands for the disquieting otherness and the unbalanced excess characterizing the Carnival scene, with its celebration of food, drink, sexuality, the heteroglot, and the topsy-turvy (A. White 167). In his bizarre and opaque polyglottism, Salvatore speaks "tutte le lingue, e nessuna" ("all languages, and no language") (54; 47):

> si era inventata una lingua propria che usava i lacerti delle lingue con cui era entrato in contatto—e una volta pensai che la sua fosse, non la lingua adamica che l'umanità felice aveva parlato, tutti uniti da una sola favella, dalle origini del mondo sino alla Torre di Babele, e nemmeno una delle lingue sorte dopo il funesto evento della loro divisione, ma proprio la lingua babelica del primo giorno dopo il castigo divino, la lingua della confusione primeva. (54; see appendix 66)

A ludicrous combination of various vernacular idioms, Salvatore's language represents carnivalesque multiplicity: "Era come se la sua favella fosse quale la sua faccia, messa insieme con pezzi di facce altrui" ("His speech was somehow like his face, put together with pieces from other people's faces") (55; 48). Grotesque like his body, Salvatore's language is a harlequinesque patchwork featuring creativity, heteroglossia, and linguistic pluralism. However, what is potentially absolute freedom in the economy of the Carnival becomes a passport to damnation in that of the abbey. Even if Salvatore's language manages to maintain a communicative efficacy of sorts, it cannot be effective on the platform of history and politics; in fact, it becomes evidence of his contacts with different sects, whose idiolects he has partially absorbed, and therefore becomes instrumental in bringing charges of heresy against him.

The extreme example of this situation is the nameless girl from the village who introduces Adso to sex. Her existence in the abbey is marked by silence—she does not speak Latin—and by a dire law of survival, as she prostitutes herself in order to provide food for herself and her family. As she cannot live in the order of language, her existence on the level of pure physicality is dictated by necessity and not by choice. What is feared as transgression by the constituted order of the abbey, she experiences not as liberation but desperate need. Just like

Salvatore, the nameless girl cannot act within the system of the Symbolic universe:

> né Bernardo, né gli arcieri, né io stesso, intendevamo cosa dicesse nella sua lingua di contadina. Per quanto parlasse, era come muta. Ci sono delle parole che danno potere, altre che rendono più derelitti ancora, e di questa sorta sono le parole volgari dei semplici, a cui il Signore non ha concesso di sapersi esprimere nella lingua universale della sapienza e della potenza. (334; see appendix 67)

Representing the totally different, the absolute otherness within the male order of the monastery, she is, as William puts it, "carne bruciata" ("burnt flesh") (334; 398). She will be burnt at the stake as a witch, a bacchanalian, a priestess of Dionysian orgies that threatens the Apollonian surface of the monastery's patriarchal order. The girl's body constitutes the maternal space of the Semiotic, as opposed to the Symbolic, of the prelogic as opposed to the logic (De Lauretis, "Il principio" 52), and her sad adventure expresses the ways in which this space is invaded, abused, and finally destroyed when the law chooses to demonstrate, in exemplary manner, its power over the carnivalesque freedom this body supposedly represents.

The dangers implicit in carnivalesque ideology become clear when the Carnival's celebration of the "upside-down world [*monde renversé*] in which fish fly and birds swim, in which foxes and rabbits chase hunters, bishops behave crazily, and fools are crowned" (Eco, "Frames" 2)[19] is combined with the apocalyptic philosophy of reversal. Apocalyptic thought is not limited, in *Il nome della rosa,* to Jorge's prophecies regarding the advent of the Antichrist, Alinard of Grottaferrata's interpretation of the timetable of his arrival, or Abo's aristocratic statements concerning the decline of civilization and his predictions of imminent disaster. *Il nome della rosa* demonstrates that apocalyptic attitudes are sociocultural occurrences permeating specific historical periods. More than by theological and philosophical reasons, apocalyptic attitudes are explainable by the empirical tools of sociohistorical analysis, as they are, to use Eco's anachronistic expression, "fenomeni di massa" ("mass phenomena") that periodically resurface when precise conditions of life and concrete situations of political instability and cultural uncertainty inspire the masses with fear of impending death and the desire for a radical reversal of the current situation ("Palinsesto" 31). For populations decimated by wars, ridden by famines, and prostrated by disease and natural disasters such as inundations and droughts, the Apocalypse seems a chronicle of the present, and the apocalyptic model provides the hope for imminent change. For the masses, interpreting the Apocalypse[20] means rewriting its message in exclusively material terms. In the popular imagination, the apocalyptic reversal takes the carnivalesque tones of the mythic land of Cockaigne, where, as Salvatore puts it, "dagli alberi, che trasudano miele, crescono forme di cacio e salsicciotti profumati" ("wheels of cheese and aromatic sausages grow on the trees that ooze honey") (192; 220). Change, in other words, refers to a better future that is attainable in this life through direct participation.

In this perspective, apocalyptic thought is recast within the mold of a confused and unrationalized anarchism, especially by the unstable elements of society (Eco, "Palinsesto" 72): the confused, polymorphous, and expanding carnivalesque body of the marginalized and disinherited masses:

> quelle bande di vaganti che poi, negli anni che seguirono, sempre più vidi aggirarsi per l'Europa: falsi monaci, ciarlatani, giuntatori, arcatori, pezzenti e straccioni, lebbrosi e storpiati, ambulanti, girovaghi, cantastorie, chierici senza patria, studenti itineranti, bari, giocolieri, mercenari invalidi, giudei erranti, scampati dagli infedeli con lo spirito distrutto, folli, fuggitivi colpiti da bando, malfattori con le orecchie mozzate, sodomiti, e tra loro artigiani ambulanti, tessitori, calderai, seggiolai, arrotini, impagliatori, muratori, e ancora manigoldi di ogni risma, bari, birboni, baroni, bricconi, gaglioffi, guidoni, trucconi, calcanti, protobianti, paltonieri. . . . (*Il nome della rosa* 192; see appendix 68)

The progressive activation of the signifier with its phonic similarities undermines semantic differences, in a linguistic mirroring of the process of indetermination characterizing this confused and menacing carnivalesque space. The ideological significance of what appears as a playful linguistic game is clear to Eco, as he interprets the birth and development of Joachim of Fiore's thought, and its appropriation by the Fraticelli and the Dolcinians, as the medieval counterpart to other anarchic aspirations to a "community of equality," a classless and stateless society, opposed to social divisions based upon power and wealth.

In this sense, the trial and conviction of Remigio of Varagine becomes exemplary because he epitomizes the threat that the Carnival poses to a given sociopolitical order when it moves from the margins to the center of the social map. As Remigio himself explains, rebellion is "understandable" in Salvatore's case because he is a serf, and Dolcino represented the destruction of the lords. For Remigio, however, who belonged to a city family and never had to suffer oppression and hunger, rebellion has been "una festa dei folli, un bel carnevale . . . e a carnevale si fanno le cose alla rovescia" ("a feast of fools, a magnificent carnival . . . and in carnival time everything is done backward") (276; 325–26). In other words, as far as Remigio is concerned, revolution becomes the illogical, unjustified, and therefore fearsome event that escapes all attempts at rationalization and interpretation, and that is seen as spreading, like a disease, upon the whole social body, causing the dissolution of all ethical criteria and the anarchic dismantling of all legal, political, and social structures.

Even more than Salvatore's and the nameless girl's, Remigio's story demonstrates that a social system accepts Carnival, and its transgressions, only as far as these transgressions are contained within a framework designed by the system. Like Adelmo's *marginalia,* in other words, Carnival can exist only within designated spaces, where its subversive drives are accepted. The *Coena Cypriani* that Bakhtin cites as an example of the Carnival spirit (Introduction 13) and that Adso relives in his erotic, Dionysian dream is "a burlesque representation based upon the subversion of topical situation of the Scriptures. [It] was enjoyed as a comic transgression only by people who took the same Scriptures seriously during the rest of the year" (Eco, "Frames" 6). The order tolerates and even thrives upon Carnival because the transgression finally acts as reminder of the existence and power of the rule: "anche la chiesa nella sua saggezza ha concesso il momento della festa, del carnevale, della fiera" ("even the church in her wisdom has granted the moment of feast, carnival, fair") (Eco, *Il nome della rosa* 477; *The Name of the Rose* 576). Carnivalization can act as a revolution when it exploits an element of surprise, as it appears suddenly, frustrating social expectations (Eco, "Frames" 6). But even in this case the subversive potential is limited, as carnivalesque revolution lacks an organized agenda, and society (what Eco has called *conservazione*) soon reabsorbs it, encompassing it within its own fixed boundaries.

Why is Aristotle's lost book on comedy so important, then, if in Eco's perspective institutionalized Carnival is ultimately only a means of social control aimed at preserving the status quo, and anarchic Carnival represents, on the other hand, a sudden eruption of irrationality and chaos unable to carry on a constructive project of social criticism and effective political change? In *Il nome della rosa* Aristotle's book represents a danger not so much because it would codify a structure of the comic parallel to that of tragedy, but because this structure would no longer be marginalized within the low framework of the Carnival scene, a scene that is drastically limited within both temporal and spatial boundaries. The ideology of the comic would be carried into the very heart of the Symbolic order, and would receive authorial foundation by the Philosopher of Philosophers, Aristotle. Jorge knows this very well, as he explains to William: "Ma il giorno che la parola del Filosofo giustificasse i giochi marginali della immaginazione sregolata, oh allora veramente ciò che stava a margine balzerebbe nel centro, e del centro si perderebbe ogni traccia" ("But on the day when the Philosopher's word would justify the marginal jests of the debauched imagination, or when what has been marginal would leap to the center, every trace of the center would be lost") (479; 578). By codifying comic theory, Aristotle gave it a profound intellectual respectability: it is this force and respectability of comedy that Jorge opposes, because it jeopardizes his ordered world (Golden 245). In this way, in fact, the ideology of the comic would act *within* the system, forcing it to modify its conceptual landscape and open itself up to the disruptive power of comedy and irony.[21]

Carnivalesque discourse marks a significant change in the ideology of the written word, and by promoting the discourse of Carnival, *Il nome della rosa* ironically unwrites and rewrites a transhistorical constant of Western tradition. As Kristeva explains, Christianity

> a rencontré le néo-platonisme et en général l'idéalisme de l'antiquité sur le terrain de l'écriture comme signe expressif

> de la vérité, de la Foi, de la Parole Divine. Dieu, Parole et Ecriture se joignent au sein du Christianisme: pour toute la culture chrétienne le livre sera le lieu du discours autoritaire, du Dire du Père. (*Le Texte* 143; see appendix 69)

Writing is submission to the order of the Law and of the Father, and it is exactly this aspect that was stressed by the monastic orders that dominated Western culture since AD 350 (Kristeva, *Le Texte* 143). In *Il nome della rosa,* intertextuality and the dialogical exchange of books within other books relativize both the text's Transcendental Signified and the singularity of meaning that the text, and all monological interpretations of the text, provide. Moreover, the discourse of Carnival envisions a different epistemological approach to reality, defining a type of knowledge that is not so much alternative as supplemental to strictly causal and logical procedures. Discussing Adelmo's vivacious imagination and his ability to create unknown and surprising images out of conventional forms, William and Adso admire his *marginalia* and their uncanny designs:

> là una grande V che dava inizio alla parola "verba" produceva come naturale viticchio del suo tronco una serpe dalle mille volute, a sua volta generante altre serpi quali pampini e corimbi. (85; see appendix 70)

The issue here is whether the Sacred Scriptures (i.e., the Word of God and the quintessential discourse of truth) originate, although at their own margins, a discourse of fallacy and falsehood, or rather whether this marginal discourse featuring an upside-down world that provokes laughter and a sense of surprise constitutes an alternative form of knowledge:

> si trattava . . . di capire in che modo si possa scoprire la verità attraverso espressioni sorprendenti, e argute, ed enigmatiche. . . . Si trattava di sapere infatti se le metafore, e i giochi di parole, e gli enigmi, che pure paiono immaginati dai poeti per puro diletto, non inducano a speculare sulle cose in modo nuovo e sorprendente. (89–90; see appendix 71)

Carnivalesque narratives, featuring semantic ambiguity and the plurality of meaning, exploiting the destabilizing force of the signifiers, disrupting conventional syntactical hierarchies, promoting analogical games and the visionary power of imagery, force us to reexamine strictly logical procedures and revise our conventional cognitive maps. By casting things in a new light and establishing surprising and unexpected connections between seemingly unrelated objects and phenomena, the discourse of Carnival frustrates ready-made interpretative procedures and establishes an approach to knowledge that differs from all unified and centered epistemologies.

While the choir begins to chant the Dies Irae of the requiem Mass in the sixth day of Adso's sojourn in the abbey, the young novice has a vision that significantly complements his first apocalyptic vision before the portal of the abbey's church. This time, however, the vision is replete with carnivalesque lore (it is based upon the *Coena Cypriani*), and it allows William to gain a fundamental clue regarding the secret of the *Finis Africae:*

> Tu hai vissuto in questi giorni, mio povero ragazzo, una serie di avvenimenti in cui ogni retta regola sembra essersi sciolta. E stamane è riaffiorato alla tua mente addormentata il ricordo di una specie di commedia in cui . . . il mondo si poneva a testa in giù. . . . Sei partito dai marginalia di Adelmo per rivivere un gran carnevale in cui tutto sembra andare per il verso sbagliato, e tuttavia, come nella *Coena,* ciascuno fa quello che ha veramente fatto nella vita. E alla fine ti sei chiesto, nel sogno, quale sia il mondo sbagliato, e cosa voglia dire procedere a testa in giù. Il tuo sogno non sapeva più dove fosse l'alto e dove il basso, dove la morte e dove la vita. Il tuo sogno ha dubitato degli insegnamenti che hai ricevuto. . . . E tuttavia, più penso al tuo sogno, più lo trovo rivelatore. (441; see appendix 72)

In *Il nome della rosa,* Carnival furnishes the other discourse that, by distorting the face of truth, inspires us to examine it more closely and more critically, thus preventing us from becoming enslaved by the rational machines that we ourselves have created.

After the Fire: *Apokalypsis* with No Revelation

What are the ideological implications of Eco's epistemological project in *Il nome della rosa?* Like the prophetic, apocalyptic thought is essentially proleptic. It extends beyond the present moment, as it binds the historical process within the perfect framework of atemporal conclusions and beginnings. While prophecy defies the scheme of causal necessity, apocalyptic thought is based on a closed sequence of "signs"; the only thing remaining open is the timetable of their occurrence. In the history of biblical exegesis, however, the change in title from the Apocalypse to the Book of Revelation suggests a change of focus from the cosmic Armageddon to the inception of a new order bestowed through Revelation. "Within the apocalyptic milieu, destruction implies redemption, the erasing of one order of being implies the creation of another, better order" (Daw 92). *Il nome della rosa* frustrates this expectation. Aristotle's book is lost; all that remains is Adso's modest reshaping of the past in the form of his gathering of the burnt relics of the once all-powerful library:

> Rovistando tra le macerie trovavo a tratti brandelli di pergamena, precipitati dallo scriptorium e dalla biblioteca e sopravvissuti come tesori sepolti nella terra; e incominciai a raccoglierli, come se dovessi ricomporre i fogli di un libro. . . . Povera messe fu la mia, ma passai una intera giornata a raccoglierla, come se da quelle disiecta membra della biblioteca dovesse pervenirmi un messaggio. . . . Alla fine della mia paziente ricomposizione mi si disegnò come una biblioteca minore, segno di quella maggiore scomparsa, una biblioteca fatta di brani, citazioni, periodi incompiuti, moncherini di libri. (501–02; see appendix 73)

The thrill of revelation gives way to a loving recollection of things past, what Vattimo refers to as *pietas,* a way to establish a link with

> the great and the beautiful of the past with whom we'd like to be and to speak, the people we have loved and who have disappeared. Inasmuch as it is a crystallization of acts of the word and of modes of experience, language itself is deposited in the coffer of death. At bottom, that coffer is also the source of the few rules that can help us to move about our existence in a nonchaotic and undisorganized way while knowing that we are not headed anywhere. Our new experiences have meaning only insofar as they carry on a dialogue with all that the coffer of death—history, tradition, language—has transmitted to us. ("Bottle" 25)

The traces of tradition and the distant voices of the past become the only kind of foundation upon which we can rely in the age of the death of metaphysics (Rosso 84). If *Il nome della rosa* leaves no space for utopian thought, the dialogue with the past is no mere sad withdrawal. The past has to be revived in order to better understand the present: writing about the past becomes, for Eco, a way to step back from our current world and our current worldviews and examine them through different filters, and as if from a distance:

> choisir d'écrire un roman historique, ce n'était pas opter pour le refuge ou l'évasion: c'était un choix politique. Vous allez me dire que l'histoire et, en particulier, le Moyen Age sont à la mode. C'est vrai. Mais pour moi, c'était une façon de mieux déchiffrer le présent. Un pays qui traverse une crise profonde dont les causes ne sont pas claires—elles le seront plus tard pour les historiens—éprouve le besoin de se ressaisir à travers son passé. (Eco, "Le Tueur" 52; see appendix 74)[22]

Historical fiction establishes a dialogue with the past that inspires an epistemological quest in the present. It questions the values and reveals the limits of the transhistorical structures that, in Western civilization, have organized knowledge and have defined our attempts to give narrative form to the world in which we live. The cognitive grids shaping our narrative understanding of the past are transferred from the absolute realm of universal constructions to the empirical spaces of specific historic and cultural occurrences. The founding precepts of identity, causality, and the narrative order—the tenets, that is, of the discourse of history—are tested not so much against as within the dialogical, citational, and polyphonic structure of carnivalesque discourse. In *Il nome della rosa* the two texts, that of the Apocalypse and that of the Carnival, meet and relativize each other in a narrative space that ironically constructs itself by subjecting them to a pitiless confrontation.

Conclusion

In *Del romanzo storico,* Manzoni maintains a dualistic approach toward history and fiction and denies that they can be combined into a single genre. Although he concedes that both history and fiction are ideological and linguistic constructs, he is nevertheless convinced that they are, both ideologically and formally, two mutually exclusive types of discourse. According to Manzoni, fiction is rooted in the universal and the transcendental, while history instead belongs to the factual and the empirical. Therefore, he concludes that fiction and history address the problems of representation, referentiality, truth, and commitment in contrasting ways.

By choosing a new form of creative historiography, however, Manzoni transcends the idealistic and absolutizing aesthetics of his age. He directly challenges the cognitive strategies implied in the process of historical emplotment and examines the subjective powers and limitations involved in the historian's reappropriation of the historical referent. By questioning the central assumption of canonical historical discourse—namely, objectivity, impersonality, and neutrality—he emphasizes the ideologically determined nature of all historical representations. Manzoni's *I promessi sposi* remains a model for the twentieth century. Although modern critical historical fiction rejects his teleological vision of history, it nevertheless takes up his commitment to narrate the unwritten histories of the marginal members of society traditionally excluded from official records. Critical historical fiction thus challenges the authority of written records, denounces their subservience to existing ideologies and power structures, and creatively reports the inverted *res gestae* of those who do not belong to the dominant orders.

In *Il Gattopardo,* Lampedusa takes up Manzoni's debate and examines the cultural and ideological codes and the cognitive and psychological patterns that interweave to reconfigure the historical past. By combining—and at times juxtaposing—the constructive strategies of the omniscient narrator with those of the novel's protagonist, Don Fabrizio, *Il Gattopardo* emphasizes that reconfigurations of the past are by no means objective and neutral, but rather dependent upon the subjective views, and historical positions, of their interpreters. Lampedusa's presentation of an episode of the Unification of Italy from the marginal and decentered point of view of a Sicilian aristocrat polemically reverses the traditional epic renderings of these historical events. *Il Gattopardo* questions the logic of linear chronology and causal connection as the founding criteria of historical reconstructions. Lampedusa reveals that these forms are by no means universal and natural, and juxtaposes them with significantly "other" forms of historical emplotment, such as analogy and repetition. *Il Gattopardo*'s alternative history questions the absolute accessibility of the historical referent; the past as it *really* was remains an absence, an elusive ghost. Its ontological void may, however, be filled by the various and transient figures that individual interpreters evoke from their cognitive involvement and emotional participation in the past. In particular, *Il Gattopardo* examines how the analogical codes and the figures of repetition that structure the novel counteract the linear rendition of historical becoming, and explores how they become ways to preserve the cultural heritage of communities about to be submerged by the flow of historical change.

Much like *Il Gattopardo,* Morante's *La Storia* confronts one of the staple concepts of traditional historiography, namely, knowledge of the past as it *really* was and faithfulness to the facts that *really* happened. The binary opposition between historical chronicle and fictional emplotment in *La Storia* is less an opposition of the "true" to the "verisimilar" than a subversion of this opposition. *La Storia* questions the validity of historical truth altogether by denouncing the omissions and the silences that plague ordinary historical chronicles. Fiction becomes a legitimate, yet alternative, form of historiography. Fiction creatively recounts the stories of those who have not been able to inscribe the public records, and by doing so denounces the biases of official versions of history exclusively geared to bolster and maintain the existing power structures and the worldviews they support. *La Storia* also teaches us that rival versions of history imply rival perceptual and cognitive schemes and alternative ways of conceptualizing and emplotting the past. A monumental, cyclical, and intersubjective notion of time alters the linear succession of teleological history, revising the universalist pretensions that make the historical continuum appear exclusively as a causal chain of meaningful political events. The utopic and prophetic tone that closes the novel not only calls for a different and better world for women to inhabit but also envisions new representations of this world, representations that would no longer subscribe to the absolutizing deterministic schemes of patriarchal history. *La Storia*'s female narrator engages in an emotional, subjective, creative, and nonomniscient relationship with the past that challenges the impersonality and objectivity of orthodox historical discourse and asserts her right to lovingly report—and invent—alternative histories in a distinctly feminine voice.

In *Il nome della rosa,* Eco puts historical fiction on trial, and self-consciously cross-examines its ability to emplot the historical past. Historical fiction becomes historiographic metafiction, a problematic genre exploiting and yet criticizing its epistemological foundations. *Il nome della rosa* affirms the resilience of narrativity as a transhistorical method of ordering and conceptualizing our knowledge of the world. At the same time, the novel ironically reveals the limits—and the traps—inherent in our narrative understanding of reality. The Aristotelian notion of plot, with its emphasis on causality and necessity, and the biblical model of the Apocalypse, with its absolute structural closure, are both successfully exploited and yet submitted to a fundamental process of self-analysis. Consequently, rational constructions are not absolutely dismissed, but rediscovered as practical cognitive tools, the validity of which is tested on empirical rather than universal grounds. Eco juxtaposes the Apocalypse and the Carnival as opposing binary discourses: closure faces openness, the monological word of the Apocalypse confronts the plurilingual babble of the Carnival, the pretense of perfect referentiality meets the ploy of the ever-shifting mask, and absolutism encounters relativism. Unlike Manzoni, however, Eco does not insist that these opposites are mutually exclusive. They exist together in textual space in order to challenge their epistemological foundations, raise questions, test their values, denounce their limits, and finally seal a paradoxical bond, that of historical fiction.

With his novel *I promessi sposi* and essay *Del romanzo storico,* Manzoni both devises the archetype for historical fiction and debates the reasons for its theoretical rejection, thus establishing the problematic and contradictory parameters that influenced the development of historical fiction in Italy. By instituting a critical dialogue with Manzoni's creative model as well as with his theoretical repudiation of the genre, Lampedusa, Morante, and Eco implicitly engage in a discussion of the cultural and historical dialectics of all literary genres, and historical fiction in particular. Lampedusa, Morante, and Eco demonstrate how genres do not objectively and neutrally catalog literary types that share certain formal and thematic characteristics in either a diachronic span or a synchronic segment. Genres are indeed part of the systems they categorize. *Il Gattopardo, La Storia,* and *Il nome della rosa* are historical novels precisely because they engage in a self-conscious analysis of their generic features. They demonstrate that these features are not universal data or natural forms, but instead reflect specific ideological choices and are grounded in the conceptual frameworks shared by cultural groups in a specific sociohistorical moment. Modern historical fiction tests its *generic* abilities —and limits—to collect, examine, evaluate, and interpret historical knowledge.

Appendix

English Translations

These English translations for the longer Italian and French quotations are keyed to the text by number. Unless identified by a title and page number referring to a published English translation, the translations are mine.

1 Novelists, you need to undeceive yourselves: there is no hope of praise in this path: if you want to live, you must invent.

2 I remember . . . that the immortal Bacon . . . affirms that, since true History narrates the outcomes of facts and events as they really happened and without any regard to the virtue or villainy of the people involved, it needs to be corrected with the inventions of the fictional; and the fictional can sagaciously present to its readers happy or adverse turns of events, according to the intrinsic value of the actions and the dictates of a vindicating justice.

3 May novels have the power to refine our souls, and from time to time detach us from the painful tediousness of real life, but may we never lose sight of the fact that we are born to search for and know the truth. The crown that the novelist may expect in Italy is beautiful, but the crown of the historian will always be more glorious, and we shall say even more eternal. Happy is Alessandro Manzoni, who has by now obtained the first, and should he but want it, can obtain the second.

4 Not for a moment must we lose sight of moral truth, and therefore if we perceive that a novel lacks it, it seems to us that its publication should be forbidden. The populace has a great reverence for all that they see in print, and it is too easy for them to be led astray into regarding as natural passion what is almost its parody. Also, the young people not yet experienced in the real movements of affections run the risk of modeling themselves on those intemperate ideas, and they enter the world convinced that the course of omnipotent passions is unstoppable.

5 when any public or private circumstances have become universally known, they must be removed forever from the liberties of fiction. . . . But would we call "history" the miserable chronicle of an obscure village, the dubious memories of an old family, the old legends that have always remained in the hands of the uneducated classes?

6 It is no wonder that a philosophy, which doubts everything and transforms axioms into problems, should strive to fight truth in its strongest trench, introducing fiction where it should never have entered. Perhaps this philosophy hopes that by rendering fiction historical we will proceed to believe that history is fictional, and if it succeeds in this, the unfortunate triumph of its systems is certain, because it will have rendered facts uncertain and dubious, and facts are the only enemies that it cannot destroy with its sophistic reasonings.

7 I do what I can to immerse myself in the spirit of the time I have to describe, to live in it. . . . As to the progress of the events, and of the plot, I think that the best way not to do like the others is to focus on considering the way in which people act in reality, and especially to consider it in its aspects which are most opposed to the spirit of romance.

8 Beauty in art requires unity because it requires harmony, and the impression deriving from it, in order to create the entire effect it is able to produce, must not be interrupted by any opposite effect. It must reach our souls unviolated.

9 In this type of novel every effort to preserve the truth will be futile or have the effect of completely distorting the work's nature. Nobody will be able to avoid the choice between these two alternatives. If the characters and the facts are historical and remain as history describes them, then the fictional account will remain totally independent from them, and instead of having a historical novel, we will have a novel and a historical text that walk side by side, like two parallel lines, without ever touching each other. If true and fictional events mutually aid each other, and the former serve to develop and unravel the story of the latter, the truth is necessarily compromised.

10 History . . . can be defined as a great painting in which all the events are outlined, in which great figures are placed, and a certain series of deeds is exposed in order, but where the multitude of historical facts is neglected or barely sketched in at random and in passing, and only the most extraordinary actions and the

greatest men are painted in isolation and almost always only in relation to public interests. The historical novel is a great lens applied to one point of that immense picture so that what was hardly visible takes on its natural dimensions; a faintly sketched outline becomes a regular and perfect drawing, or rather a painting in which all the objects recover their true colors. No longer are kings, captains, and magistrates alone displayed, but so are common people, women, and children: vices and domestic virtues are put into action, and the influence of public institutions on private customs, on the needs and joys of life, is revealed; which is what in the end must interest all men.

11 The purpose of history is to narrate the truth; yet, having to narrate the facts in the manner and order in which they happened, history, unlike the novel, is not free to use invention to organize, stretch and pull, and shorten the threads of the plot so that the mind of every common reader is necessarily and irresistibly guided to the conclusion that it is good for him to reach.

12 The superstitious and meticulous religion of facts has run its course: we are now ripe for the religion of principles. . . . Until today facts were gathered and lined up as time gave them, or they were ordered into groups as suggested by the isolated observation of one year, one century, or one people. The connection existing among the facts forming the different groups was traced without considering whether a superior link united one group to the other: partial consequences were deduced. . . . It is now time . . . to establish a series of general formulae for the operations of the mind:—find the way to verify these formulae in history.

13 Like all others, this subject can be portrayed in a new form, according to the variety of perspectives caused by the variety of the imaginations and the changing times. . . . The new experiences made by a man, a people, or an age may, suddenly, shed new light on well-known ancient facts and illuminate them with a new moral sense.

14 is a work in which the necessary turns out to be impossible, and in which two essential conditions cannot be reconciled, or even one fulfilled. It inevitably calls for a combination that is contrary to its subject matter and a division contrary to its form. Though we know it is a work in which history and fable must figure, we cannot determine or even estimate their proper measure or relation. In short, it is a work impossible to achieve satisfactorily, because its premises are inherently contradictory. (Manzoni, *On the Historical Novel* 72)

15 Art is art to the extent that it produces, not just any effect, but a definitive one . . . for the verisimilar (the raw material of art) once offered and accepted as such, becomes a truth that is altogether different from the real, but one that the mind perceives forever, one whose presence is irrevocable. Though it is an object that might come to be forgotten, it can never be destroyed through disillusionment. (Manzoni, *On the Historical Novel* 70–71)

16 One of the most important faculties of the human spirit is that of grasping the relations of cause and effect, and anteriority and posteriority that link events together; of tracing back to a single point of view, as if by a single intuition, several facts separated in time and space while setting aside the other facts that are related only by accidental circumstances. This is the task of the historian. The historian sorts out the events in order to reach this unitary view; he leaves aside all that does not have any relation with the most important facts and, availing himself of the rapidity of the thought process, brings these facts as close together as possible, so as to present them in that order that the spirit loves to find there and of which it bears the archetype within itself.

17 History may truly be defined as a famous War against Time; for she doth take from him the Years that he had made Prisoner, or rather utterly slain, and doth call them back into Life, and pass them in Review, and set them again in Order of Battle. (Manzoni, *The Betrothed* 19)

18 When, on a summer evening, the melodious sky growls like a tawny lion, and everyone is complaining of the storm, it is the memory of the Méséglise way that makes me stand alone in ecstasy, inhaling, through the noise of the falling rain, the lingering scent of invisible lilacs. (Proust 222)

19 Its goal . . . is to uproot all forms of "positionalism" through a constant check and struggle against latent tendentiousness. . . . This same philological spirit also presides over our political attitude, and our difficult, painful, and even humiliating attitude of independence, which cannot accept any historical and practical forms of ideology and, at the same time, suffers as if from remorse, from the unclear and irrational moral trauma of being excluded from all praxis or, in any case, from action.

20 It is one thing . . . to refuse to transform the history of the Risorgimento into the hagiography and oleography of a "miracle of Italian patriotism," it is another thing to purely and simply ignore the sum of ideas, feelings, and passions that history brought about,

especially the sum of ideas, feelings, and passions linked to the formation of a national consciousness.

21 The neorealist movement did not ignore the process that the avant-garde terms the "reduction of the Self"; on the contrary, neorealism considered it an unmistakable innovation in relation to prewar narrative prose; . . . [in neorealism] the individual consciousness was emblematic of the social consciousness. In the neo-avantgarde the problem of the reduction of the Self becomes more subtle and complex, because it a priori excludes personal experience. . . . The objection here is addressed to subjectivity as a poetic category.

22 The point of reference is always the hidden character who says I, the writer, who enriches himself in a certain sense with the experience of all that has occurred between the narrated facts and *his own* present. . . . In the course of the story the character . . . loses, little by little, his historical traits, in order to acquire the relevance and paradigmatic drama of a man crushed by time, of a man alone in the face of destiny.

23 The historical novel flourishes in periods during which history rests and has no popular continuity, but is a study of the past by the educated classes. The authors of epics, then, address the past through their imagination, because they need vast scenarios in which to place characters worthy of their dreams and visions of the world. But he who did not have the epic voice to narrate what happened around him . . . how will he have it to describe obscure events that seem epic only because the arguments of Marxist historians say they are?

24 Rosary and Introduction to the Prince - The Garden and the Dead Soldier - Royal Audiences - Dinner - A Carriage to Palermo - Going to Mariannina's - [Return to S. Lorenzo] - Conversation with Tancredi - In the Office; Estates and Politics - In the Observatory with Father Pirrone - Relaxation at Luncheon - Don Fabrizio and the Peasants - Don Fabrizio and His Son Paolo - News of the Landing and Rosary Again. (Lampedusa, *The Leopard* 11)

25 they turned up a slope and found themselves in the immemorial silence of pastoral Sicily. All at once they were far from everything in space and still more so in time. Donnafugata with its palace and its newly rich was only a mile or two away, but it seemed a dim memory like those landscapes sometimes glimpsed at the distant end of a railway tunnel; its troubles and splendors appeared even more insignificant than if they belonged to the past, for

compared to this remote unchangeable landscape they seemed part of the future. (Lampedusa, *The Leopard* 98)

26 When the sportsmen reached the top of the hill, there among the tamarisks and scattered cork trees appeared the real Sicily again, the one compared to which baroque towns and orange groves are mere trifles: aridly undulating to the horizon in hillock after hillock, comfortless and irrational, with no lines that the mind could grasp, conceived apparently in a delirious moment of creation; a sea suddenly petrified at the instant when a change of wind had flung waves into frenzy. (Lampedusa, *The Leopard* 108–09)

27 Supported, guided, it seemed, by calculations which were invisible at that hour yet ever present, the stars cleft the ether in those exact trajectories of theirs. The comets would be appearing as usual, punctual to the fraction of a second, in sight of whoever was observing them. They were not messengers of catastrophe as Stella thought; on the contrary, their appearance at the time foreseen was a triumph of the human mind's capacity to project itself and to participate in the sublime routine of the skies. (Lampedusa, *The Leopard* 47–48)

28 Sleep, my dear Chevalley, sleep, that is what Sicilians want, and they will always hate anyone who tries to wake them, even in order to bring them the most wonderful of gifts; and I must say, between ourselves, I have strong doubts whether the new Kingdom will have many gifts for us in its luggage. All Sicilian expression, even the most violent, is really wish-fulfillment: our sensuality is a hankering for oblivion, our shooting and knifing a hankering for death . . . novelties attract us only when they are dead, incapable of arousing vital currents; that is what gives rise to the extraordinary phenomenon of the constant formation of myths which would be venerable if they were really ancient, but which are really nothing but sinister attempts to plunge us back into a past that attracts us only because it is dead. (Lampedusa, *The Leopard* 183)

29 As soon as he got into the house he was assailed as always by sweet youthful memories; nothing was changed, from the red-brick floor to the sparse furniture; the same light entered the small narrow windows; Romeo, the dog, barking briefly in a corner, was exactly like another hound, its great-great-grandfather, his companion in violent play. (Lampedusa, *The Leopard* 197)

30 Until today, on the rare occasions when she thought over what had happened at Donnafugata that distant summer, she had felt

upheld by a sense of being martyred, being wronged. . . . Now, however, these second-hand feelings which had formed the skeleton of her whole mode of thought were also collapsing. There had been no enemies, just one single adversary, herself; her future had been killed by her own imprudence, by the reckless Salina pride; and now, just at the moment when her memories had come alive again after so many years, she found herself even without the solace of being able to blame her own unhappiness on others, a solace which is the last deceiving philter of the desperate. (Lampedusa, *The Leopard* 279–80)

31 But was it the truth? Nowhere has truth so short a life as in Sicily; a fact has scarcely happened five minutes before its genuine kernel has vanished, been camouflaged, embellished, disfigured, squashed, annihilated by imagination and self-interest; shame, fear, generosity, malice, opportunism, charity, all the passions, good as well as evil, fling themselves onto the fact and tear it to pieces; very soon it has vanished altogether. (Lampedusa, *The Leopard* 280)

32 As the carcass was dragged off, the glass eyes stared at her with the humble reproach of things discarded in the hope of final riddance. A few minutes later what remained of Bendicò was flung into a corner of the courtyard visited every day by the dustman. During the flight down from the window his form recomposed itself for an instant; in the air one could have seen dancing a quadruped with long whiskers, and its right foreleg seemed to be raised in imprecation. Then all found peace in a little heap of livid dust. (Lampedusa, *The Leopard* 285)

33 It was useless to try to avoid the thought, but the last of the Salinas was really he himself, this gaunt giant now dying on a hotel balcony. For the significance of a noble family lies entirely in its traditions, that is in its vital memories; and he was the last one to have any unusual memories, anything different from those of other families. . . . He had said that the Salinas would always remain the Salinas. He had been wrong. The last Salina was himself. That fellow Garibaldi, that bearded Vulcan, had won after all. (Lampedusa, *The Leopard* 255)

34 He is the Adam who gives a name to everything he sees and hears. He discovers the most ingenious resemblances and relations among things. . . . He is the one . . . who is afraid in the dark, because in the dark he sees or believes he sees; the one who seems to be dreaming in the light, remembering things he has never seen; the one who speaks to animals, to trees, to stones, to clouds, and to

stars; who peoples the shadows with ghosts and the sky with gods.

35 It seems to me that a crucial problem in these regards is the following: if, as it seems, the orthodox historiography that we have inherited was founded on a very rigid distinction between history and fiction, today we are challenged to critically rethink this distinction over again. Our problem is not only *what* to write (to renew, that is, the material contents of history) but also, and perhaps most of all, *how* to write: to experiment with new forms of historical narration that would be more suitable to achieving the knowledge pertaining to women's history.

36 The value, also *historical,* of a novel does not depend upon its narrative pretexts, but upon its truths. It takes the intelligence, freedom of judgment and attention of the contemporaries to recognize these truths—even the most occult and unrevealed—in their poets' representations.

37 The predicaments caused by characters deliberately forced into a position of social and psychical inferiority are related to an even more dangerous [sentimentalism] consisting in the adoption of the so-called omniscient narrator: the almighty narrator who sees and knows everything about his characters, who dominates them with his Olympian gaze, hypocritically hiding the fundamental fact that even before understanding them, he makes and creates them.

38 Allow me, then, to stay a bit longer in the company of my little kid, before coming back alone to the secular life of the others. (Morante, *History* 529)

39 As she defines her own *truth* by examining the real world, the modern novelist, instead of invoking the Muses, is prompted to create a reciting "*I*" (protagonist and interpreter) that functions as her alibi, almost as if to say, in her own defense: "Naturally what I represent is not *reality,* but a reality that is relative to my own self, or to another self, apparently different from my own, but which, in substance, belongs to me and in which I now completely identify myself." Thus, through the use of the first person, a newly invented reality expresses [itself by creating] a new truth. This *responsible first person,* then, is a modern condition.

40 She felt drawn there by a summons of sweetness, like the stable's smell for a calf, or a souk's for an Arab woman; and also by an impulse of obsessive necessity, like a planet gravitating around a star. (Morante, *History* 81)

41 And Ida recognized this confused chorus. . . . all this wretched human sound from the cars caught her in a heart-rending sweetness, because of a constant memory that didn't return to her from known time, but from some other channel: from the same place as her father's little Calabrian songs that had lulled her, or the anonymous poem of the previous night, or the little kisses that whispered *carina, carina* to her. It was a place of repose that drew her down, into the promiscuous den of a single, endless family. (Morante, *History* 209)

42 He was a male, no doubt about it, he lacked nothing; but for the present (and you can believe my sworn testimony) he took absolutely no interest in his own virile organ, any more than in his ears or his nose. (Morante, *History* 345)

43 A merrier baby than he had never been seen. Everything he glimpsed around him roused his interest and stirred him to joy. He looked with delight at the threads of rain outside the window, as if they were confetti and multicolored streamers. . . . he didn't see things only in their usual aspects, but as multiple images of other things, varying to infinity. (Morante, *History* 103)

44 One of the first words he learned was *ttars* (stars). However, he also called the lightbulbs in the house ttars, and the derelict flowers Ida brought from school, the hanging clusters of onions, even the door knobs, and later also swallows. Then when he learned the word *wallows* (swallows) he called wallows also his underpants hanging out on a line to dry. . . . Articles of furniture and domestic objects became for him houses, trains. Towels, rags, even clouds were *lags* (flags). The lights of the stars were grass, and the stars themselves were ants around a crumb (the moon). (Morante, *History* 104, 113)

45 The sun is like a big tree
that has nests inside.
And it sounds like a male cicada and like the sea
and it plays with the shadow like a little cat.
(Morante, *History* 534)

46 it's a fact that, while he was thinking in this way, the ordinary time of other people was reduced for him almost to zero. In Asia there exists a little creature known as the *lesser panda,* which looks like something between a squirrel and a teddy-bear and lives on the trees in inaccessible mountain forests; and every now and then it comes down to the ground, looking for buds to eat. Of one of these panda it was told that he spent millennia thinking

on his own tree, from which he climbed down to the ground every three hundred years. But in reality, the calculation of such periods was relative: in fact, while three hundred years had gone by on earth, on that panda's tree barely ten minutes had passed. (Morante, *History* 240–41)

47 At the end of the fields, the terrain sloped down and a little wooded area began. It was there that Useppe and Bella at a certain point slowed their pace and stopped chatting.

They had entered a round clearing, closed off by a circle of trees whose highest boughs became tangled so as to form a kind of room with a roof of leaves. The floor was new grass, just born after the rains, perhaps not yet trampled by anyone, and with only a kind of minuscule daisy flowering in it. The flowers looked as if they had all blossomed together at that moment. . . . It really was like being in an exotic tent, far from Rome and from every other city, who knows where, having arrived after a great journey; and outside an enormous space seemed to stretch, with no other sound but the calm movement of the water and the air. (Morante, *History* 431)

48 [F]or him there existed no differences of age, or of beauty and ugliness, or sex, or social station. Tole and Mémeco were, really, two misshapen, stubby boys, of uncertain profession (black marketeers, or thieves, according to circumstances), but for him they were the same as two Hollywood strong men or two patricians of high degree. Sora Mercedes stank; but when he was playing hide-and-seek, his favorite hiding-place was the blanket she kept over her lap. (Morante, *History* 159)

49 For some time, Vilma brought back to the Ghetto from her daily laboring rounds strange, unheard-of information, which the other women rejected as fantasies of her brain. And in fact, her imagination was always toiling, like a convict, in Vilma's head; however, later, certain *fantasies* of hers were to prove far less fantastic than the truth. (Morante, *History* 51)

50 Between 1965 and today, two ideas have been definitively clarified: that plot could be found also in the form of quotation of other plots, and that the quotation could be less escapist than the plot quoted. (Eco, *Postscript* 65)

51 It is in a state of crisis because the order of words no longer corresponds to the order of things (words are still articulated according to traditional ordering systems, while science inspires us to see things as organized according to other ordering principles, and

even according to principles of disorder and discontinuity); . . . by adopting a new grammar that rests not on a system of organization but on a permanent assumption of disorder, [the intellectual] has accepted the world in which he lives as it is, in full crisis. By doing so, he has *compromised* himself anew in the world in which he lives, speaking a language he thinks he has invented but that instead is suggested by the existential situation in which he finds himself; this, however, was the only option that remained to him.

52 In any case, however, the artistic process that attempts to confer a form on what may appear as disorder, amorphousness, dissociation, and the absence of relationships is nothing but the effort of a reason that attempts to lend a discursive clarity to things; and when its discourse is obscure, it is because things themselves, and our relationship to them, are still very obscure.

53 The great season of the nineteenth-century plot was also the great season of consolation by installments. Every return to pure narrative contains something equivocal, as it represents an escape from all that is problematic.

54 One constant element will continue to distinguish the popular novel from the problematic novel: it is that the former will always unravel a struggle between Good and Evil and will always resolve it, whether the denouement is filled with sorrow or with happiness, in favor of the Good, and the Good will remain defined in the terms of the contemporary morality, values, and ideology. The problematic novel instead proposes ambiguous endings precisely because both Rastignac's happiness and Emma Bovary's desperation punctually and fiercely question the acquired notion of "Good" (and "Evil").

55 One can no longer "tell" a story in an innocent manner, it has never been possible, either in the age of Sterne or today. From *Tristram Shandy* to *If on a Winter's Night a Traveler* by Calvino . . . one has wished to write the novel about the novel; one has theorized about the plot through another plot. In *The Name of the Rose* the story is intertwined with History a little as if it were a matter of reconciling Alexandre Dumas with the *Annales* School.

56 In the past men were handsome and great (now they are children and dwarfs), but this is merely one of the many facts that demonstrate the disaster of an aging world. The young no longer want to study anything, learning is in decline, the whole world walks

on its head, blind men lead others equally blind and cause them to plunge into the abyss, birds leave the nest before they can fly, the jackass plays the lyre, oxen dance. Mary no longer loves the active life, Leah is sterile, Rachel has a carnal eye, Cato visits brothels, Lucretius becomes a woman. Everything is on the wrong path. (Eco, *The Name of the Rose* 8)

57 I prepare to leave on this parchment my testimony as to the wondrous and terrible events that I happened to observe in my youth, now repeating verbatim all I saw and heard, without venturing to seek a design. . . .

May the Lord grant me the grace to be the transparent witness of the happenings that took place in the abbey whose name it is only right and pious now to omit, toward the end of the year of our Lord 1327. (Eco, *The Name of the Rose* 3–4)

58 But I have determined to tell, of those remote events, the whole truth, and truth is indivisible, it shines with its own transparency and does not allow itself to be diminished by our interests and our shame. The problem is, rather, of telling what happened not as I see it now and remember it . . . but as I saw it and felt it then. And I can do so with the fidelity of a chronicler, for if I close my eyes I can repeat not only everything I did but also what I thought in those moments, as if I were copying a parchment written at the time. (Eco, *The Name of the Rose* 288–89)

59 The library was laid out on a plan which has remained obscure to all over the centuries, and which none of the monks is called upon to know. Only the librarian has received the secret, from the librarian who preceded him, and he communicates it, while still alive, to the assistant librarian. . . . And the secret seals the lips of both men. (Eco, *The Name of the Rose* 35)

60 There follows an investigation conducted by a mind, the detective, uncompromised by the disorder that caused the crime, but inspired by the paradigmatic order; the detective discerns from the actions of the suspects those that fit the paradigm and those that deviate from it; he separates the apparent deviations from the real ones, and eliminates the false clues, . . . he identifies the real causes that, according to the laws of order, . . . have provoked the crime; he identifies the person who was driven by personal characteristics and circumstances to commit the crime: the culprit is discovered and punished. Order reigns again.

61 reasoning about causes and effects is a very difficult thing, and I believe the only judge of that can be God. We are already hard

put to establish a relationship between such an obvious effect as a charred tree and the lightning bolt that set fire to it, so to trace sometimes endless chains of causes and effects seems to me as foolish as trying to build a tower that will touch the sky. (Eco, *The Name of the Rose* 27)

62 I had always believed logic was a universal weapon, and now I realized how its validity depended on the way it was employed. Further, since I had been with my master I had become aware . . . that logic could be especially useful when you entered it but then left it. (Eco, *The Name of the Rose* 312–13)

63 And once he had shown the connection between those ideas, which were also those of the chapter of Perugia, and the ideas of the Fraticelli and the Dolcinians, and had shown that one man in that abbey subscribed to all those heresies and had been the author of many crimes, he would thus have dealt a truly mortal blow to his adversaries. (Eco, *The Name of the Rose* 461)

64 I . . . find the most joyful delight in unraveling a nice, complicated knot. And it must also be because, at a time when as philosopher I doubt the world has an order, I am consoled to discover, if not an order, at least a series of connections in small areas of the world's affairs. (Eco, *The Name of the Rose* 476)

65 I set about reading or rereading medieval chroniclers, to acquire their rhythm and their innocence. They would speak for me, and I would be freed from suspicion. Freed from suspicion, but not from the echoes of intertextuality. Thus I rediscovered what writers have always known (and have told us again and again): books always speak of other books, and every story tells a story that has already been told. . . . My story, then, could only begin with the discovered manuscript, and even this would be (naturally) a quotation. So I wrote the introduction immediately, setting my narrative on a fourth level of encasement, inside three other narratives: I am saying what Vallet said that Mabillon said that Adso said . . . (Eco, *Postscript* 19–20)

66 he had invented for himself a language which used the sinews of the languages to which he had been exposed—and once I thought that his was, not the Adamic language that a happy mankind had spoken, all united by a single tongue from the origin of the world to the Tower of Babel, or one of the languages that arose after the dire event of their division, but precisely the Babelian language of the first day after the divine chastisement, the language of primeval confusion. (Eco, *The Name of the Rose* 47–48)

67 neither Bernard nor the archers nor I myself could understand what she was saying in her peasant tongue. For all her shouting, she was as if mute. There are words that give power, others that make us all the more derelict, and to this latter category belong the vulgar words of the simple, to whom the Lord has not granted the boon of self-expression in the universal tongue of knowledge and power. (Eco, *The Name of the Rose* 398)

68 those bands of vagrants that in the years that followed I saw more and more often roaming about Europe: false monks, charlatans, swindlers, cheats, tramps and tatterdemalions, lepers and cripples, jugglers, invalid mercenaries, wandering Jews escaped from the infidels with their spirit broken, lunatics, fugitives under banishment, malefactors with an ear cut off, sodomites, and along with them ambulant artisans, weavers, tinkers, chair-menders, knife-grinders, basket-weavers, masons, and also rogues of every stripe, forgers, scoundrels, cardsharps, rascals, bullies, reprobates, recreants, frauds, hooligans. . . . (Eco, *The Name of the Rose* 221)

69 has met Neoplatonism and, in general, the idealism of antiquity on the ground of writing as the expressive sign of truth, Faith, and the Divine Word. God, Word, and Writing are united in the bosom of Christianity: for all Christian culture, the book will be the place of authoritative discourse, of the Word of the Father.

70 there a great *V,* which began the word "verba," produced as a natural shoot from its trunk a serpent with a thousand coils, which in turn begot other serpents as leaves and clusters. (Eco, *The Name of the Rose* 86)

71 we were discussing the question of understanding how the truth can be revealed through surprising expressions, both shrewd and enigmatic. . . . The question, in fact, was whether metaphors and puns and riddles, which also seemed conceived by poets for sheer pleasure, do not lead us to speculate on things in a new and surprising way. (Eco, *The Name of the Rose* 91–92)

72 In these past days, my poor boy, you have experienced a series of events in which every upright rule seems to have been destroyed. And this morning, in your sleeping mind, there returned the memory of a kind of comedy in which . . . the world is described upside down. . . . From the marginalia of Adelmo you went on to relive a great carnival where everything seems to proceed in the wrong direction, and yet, as in the *Coena,* each does what he really did in life. And finally you asked yourself, in the dream, which world is the false one, and what it means to walk head down.

Your dream no longer distinguished what is down and what is up, where life is and where death. Your dream cast doubt on the teachings you have received. . . . And yet, the more I think of your dream, the more revealing it seems to me. (Eco, *The Name of the Rose* 531–32)

73 Poking about in the rubble, I found at times scraps of parchment that had drifted down from the scriptorium and the library and had survived like treasures buried in the earth; I began to collect them, as if I were going to piece together the torn pages of a book. . . . Mine was a poor harvest, but I spent a whole day reaping it, as if from those disiecta membra of the library a message might reach me. . . . At the end of my patient reconstruction, I had before me a kind of lesser library, a symbol of the greater, vanished one: a library made up of fragments, quotations, unfinished sentences, amputated stumps of books. (Eco, *The Name of the Rose* 608–09)

74 Choosing to write a historical novel did not mean opting for a retreat or an evasion: it was a political choice. You would say to me that history and in particular the Middle Ages are fashionable. This is true. But for me it was a way to better decipher the present. A country that finds itself in a profound crisis, the causes of which are not clear—they will become clear later to the historians—feels the need to regain possession of itself through its own past.

Notes

Introduction: The Historical Novel and the Dialectics of Genre

1. Throughout the text I have provided translations for titles and passages quoted in languages other than English. I used published translations when they were available, sometimes slightly altering them for accuracy. Page numbers are included in the text: the first page number refers to the work in the original language and the second to the published English translation (see bibliography for references). In all other instances, the translations are mine. English translations to the longer quotations are located in the appendix, keyed by number. In all quotations, emphasis is as in the original.

2. In Georg Lukács's words, "If literature is a particular form by means of which objective reality is reflected, then it becomes of crucial importance for it to grasp that reality as it truly is, and not merely to confine itself to reproducing whatever manifests itself immediately and on the surface. If a writer strives to represent reality as it truly is, i.e. if he is an authentic realist, then the question of totality plays a decisive role" ("Realism in the Balance" 33).

3. The years that immediately preceded and followed the definitive edition of *I promessi sposi* were the golden age of Italian historical fiction. S. Agrati's *Storia di Clarice Visconti, duchessa di Milano* (*Story of Clarice Visconti, Duchess of Milan,* 1817) and Ambrogio Levati's *I viaggi di Francesco Petrarca in Francia, in Germania ed in Italia* (*Francis Petrarch's Travels in France, Germany and Italy,* 1820) may be counted among the precursors of historical fiction. In 1823, Davide Bertolotti wrote *La calata degli Ungheri in Italia nel Novecento* (*The Hungarian Invasion of Italy in the Tenth Century*). Vincenzo Lancetti's *Cabrino Fondulo* appeared in 1827 with Giambattista Bazzoni's *Il castello di Trezzo* (*The Castle of Trezzo*) and Angelica Palli's *Alessio o gli ultimi giorni di Psara* (*Alessio, or The Last Days of Psara*). In 1829, Giovanni Rosini published *La monaca di Monza: storia del secolo XVII* (*The Nun of Monza: A Story of the XVII Century*) followed by *Luisa Strozzi* (1833) and *Il conte Ugolino della Gherardesca e i Ghibellini di Pisa* (*Count Ugolino della Gherardesca and the Ghibellines of Pisa,* 1843). Defendente Sacchi published *I Lambertazzi e i Geremei, cronaca di un trovatore* (*The Lambertazzi and the Geremei, A Troubadour's Chronicle,* 1830) and *Teodote o storia del secolo VIII* (*Teodote, or A Story of the VIII Century*, 1832). Carlo Varese's *Sibilla Odaleta* appeared in 1827 and *I Torriani e i Visconti* in 1839; Giovanni Campiglio set his novels *La figlia d'un ghibellino* (*A Ghibelline's Daughter,* 1830) and *Lodovico il Moro* (1837) in the Milanese *Quattrocento,* while *Il conte di Lavagna* (*The Count of Lavagna,* 1832) is set in sixteenth-century Genoa. Massimo D'Azeglio published *Ettore Fieramosca ossia la disfida di Barletta* (*Ettore*

Fieramosca, or The Challenge of Barletta) in 1833 and Tommaso Grossi's *I Lombardi alla prima crociata* (*The Lombards at the First Crusade*) and *Marco Visconti* appeared, respectively, in 1826 and 1834. Niccolò Tommaseo published *Il duca d'Atene* (*The Duke of Athens*) in Paris in 1837. The year 1838 saw the publication of Cesare Cantù's *Margherita Pusterla.* Lorenzo Ercoliani's *I Valvassori bresciani o i feudatari del secolo XI* (*The Vavasours of Brescia, or The Feudatories of the XI Century*) and *Leutelmonte* were published, respectively, in 1842 and 1844. Francesco Domenico Guerrazzi wrote, among others, *La battaglia di Benevento* (*The Battle of Benevento*) in 1827, *L'assedio di Firenze* (*The Siege of Florence*) in 1836, *La duchessa di San Giuliano* (*The Duchess of San Giuliano,* later entitled *Veronica Cybo*) in 1837, *Isabella Orsini* in 1844, and *Beatrice Cenci* in 1853. Giuseppe Rovani's *Cento anni* (*One Hundred Years*) was published in installments in the *Gazzetta di Milano* between 1857 and 1864 (Romagnoli 7–87 and Morawski 20).

4. Apart from classical and neoclassical genre theories such as those by Aristotle, Horace, Boileau, and Hugh Blair (Wellek and Warren 227–32), the most influential normative philosophy of genre is probably Johann Wolfgang von Goethe's, who, in the *Westöstlicher Divan,* made the famous distinction between "Dichtarten" and "Naturformen der Dichtung." The former include heterogeneous genres such as the elegy, the sonnet, the ballad, and the ode. The latter identifies the epic, lyric, and dramatic forms as the three universal genres that are present, alone or in combination, in each and every poetic composition. More recently, Mario Fubini recalled Goethe's distinction, arguing that genres are based on certain "stylistic traditions," while Goethe's "Naturformen" are founded instead on psychological categories (142). In turn, within the normative category of genre, Maria Corti sees a further subdivision between anthropological structures (Goethe's "Naturformen" and Fubini's "psychological categories") and rhetorical structures (Goethe's "Dichtarten" and Fubini's "stylistic traditions"). "In the [anthropological] approach," Corti observes, "a reflection on anthropological structures (for example, on the fantastic) leads to the discovery of fundamental properties from which the genre is deduced—lyric, dramatic, epic, fantastic, etc.—and, consequently, to the typology of literary 'discourse,' or better, of literary types that correspond to anthropological structures. . . . In the second approach . . . it is basic rhetorical structures that are responsible for conferring a normative character to genre theory: literary genre is the place of encounter for certain thematic and formal possibilities" (*An Introduction* 115–16).

5. Gérard Genette observes that the "norm of genre" does not exist as an a priori assumption or innate concept and cannot precede the specific historical forms from which it is deduced. A genre is the product of the critical analysis of literary history: "[les] genres . . . sont des classes empiriques, établies par observation du donné historique, à la limite . . . par extrapolation à partir de ce donné, c'est-à-dire par un mouvement déductif superposé à un premier mouvement toujours inductif et analytique" ("Genres . . . are empirical classes, established by observing historical data, even by extrapolating from that data, that is, through a deductive operation superimposed on an initial operation that is always inductive and analytical") ("Genres" 419).

6. As Karl Viëtor points out, "On sait quel pouvoir exerçaient, dans les littératures antiques, la tradition et la forme canonique, transindividuelle, des ouvrages que la tradition préservait . . . et combien, d'autre part, depuis le Romantisme, l'élément formel qui se rattache au genre n'a cessé . . . de perdre en importance" ("We know what kind of power was exercised in ancient literatures by tradition and by the canonic, transindividual form of the works that tradition preserved . . . and, conversely, how much the importance of the formal element relating to genre has continued . . . to decline since the romantic period") (493).

7. "Though at all times they remain separate from each other," Horst Steinmetz argues, "the genres are immanently interwoven and constantly attempt to supplement each other in order to create a system. Every genre as a convention is dependent on all other genre-conventions" (253).

8. A case in point would be the profoundly revolutionary influence of a text like James Joyce's *Ulysses* on the genre of the novel (Głowiński, "Les Genres" 93). The artist who is an innovator does not view the law of a literary genre as the operating principle within which he or she has to work, but subjects this very law to interpretation, revision, and, eventually, re-institutionalization (Corti, *An Introduction* 136).

9. Claudio Guillén defines a genre as "an invitation to the matching of matter and form" (112), and Corti argues that the laws of genre pertain "to the dynamic relation between certain thematic-symbolic levels and certain formal levels of the genre" (*An Introduction* 121). In a similar vein Alastair Fowler argues that "it may be a mistake to identify genre primarily with thematic motifs. . . . Strictly speaking only motifs with a formal basis . . . are securely genre-linked" (81). These definitions can be easily applied to strictly codified genres such as the sonnet or the ode, where specific themes are always matched with specific formal requirements. In the case of historical fiction, however, the mingling of factual and fictional worlds need not adhere to specific formal guidelines.

10. For a similar interpretation see the discussion on historical fiction in Umberto Eco's "Postille a *Il nome della rosa*" ("Postscript to *The Name of the Rose*"). Eco includes the form of the *romance* within the genre of historical fiction, explaining, however, that in romance the past is "scenografia, pretesto, costruzione favolistica" ("scenery, pretext, fairy-tale construction") (531; 74). Romance, in other words, renounces every aspect of historical accuracy: the past becomes a metaphor for the *elsewhere.* The definition of historical fiction that I have proposed, then, cannot include the romance, which is a genre in its own right, a genre contingent upon but not coexistent with that of historical fiction.

11. "Le système des genres," Michał Głowiński writes, "détermine d'une manière spécifique les pratiques littéraires tant sur le plan de l'émission que celui de la réception" ("The genre system determines literary practices in a specific manner, both on the level of transmission and on that of reception") ("Les Genres" 85). In a similar tone, René Wellek and Austin Warren define a genre as "a sum of aesthetic devices at hand, available to the writer and already intelligible to the reader. The good writer partly conforms to the genre as it exists, partly stretches it" (235).

12. "[T]oute œuvre littéraire," Hans-Robert Jauss explains, "appartient à un genre, ce qui revient à affirmer purement et simplement que toute œuvre suppose l'horizon d'une attente, c'est-à-dire d'un ensemble de règles préexistant pour orienter la compréhension du lecteur . . . et lui permettre une réception appréciative. . . . [L]a relation du texte singulier avec la série de textes constituant le genre apparaît comme un processus de création et de modification continue d'un horizon. Le nouveau texte évoque pour le lecteur . . . l'horizon d'une attente et de règles qu'il connaît grâce aux textes antérieurs, et qui subissent aussitôt des variations, des rectifications, des modifications ou bien qui sont simplement reproduits. La variation et la rectification délimitent le champ, la modification et la reproduction définissent les limites de la structure d'un genre. . . . L'historicité d'un genre littéraire se manifeste dans le processus de création de la structure, ses variations, son élargissement et les rectifications qui lui sont apportées" ("Every work of literature belongs to a genre, which means quite simply that every work presupposes a set of expectations, that is, a group of preexisting rules to orient the reader's comprehension . . . and enable him to undertake a critical evaluation. . . . The relationship of the single text to the series of texts constituting the genre appears as a process of creation and continuous modification of a range of expectations. The new text evokes for the reader . . . the set of expectations and rules that he knows from prior texts, expectations and rules that are subject to immediate variations, corrections, modifications or that may simply be reaffirmed. The variations and corrections delimit the field, the modifications and reaffirmations define the limits of the structure of a genre. . . . The historicity of a literary genre manifests itself in the process of creation of the structure, its variations, its expansion and the corrections made to it") (82, 85–86).

13. The systematizing efforts should be made with the awareness that "the genre that binds a reader's understanding is always the latest state of it that he knows, or at best the most inclusive conception he can realize" (Fowler 83).

14. Fubini views genres as provisionary classificatory devices, practical tools that provide the literary historian with, at best, a useful set of guidelines. Genre classifications remain, however, unable to grasp the true essence of a literary work, which always remains above and beyond all attempts at classification. While Fubini accepts Benedetto Croce's idealistic legacy in this definition of genre, he emphasizes the fact that genres are historically changeable constructions that must be studied as cultural (rather than aesthetic) objects, as they reveal fundamental aspects of taste and culture (123, 139).

15. Even a critic like Fowler falls prey to the organic theory. After agreeing with Wellek's criticism of the organic model, Fowler ends up accepting the model's founding correlation between biological and literary forms: "It would be strange if literature, life's image, contained no correlate to the evolution of biological forms. By organizing forms into complexes, a genre falls subject to such historical laws as govern all organizations in time. Like any other, it is bound to evolve" (85).

16. Critic Leone De Castris furnishes one of the most comprehensive analyses of the evolution of historical fiction, starting from the eighteenth-century "novel of ideas," which liberated fiction from aristocratic and escapist tendencies by giving it didactic, moral, and popular functions. The "archeological novels" such as Alessandro Verri's *Le avventure di Saffo* (*Sappho's Adventures,* 1780), *Le notti romane* (*Roman Nights,* 1804), and *La vita di Erostrato* (*Erostratus's Life,* 1815) took up this legacy together with Vincenzo Cuoco's *Platone in Italia* (*Plato in Italy,* 1804–06), which was explicitly aimed at forming the "public morality" of the Italian people (De Castris 21). Ugo Foscolo's *Le ultime lettere di Jacopo Ortis* (*Love and Suicide, or Letters of Ortis to Lorenzo,* 1817) also represents an important link in the chain leading to historical fiction, because of its interplay between private events and public history, and to its canonization of a number of formal and stylistic rules regarding prose writing in Italian (De Castris 22–23).

17. For an exhaustive survey of the concept of evolution in literary history, see Wellek 37–53.

18. The political and patriotic themes of the Italian Risorgimento emerge in the historical novels of Guerrazzi, D'Azeglio, Giovanni Ruffini, and Ippolito Nievo, and are announced in the novels of historian Cesare Balbo, author of *Giulio II* (1811) and *La lega lombarda* (*The Lombard League,* 1815–16), and in those of historian Santorre di Santarosa, who wrote *Lettere siciliane* (*Sicilian Letters*), a story mingling love and politics based on the historical occurrences of the Sicilian *Vespri* (De Castris 25–26).

19. Several Italian writers such as Giambattista Bazzoni, Niccolò Tommaseo, and Tommaso Grossi translated Walter Scott's novels. In 1821 the Milanese publisher Vincenzo Ferrario started a successful series entitled Romanzi storici di Walter Scott ("Historical Novels by Walter Scott") that included all of Scott's major novels translated by Gaetano Barbieri. On Scott's success in Italy see De Castris 8–9 and Romagnoli 7–9.

20. According to Viëtor, a literary genre always transcends the individual works or group of works that belong to its system (505). By arguing that no particular text can be the model for a genre, Viëtor insists that "on obtient le type d'un genre littéraire donné grâce à l'examen d'ensemble de toutes les œuvres individuelles qui appartiennent à ce genre; le type est une abstraction, autrement dit c'est la définition, le schème conceptuel de ce qui, pour ainsi dire, fait la structure fondamentale (qui n'existe que sous la forme de particularités pures), la 'généricité' du genre" ("The type of a given literary genre is given by examining as a group all the individual works belonging to that genre; the type is an abstraction, in other words, it is the definition, the conceptual form of that which, so to speak, constitutes the fundamental structure—which exists only in the form of pure particulars—the 'genericalness' of the genre") (500). This view idealizes the concept of genre, which becomes a purely abstract and theoretical model that never fully translates itself in the concrete literary system. For a similar perspective, one that refuses to see genre as traceable back to a single text or even a group of texts or a historian's codification, see Głowiński ("Les Genres" 84–85).

21. In this sense, Wellek and Warren's definition of literary genres as "institutions" seems particularly useful: "One can work through, express oneself through, existing institutions, create new ones, or get on, so far as possible, without sharing in polities or rituals; one can also join, but then reshape, institutions" (226). See also Harry Levin, "Literature as an Institution."

22. Steinmetz concludes that genres should not be seen as merely formal units, but, rather, as semantic, thematic, and ideological units (253). Formalistic and ideological approaches to genre do not contradict, but complement one another. As shown in the following chapters, the problem of genre definition implies an analysis of both the ideology and the aesthetics of form, that is, in the case of the historical novel, of the ideological and aesthetic implications of combining history with fiction.

23. I am referring to Roland Barthes's eloquent proclamation in "The Death of the Author" (1968): "[W]riting is the destruction of every voice, of every point of origin. Writing is that neutral, composite, oblique space where our subject slips away, the negative where all identity is lost, starting with the very identity of the body writing. . . . As soon as a fact is *narrated* no longer with a view to acting directly on reality but intransitively, that is to say, finally outside of any function other than that of the very practice of the symbol itself, this disconnection occurs, the voice loses its origin, the author enters into his own death, writing begins" (142). Barthes's deconstruction of the monolithic Author who controls his text from above depends upon the revision of the subject-language relationship operated by structuralist linguistics. The Author is subject to the language that "owns" and defines him; he does not preexist his work, but is born and exists within it. The only reality is that of the text, which is a multiple and composite space where different voices are combined, each of them pointing back to anterior voices and diverse cultural spaces, and none of them claiming to be the original one. If the Author is no longer the all-controlling source of his writing, and if the text itself is a "composite dictionary" refusing to be univocally deciphered, do we have to renounce, as a consequence, any attribution of authorial and/or textual responsibilities? In "What Is an Author?" (1968), Michel Foucault makes a significant point when he argues that the "author function" is not the mere attribution of a specific discourse to a specific individual, but is the result of a complex intellectual operation that "constructs" a being called author. This construct "is characteristic of the mode of existence, circulation, and functioning of certain discourses within a society" (108), and therefore is subject to change in different times and different types of civilizations. Furthermore, the "author function" does not refer to a real individual: in a novel narrated in the first person, for example, the first-person pronoun does not refer to the writer but to "an alter ego, whose distance from the author varies, often changing in the course of the work. It would be just as wrong to equate the author with the real writer as to equate him with the fictitious speaker; the author function is carried out and operates in the scission itself, in this division and distance" (112). If we get rid of the "author-and-his-work" category with all its biographical and psychological connotations, and we agree that the author function (which changes according to its sociocultural placement) implies the recognition of a discontinuous plurality of selves within a text, do we also subscribe to the ultimate refusal of ideology? With the breakdown of the notions of genesis, totality, and continuity, the subject becomes a multiple and decentered site and a "constructed," historically changeable entity. This breakdown also implies the end of ideology in the sense of a totalizing mode of thought. Ideology is replaced by perspectivism, and by the idea that the world has no unique or ultimate meaning, that there is no universal truth but only diverse interpretative discourses, each reflecting the "institutional sites where subjects are produced within power relations" (Best and Kellner 51).

24. Critical historical novels emphasize the fact that history and fiction are "themselves historical terms and that their definitions and interrelations are historically determined and vary with time" (Hutcheon 105). They self-consciously test the generic features they have inherited from our narrative tradition, often exploiting and subverting them at the same time. Novels like Claude Simon's *Histoire* (1967), Salman Rushdie's *Midnight Children* (1981) and *Shame* (1983), Robert Coover's *The Public Burning* (1977), Maxine Hong Kingston's *China Men* (1976), Toni Morrison's *Song of Solomon* (1977), and P. M. Pasinetti's *Melodramma* (1993) question the conventions of historical fiction, especially the issues of referentiality, representation, and "objective" truth upon which the genre of historical fiction has been founded. Sebastiano Vassalli's *La chimera* (1990) constitutes a significant example of utilization and transgression of the Manzonian model of *I promessi sposi* on both thematic and formal grounds. Like Alessandro Manzoni, Vassalli sets his novels in seventeenth-century Lombardia and chooses marginal figures as the story's main characters. In doing so, however, Vassalli polemically unearths a historical theme that the Catholic Manzoni had only cursorily hinted at in *I promessi sposi:* the Church's involvement in the witch hunts culminating in the persecutions and public burnings of thousands of women accused of witchcraft, and the role played by Catholic intellectuals in the eradication of a rich folkloric culture of pre-Christian origins. Narrating the story of Antonia, a young woman accused of witchcraft and burnt at the stake in 1610, is a way, for Vassalli, to revise the teleological orientation of Manzoni's novel. If Manzoni believed that historical discourse could objectively reflect history's deep providential order, Vassalli argues that history-as-it-really-is remains a chimera, an elusive ghost. All we can retrieve from the past is a "plot," a tale informed and deformed by its interpreter's ideological filters and historical imagination. In spite of his anti-idealistic and relativistic philosophy, Vassalli shares with Manzoni the belief in writing's ethical function to teach about the past in order to help people live, if not in view of a transcendental future, in the *hic et nunc* of a better present.

Chapter One
Alessandro Manzoni's *J'accuse:* Literary Debates, the Essay *Del romanzo storico,* and a Theory of Creative Historiography

1. In 1816 the first issue of the *Biblioteca italiana* published the famous letter by Mme de Staël that formally launched the arguments between Classicists and Romantics.

2. The essay was "promesso in un manifesto" ("promised in a manifesto") of January 2, 1845 (Manzoni, *Opere* 7.2: 505, 936; see n13 below) and was published in 1850 in the *Opere varie,* the publication of which took ten years, from 1845 to 1855 (Cottignoli 155). Manzoni was actually planning the essay long before that date. In 1830 critic Paride Zaiotti wrote: "noi abbiamo udito con vero sentimento di gioja quello che la fama racconta del nostro Manzoni, che non solo egli abbia dentro sè conosciuta la falsità del sistema cui ne' *Promessi sposi* si era appigliato, ma voglia ben anche far palese il suo disinganno, e dimostrare con lunghe e vigorose parole, come il romanzo storico sia nemico alle intenzioni morali dell'alta letteratura, e riesca altresì di gran pregiudizio agli avanzamenti dell'arte e alla piena e libera rappresentazione del bello" ("we have heard with a true feeling of joy what is being reported about our Manzoni, that not only has he recognized the falsity of the system he had embraced in *I promessi sposi,* but that he wants to disclose his disillusionment and demonstrate with an exhaustive and vigorous argument how the historical novel is a foe to the moral aims of high literature and greatly prejudices the advancement of art and the full and free representation of beauty") ("De' romanzi storici" 164–65).

3. Goethe's review was actually written by Adolf F. Streckfüss, who acted as spokesman for Goethe's ideas on Manzoni's novel (Negri 309 and Vittori 22–23). As J. F. Beaumont discovered, Carlo Cattaneo wrote to Goethe on June 3, 1829, to report Manzoni's growing skepticism concerning the coexistence of historical and fictional systems in his novel. Cattaneo explained that Manzoni's doubts regarding the system he had used to tie history to fiction had forced him to reevaluate the system and question its foundations (Manzoni, *Carteggio* 520).

4. Goethe claimed that from chapter 25 onward, all the detailed reports of the plague, the war, and the famine had quenched the poetic inspiration with an excessive care for exact documentation (Negri 310). In 1828, the Parisian *Revue Encyclopédique* published a review that vehemently attacked the historical accuracy of *I promessi sposi:* "Le roman . . . est tout-à-fait subordonné [à l'histoire] . . . ; le peu même que l'auteur a imaginé tient tellement du caractère des lieux et des temps auxquels il se rapporte, qu'on pourrait le regarder comme plus ou moins historique. . . . [A]u lieu de faire servir l'histoire au roman, [Manzoni] a consacré et même sacrifié le roman à l'histoire" ("the novel is entirely subordinated [to history] . . . ; and even the few things that the author has invented maintain so much of the character of the places and times to which they refer that the novel can be considered as more or less historical. . . . Instead of making history serve the novel, [Manzoni] has dedicated and even sacrificed fiction to history") (Salfi 380).

5. On October 29, 1827, Lamartine wrote to Manzoni: "Je ne vous ferai qu'un reproche, c'est de n'avoir pas crée le genre où vous vouliez exercer un si beau et si puissant talent. Une autre fois, faites-le. Sortez du Roman historique, faites nous de l'histoire dans un genre neuf. Vous le pouvez: vous l'avez fait, votre troisième volume est cela même" ("I will reproach you for only one thing—for not creating the genre in which you have employed such beautiful and powerful talents. Next time, do it. Abandon historical fiction, give us history in a new genre. You can do it: you have done it, your third volume is exactly that") (Manzoni, *Carteggio* 351).

6. The Classicists' attacks against the immorality of fiction soon became one of the clichés in the debate over the historical novel. In an article written in 1818 for *Il Conciliatore,* Silvio Pellico exploited the Classicists' appeals to the authority of the great writers of the past in order to counteract their accusations that the novel was immoral because it depicted amorous passions: "E giacchè l'Italia non arrossisce delle oscenità onde son ricche le prose e le rime di parecchi fra' suoi celebratissimi scrittori, l'Italia può anche desiderare d'acquistare un genere di letteratura di cui è povera, e permettere che, come Petrarca e Metastasio in versi, così altri in prosa si prenda la libertà di commuoverci parlando d'amore senza offendere i costumi" ("Since Italy does not blush at the obscenities that abound in the verse and prose of several of her celebrated writers, Italy can also seek a missing literary genre and, like Metastasio and Petrarch in their poetry, permit others to take the liberty in prose to speak to us movingly of love without offending our customs") (16). Love is so much a part of the contemporary world, Pellico continues, that it deserves to be seriously investigated and faithfully represented. The moral value of a novel depends on its ability to portray the contemporary world and narrate "the natural history of human passions" (20).

7. The criticism against the amphibious nature of historical fiction, which only Manzoni studied with aesthetic and philosophical rigor, was one of the commonplaces of the Classicists' assaults on the historical novel. See, for example, the anonymous review of Levati's *Viaggi di Francesco Petrarca in Francia, in Germania ed in Italia* that appeared in the *Biblioteca italiana* in 1821. The reviewer denounced the "monstrous coupling" of history and fiction and stated that "dalla confusione di due generi opposti non può alle arti derivare che danno e vergogna" ("the confusion of two opposite genres can only bring damage and shame to art") (148). Domenico Biorci, owner of the Veronese magazine *Il Poligrafo* (De Castris 70), dismissed D'Azeglio's *Ettore Fieramosca* on the usual assumptions that instead of a good story or a useful novel, *Ettore Fieramosca* was a prolix and boring chronicle, full of sad tales and false stories: "Che stravaganza di gusti è quella d'oggidì, voler rinunciare alla verità per la menzogna; al bello per l'orrido; alla pietà ed alla compassione, per la ferocia e lo strazio, al naturale per l'esagerato; alla gravità della storia per la leggerezza del romanzo, o meglio di un componimento che non è né romanzo né storia! Non si confonda un genere coll'altro. Perocché, se è un romanzo, perchè mancante d'un ingegnoso verosimile? . . . Se è una storia, perchè alterare tanti fatti, sfigurare tanti caratteri?" ("What extravagance of taste is that which, nowadays, seeks to renounce truth for lies; beauty for the horrid; piety and compassion for ferocity and torment; the natural for the exaggerated; the gravity of history for the lightness of the novel or, rather, of a work which is neither novel nor history! Do not confuse one genre with another. If it is a novel, why does it lack an ingenious verisimilitude? . . . If it is history, why alter so many facts, disfigure so many characters?") (198–99).

8. Zaiotti's 1827 article was divided into two parts that appeared in consecutive issues of the *Biblioteca italiana.* As its title suggests, the first part focused on fiction in general, while the second concentrated on *I promessi sposi.*

9. On this subject, see also the anonymous review of Levati's *Viaggi* (145–46).

10. François Guizot and Augustin Thierry advocated a "school of historical science for which dynasties and battles were distinctly not enough. These early Romantic historians, not unlike Voltaire some seventy-five years before, made customs, art, and literature their field" (Bermann 13).

11. Tommaseo complained that most novels catered to the lowest intellectual denominator, titillating the curiosity "delle donne, e de' galanti, e degli sfaccendati" ("of women, gallants, and loafers"), and proposed that novels should abandon light amorous themes for more engaged and serious topics of moral and political interest ("Del romanzo storico" 49).

12. Only a few years earlier Gaetano Angeli, in *Contro il leggersi romanzi dei giovani* (*Against Young People Reading Novels,* 1821), had attacked fiction, claiming it was "la peste dei giovani, il disonore degli studi" ("the plague of youths, the dishonor of studies") (66). In his introduction to *Fermo e Lucia* (1821–23), Manzoni ironically wrote that he would be accused of "niente meno che di aver fatto un romanzo, genere proscritto nella letteratura italiana moderna, la quale ha la gloria di non averne o pochissimi" ("nothing less than having written a novel, a proscribed genre in modern Italian literature, which has the glory of having none or very few") (*Opere* 2.3: 5).

13. The Chiari and Ghisalberti edition of Manzoni's works from which I am citing consists of several volumes, and each volume is divided into a series of books. In all my references to this edition, the first number refers to the volume and the second to the book in question.

14. The character of Lucia is not exclusively the product of Manzoni's ethical preoccupations and literary borrowings, but also of his socioeconomic meditation on the role of women in a society that was rapidly transforming under the effects of the democratic revolutions and the advent of the industrial age (Giannantonio 226–27).

15. Manzoni's defense of the truth and morality of historical fiction may be juxtaposed with the views held by Costanza Moscheni, a member of the Regia Accademia Lucchese (Royal Academy of Lucca) and the author of the essay *Dei moderni romanzi* (*On Modern Novels,* 1828). Attributing the suicide of two Milanese lovers to their reading of popular novels, Moscheni attacks those novels that "prendendo ad argomento la vita privata degli uomini, e penetrando ne' più segreti nascondigli del cuore, tessono veramente la storia delle passioni, raggirandosi principalmente intorno ad amori, e col dilicato maneggio della più seducente e pericolosa fra le tendenze del cuore umano, trascinano i leggitori in massime erronee, ed al buon costume fatali" ("by choosing as their subject people's private lives, and penetrating into the most hidden recesses of the heart, faithfully weave the story of their passions, mainly revolving around affairs, and with the delicate manipulation of the most seductive and dangerous of the tendencies of the human heart, draw their readers into erroneous principles, fatal to good customs") (6).

16. The first forty years of the nineteenth century marked the flourishing of the publishing trade in Milan and witnessed its development along modern entrepreneurial lines. This phenomenon resulted from the timely combination of several factors. The mandatory elementary instruction enlarged the reading public and contributed to the diffusion of popular literature such as almanacs, devotional texts, and popular novels. Milan became the gathering point for intellectuals and scholars converging in what became Italy's foremost cultural center. If faithful to the Austrian government, these intellectuals were granted teaching careers in universities or high schools or invited to fill other governmental positions. If suspected of disseminating *massime impolitiche,* they were excluded from those official positions. They frequently offered their intellectual workmanship to the publishing trade, and earned a living according to the variable fortunes of a volatile book market. For these reasons, the publishing world of the Restoration period mainly consisted of politically liberal intellectuals. Several officers of the dissolved Napoleonic army became writers, booksellers, typographers, and publishers. The cultivated bureaucrats of the Napoleonic government, now unemployed, formed a society of *gente di lettere* that was also integrated in the publishing business. All these factors contributed to the progressive transformation of the traditional publishing trade into the modern, capitalistic, and speculative enterprises such as those of Vincenzo Ferrario, Felice Rusconi, and Anton Fortunato Stella. The vitality of the burgeoning industry coincided with its unruliness; this was the age of literary piracy, and of the hasty, untidy publications that embittered Zaiotti and made Austria's censoring tasks close to impossible. This situation affected especially the historical novel. It is well known that no book was more pirated than *I promessi sposi,* and none of the twelve publications of *Sibilla Odaleta* that followed the first were authorized by Varese (Berengo 3–49; 289–90).

17. See also Zaiotti, "Del romanzo" (43).

18. "Il governo," wrote governor Bellagarde to Giuseppe Acerbi, the founder of the *Biblioteca italiana,* "vuole servirsi di questo giornale, il quale . . . presenta un punto di riunione a tutta l'Italia letteraria, per parlare al pubblico e per rettificare le opinioni erronee sparse in tutte le forme dal cessato governo" ("The government wants to use this magazine, which . . . offers a meeting point for all of literary Italy, to speak to the public and rectify the erroneous opinions spread in every form by the previous government") (Mazzoni 183–84).

19. Imitating Pietro Borsieri's text, and anticipating Manzoni's, Ferdinando Orlandi's essay stages a debate in which, after reporting the arguments in favor of and against historical fiction, Orlandi intervenes to convey his own conclusions on the subject.

20. In the introductory article to *Preziosa di Sanluri,* Varese argued that the historical novel does not claim to teach history but, at the most, hopes to induce some of its readers to consult the history books (lx–lxi). See also Sansone Uzielli's "Del romanzo storico, e di Walter Scott" (121).

21. In Borsieri's *Avventure,* Pellico contended that the great Italian historians such as Machiavelli, Guicciardini, and Sarpi were more useful in instructing "statesmen, leaders and princes" rather than obscure folks, who would rather profit from the pleasing and uncomplicated lessons of the historical novel (360–61). Even the Classicist reviewer of Levati's *Viaggi* conceded that the "cautious reading" of fiction furnishes a useful supplement to the lofty teachings of history. The common reader, unable to apply the examples of national government to the management of the family, will be able to profit from a "domestic preceptor" in the form of the novel (146–47). In the romantic arena, the didactic role of the historical novel was not limited to the cautious teachings of private and domestic lessons. Critic Giuseppe Bianchetti insisted that the topics and the readability of the historical novel responded to the commitment of modern literature to participate in its country's social development and political evolution (84–85). See also Giuseppe Mazzini's similar views in "Del dramma storico" (277–78).

22. Originally written for the *Giornale delle province venete* (Sept./Oct. 1830), Bianchetti's essay was reprinted as the "Discorso secondo" of a volume in defense of the historical novel that also included Tommaseo's essay "Del romanzo storico."

23. Starting from this concept, Bianchetti addresses the shift from *fiction* to *falsity* that had marked Zaiotti's condemnation of the historical novel. A change in the extrinsic literary medium (from poetry to prose) cannot alter the intrinsic value of the truth it conveys. It is absurd to argue, Bianchetti concludes, that the combination of true and invented facts in poetry results in a useful fiction; and the same combination in historical fiction results in pernicious falseness (97–98).

24. Bianchetti's discussion anticipates Lukács's distinction between realism and naturalism, which the latter developed in the 1930s. Realism, Lukács explains, does not catalogue surface phenomena, but selects and organizes the most meaningful examples of what is essential in a historical period, the crucial events that shape the present and anticipate the future. Naturalism, instead, inventories the immediate phenomena of everyday life without any sense of the real causality of events ("Narrate or Describe?" 139).

25. Mazzini engaged in the debate on the historical novel with a review of Zaiotti's 1827 essay that appeared in the *Indicatore genovese* in 1828. Mazzini's most systematic analysis of history and fiction is contained in "Del dramma storico," originally published in Vieusseux's *Antologia* in 1830.

26. Opposing the Classicists, Mazzini writes: "L'*ideale* è sacro e supremo intento all'Arte come ad ogni altra manifestazione della Vita; e il problema è per noi tutti d'intravvederne nei *fatti* quel tanto che v'è racchiuso e guidare altrui a indovinarlo e adorarlo. Ma l'*ideale* che noi cerchiam d'afferrare è la Verità eterna, dominatrice, la Legge che governa le cose umane, il concetto di Dio ch'è l'anima dell'Universo. E il valore della parola era assolutamente ignoto ai *classicisti:* ciò ch'essi chiamavano *ideale* a contrasto col *reale* era il concetto astratto, arbitrario, d'un individuo, o d'una scuola negatrice d'ogni progresso" ("The *ideal* is the sacred and supreme goal of Art as well as of any other manifestation of Life; and the problem for all of us is to perceive that part of the ideal that is contained in the *facts,* and lead others to divine and adore it. But the *ideal* that we try to grasp is the eternal dominating Truth, the Law that governs human matters, the concept of God that is the soul of the Universe. The value of this word was totally unknown to the *classicists:* what they called *ideal* as opposed to the *real* was the abstract, arbitrary concept of an individual and a school that denied all progress") ("Del dramma storico" 264–65).

27. Mazzini's theory is best exemplified by Manzoni's juxtaposition between the secret providential law that governs historical progress and the arbitrary legal system of the Italian *Seicento* in *I promessi sposi.*

28. The *Antologia* played a leading role in the debate on fiction and the historical novel, particularly with articles by critics Uzielli, Giuseppe Montani, and Tommaseo himself. Mazzini, who published "Del dramma storico" and "D'una letteratura europea," in the *Antologia,* subsequently declined any further contributions because he was discontented with the journal's exceedingly moderate and accommodating tone, which failed to support the Romantics' agenda. Mazzini's two articles were harshly criticized by conservative members of the magazine such as Mario Pieri and G. B. Niccolini (Savini 14).

29. This idea parallels the second part of Manzoni's *Del romanzo storico,* which examines the genre of the historical novel from a diachronic perspective. Manzoni attributes the origins of the genre to the epic and the historical tragedy and follows the evolution of these two literary forms into the historical novel.

30. Critic Montani made a similar point in 1827 when he argued that the fashion of the historical novel was the direct result of an increased interest in historical truth and a declining fascination with fantastic constructions, which he related to civilization's progress toward maturity (76).

31. Tommaseo's position on this subject was unprecedented and remained unparalleled. In 1827, Montani voiced the Romantics' conviction that historical novels create a perfect fusion of historical matters and fictional inventions, and strike a balance between *vero* and *mirabile,* which Montani saw as two constant needs of human nature (75). Replying to Manzoni's *Del romanzo storico* in 1850, Carlo Tenca reinforced the idea of the superior synthesizing nature of the historical novel and defended the harmonious unity resulting from its combination of historical and fictional themes (89).

32. At the origins of the debate on the historical novel, the Classicists highlighted, like Tommaseo, the didactic function of history: the reviewer of Levati's *Viaggi* claimed that the examples of the past, by establishing analogies with the present, are ways of teaching practical lessons and guiding our actions in the historical world (145–46). The Classicists abandoned this argument after it was appropriated by the Romantics to praise the political urgency of novels such as D'Azeglio's *Ettore Fieramosca.* In *Storia della Colonna Infame* (*Story of the Column of Infamy,* 1840), Manzoni argued, in more general terms, for conducting studies of the past in order to address concerns of the present: "non è forse l'interesse delle cose presenti che principalmente ci muove ad esaminare le passate? . . . E quando ci vien proposto di esaminare qualche avvenimento che non abbia una relazione diretta colle cose nostre presenti . . . non diciamo che la ricerca non è interessante?" ("It is the interest of present matters that mainly inspires us to examine the past, is it not? . . . And when we are asked to examine some event that does not have a direct relation with our present circumstances . . . don't we say that the research is uninteresting?") (*Opere* 2.3: 874).

33. On the literary discussions between Tommaseo and Manzoni, see Giuseppe Titta Rosa's *Colloqui col Manzoni.*

34. The Classicist reviewer of Levati's *Viaggi* required that the historical novelist always distinguish true from fictional events by means of "notes and citations" in order to allow the reader to know all the sources from which the story is taken (161).

35. Twentieth-century literary criticism displays a number of approaches that derive from this critical perspective: structural, rhetorical, or stylistic, they all see the work of art as a self-contained linguistic system (McGann 114).

36. Treating the historical text as "a verbal structure in the form of a narrative prose discourse," Hayden White argues that historians emplot the past according to the Fryean archetypes of Romance, Comedy, Tragedy, and Satire. Each of these archetypes purports to be a model of past structures "in the interest of *explaining what they were by representing* them" (*Metahistory* 2).

37. Mazzini did not discuss how the fusion of real and ideal spheres is achieved in the historical novel. Untrained in the craft of fiction and deprived of Manzoni's narratological sophistication, Mazzini attributed it all to the secret workings of the genius's mind ("Del dramma storico" 307).

38. Manzoni was not entirely appreciative of this artificial unity, which he related to the despotism of long-ingrained aesthetic rules (*Opere* 7.1: 271).

39. In *Del romanzo storico,* Manzoni encourages the historian to select, connect, contrast, deduce, and infer in order to arrive at a more precise and more comprehensive understanding of a specific historical moment (*Opere* 5.3: 307).

40. "Dopo un lungo dibattere e cercare insieme, conclusero che i guai vengono bensì spesso, perché ci si è dato cagione; ma che la condotta più cauta e più innocente non basta a tenerli lontani; e che quando vengono, o per colpa o senza colpa, la fiducia in Dio li raddolcisce, e li rende utili per una vita migliore" ("[A]fter a long debate, and much heart-searching they came to the conclusion that troubles very often come because we have asked for them; but that the most prudent and innocent of conduct is not necessarily enough to keep them away; also that when they come, through our fault or otherwise, trust in God goes far to take away their sting, and makes them a useful preparation for a better life") (*Opere* 2.1: 673; *The Betrothed* 720).

41. Paul Ricoeur attributes this "proud claim" to Lucien Febvre and argues that it restores to the historian the initiative of "posing pertinent questions" and "inventing fruitful hypotheses," opposing the notion that the historian "finds his work already done for him in the documents" (*Contribution* 9).

42. For a discussion of Manzoni's distinction between the level of historical narrative (*histoire*) and that of the verisimilar (*discours*) see Sandra Bermann 37–39.

Chapter Two
Historical Reconfigurations and the Ideology of Desire: Giuseppe Tomasi di Lampedusa's *Il Gattopardo*

1. For an exhaustive analysis of *Il Gattopardo*'s significance as an autobiography, and in terms of relevance to Lampedusa's own historical present, see Tom O'Neill's "Ants and Flags: Tomasi di Lampedusa's *Gattopardo.*"

2. Literary debates in Italy often originate and revolve around what is popularly defined as a *caso letterario,* usually a novel engaging and polarizing discussions of intellectuals, academics, journalists, and sociologists in literary journals as well as weekly magazines and newspapers' *terze pagine.* Historical "cases" were built around the long-delayed recognition of Italo Svevo's novels and around the official proscription of Ignazio Silone's works in Fascist Italy. Giovanni Verga became a *caso* in the reassessment of Italian *verismo* after 1968, and *Il Gattopardo,* along with Vasco Pratolini's *Metello* (1955) and Carlo Cassola's *La ragazza di Bube* (*Bube's Maid,* 1960), constituted a *caso* when critical attention focused on their unprecedented success (*Il Gattopardo* sold 100,000 copies in only a few months). *Casi letterari* are often artfully constructed and orchestrated by writers and publishers in order to launch a newly published novel toward the top of the best-seller lists. This happened with Elsa Morante's *La Storia,* which sold 465,000 copies in one year (Lucente, "*Scrivere*" 228, 231), and Alberto Moravia's *Vita interiore* (*The Inner Life*) and *1934,* which Bompiani acclaimed as best-selling novels even before their publication (Ferretti 23–24).

3. In May 1956 Lampedusa submitted his novel to Mondadori, which turned it down after Elio Vittorini, who worked as a consultant for Mondadori, had commented on its lack of unity and completeness (Gilmour 141). In 1957, Lampedusa tried again with Einaudi, hoping that *Il Gattopardo* would have better luck in Vittorini's series I Gettoni. After further disappointment, *Il Gattopardo* was finally accepted for publication a year after Lampedusa's death, in Giorgio Bassani's series I Contemporanei for Feltrinelli. In November 1958 the first edition of *Il Gattopardo* was published in Milan; by the following March, a year after it won the Strega prize, it had already been republished in fifty-two editions (Gilmour 159–62).

4. Both Einaudi and Mondadori, in fact, relied on Vittorini's negative evaluation of *Il Gattopardo.* Bassani, who was then the editor of Feltrinelli's series I Contemporanei, liked the novel very much and published it with an enthusiastic foreword. As Gregory Lucente points out, Vittorini took "Bassani's laudatory introduction . . . not just as a 'nota introduttiva' but also as a professional *sfida*" ("*Scrivere*" 223). From then on, *Il Gattopardo* became the pretext more for retaliations involving publishing intrigues and personal interests than for unbiased critical interpretations.

5. The Jesuit literary critic Giuseppe De Rosa, in particular, saw a moral danger in the novel's hopeless pessimism (174).

6. Louis Aragon and E. M. Forster were among the most prominent foreign critics who praised *Il Gattopardo.* After their positive reviews, several Italian critics revised their previous interpretations. The Sicilian writer Leonardo Sciascia, in particular, openly admitted to a hurried and biased first reading of the novel and even favorably quoted passages that he had criticized before (Gilmour 188).

7. The avant-garde literary journal *Il Verri* introduced in Italy the first discussion on the *nouveau roman.* The April 1959 issue of the journal included the translation of Robbe-Grillet's "Une Voie pour le roman futur" ("A Path for the Future Novel") and articles on Michel Butor, Samuel Beckett, and Robbe-Grillet as well as excerpts from their works.

8. By the late 1950s the magazine *Officina* was publishing Edoardo Sanguineti's and Elio Pagliarani's experimental texts. In November 1956 *Il Verri* was founded. It soon became the headquarters of the neoavantgarde group I Novissimi, publishing works and critical pieces by Renato Barilli, Angelo Guglielmi, Nanni Balestrini, Sanguineti, and Antonio Porta.

9. Italian neorealism was deeply concerned with the issue of ideological commitment in art, and promoted aesthetic practices that would be both historically and politically engaged. The methods and conditions of this commitment were widely addressed, particularly in the pages of Vittorini's *Il Politecnico,* which published translations of the works by Lukács, Bertolt Brecht, and Jean-Paul Sartre. Sartre's 1946 essay *What Is Literature?* was especially influential, as it intensified the debate on the relationship of literature to history, politics, and aesthetics, the role of the intellectual and the masses, and literature's potential for social change.

10. Pier Paolo Pasolini defines neo-experimentalism as the "free" territory wherein the neorealist and hermetic experiences meet and influence each other ("Il neo-sperimentalismo" 170).

11. Crocean idealism and Gramscian materialism were, according to Guglielmi, the most obtrusive of these ideological grids. The controversy was far from being resolved, and in the years that followed the publication of *Il Gattopardo* the positions tended instead to be absolutized. In the famous meeting in Palermo of the Gruppo 63, five years after the publication of Lampedusa's novel, Guglielmi reiterated in even stronger terms the nonideological, noncommittal, and antihistorical nature of contemporary culture. Sanguineti took exactly the opposite view and claimed that the literary operation is, in its own nature, the expression of an ideology in the form of language (Balestrini and Giuliani 377–85).

12. According to Aragon, Lampedusa had created a novel that was "l'immagine perfetta della perdizione di questa aristocrazia, l'immagine consapevole, *politica,* di questa perdizione, come poteva descriverla solo un uomo che della sua classe avesse fatto una critica spietata, *una critica di sinistra*" ("the perfect image of this aristocracy's agony, the conscious, *political* image of this agony as it could be depicted only by a man who had provided a merciless critique of his own class, *a critique from the left*") (224).

13. Olga Ragusa makes a similar point in the survey of Lampedusa criticism that precedes her intelligent reading of *Il Gattopardo* in the light of Lampedusa's *Lezioni su Stendhal* (*Lessons on Stendhal,* 1959) (195–200).

14. By concentrating on an episode from the Unification of Italy, Lampedusa, unlike the *Annales* historians, did not utterly dismiss the history of events, but rather explored the connections between the time of single pivotal events and other time spans, from the "geo-time" of the Sicilian territory to the inner time of the characters' psychological drives.

15. This reevaluation was undertaken at the meeting dedicated to "I problemi del realismo in Italia" ("The Problems of Realism in Italy"), which took place at the Istituto Gramsci in January 1959, and which featured, among others, the essays by Carlo Salinari and Mario Alicata (Caputo 37). On this topic see also *Il Contemporaneo* 11 (1959).

16. "In doing this," Terry Eagleton writes, commenting on Lukács's interpretation, "great art combats the alienation and fragmentation of capitalist society, projecting a rich, many-sided image of human wholeness" (28).

17. In the years that immediately followed World War II, Italy's moral and political climate presented "singular analogies" with that of the post-Unification period (Trombatore 5). The foundation of the new national government brought to the foreground the issue of national unity and, with it, the difficult and contrasted problem of the *Mezzogiorno*'s insertion in the unitary state. Gaetano Trombatore contends that Lampedusa's representation of the Risorgimento in Sicily, with his cynical upturning of the Risorgimento's myths and ideals, was a loose allegory of what had happened around him during the concluding chapters of World War II, with the fall of the Fascist regime, the Reunification, and the foundation of the democratic state (5–8).

18. As Italo Calvino observed in his 1964 preface to *Il sentiero dei nidi di ragno* (*The Path to the Nest of Spiders,* 1947), after the Liberation, short-stories of the Resistance such as those by Angelo Del Boca, Marcello Venturi, and Silvio Micheli offered a kind of hagiography, a tendentious celebration of the Resistance and an idealization of the epic undertakings of the partisan "positive heroes" (xiii–xiv).

19. In the famous letter to Mrs. Harkness, Friedrich Engels argued that critical realism could manifest itself in spite of and even against its author's ideological convictions. Balzac, for example, gave a complete realistic account of French society in his *Comédie humaine* that went far beyond his personal Catholic and legitimist views (Marx and Engels 161).

20. An example of an epic rendering of the Unification of Italy is Alessandro Blasetti's historical film *1860* with its heroic celebration of Garibaldi's liberation of Sicily. *Il Gattopardo* exploits as well as undermines the forms of the epic. Apart from the homage to Ludovico Ariosto's and Torquato Tasso's epic poems in using the characters Angelica and Tancredi, Lampedusa utilizes, often with an ironic and melancholic tone, other typical devices of epic narratives such as those of the catalogue and the enumeration. One of the most touching examples occurs in the scene of the Prince's death. Don Fabrizio enumerates, by recollecting them, the people and those personal and public events that have left an ineffaceable trace in his life: "Tancredi: la sua comprensione tanto piú preziosa in quanto ironica, il godimento estetico nel vederlo destreggiarsi fra le difficoltà della vita, l'affettuosità beffarda come si conviene che sia. Dopo, i cani: Fufi, la grossa Mops della sua infanzia, Tom l'irruento barbone confidente ed amico, gli occhi mansueti di Svelto, la balordaggine deliziosa di Bendicò; . . . qualche cavallo, questi già piú distanti ed estranei. Vi erano le prime ore dei suoi ritorni a Donnafugata, il senso di tradizione e di perennità espresso in pietra ed in acqua, il tempo congelato; lo schioppettare allegro di alcune cacce, il massacro affettuoso delle lepri e delle pernici, alcune buone risate con Tumeo, alcuni minuti di compunzione al convento fra l'odore di muffa e di confetture" ("Tancredi: that sympathy of his, all the more precious for being ironic; the aesthetic pleasure of watching him maneuver amid the shoals of life, the bantering affection whose touch was so right. Then, the dogs: Fufi, the fat Mops of his childhood, the impetuous poodle Tom, confidant and friend, Speedy's gentle eyes, Bendicò's delicious nonsense; . . . then a horse or two, those already more distant and extraneous. There were the first few hours of returns to Donnafugata, the sense of tradition and the perennial expressed in stone and water, time congealed; a few carefree shoots, a cozy massacre or two of hares and partridges, a few good laughs with Tumeo, a few minutes of compunction at the convent amid odors of musk and confectionery" (295–96; 258). For a more detailed analysis of the techniques of enumeration in *Il Gattopardo,* see Karl-Ludwig Selig's "*Il Gattopardo:* Observations" (34–41); and on the topos of the so-called catalogue in the epic, see Ernst-Robert Curtius's study in *Europäische Literatur und lateinisches Mittelalter.*

21. Apart from the initial grandiose presentation of Don Fabrizio as a giant whose footsteps make the floors tremble and whose head touches the lowest rosette on the chandeliers in the common people's houses, one should note the semiserious description of the Prince arising from the bathtub under the eyes of a shocked Father Pirrone: "[Il Principe] si ergeva interamente nudo, come l'Ercole Farnese, e per di più fumante, mentre giù dal collo, dalle braccia, dallo stomaco, dalle coscie, l'acqua gli scorreva a rivi, come il Rodano, il Reno, il Danubio e l'Adige traversano e bagnano i gioghi alpini" ("[The Prince] was emerging quite naked, like the Farnese Hercules, and steaming as well, while the water flowed in streams from neck, arms, stomach, and legs like the Rhone, the Rhine, the Danube, and the Adige crossing and watering Alpine ranges") (85; 73).

22. "[T]ime becomes human," Ricoeur argues, "to the extent that it is articulated through a narrative mode, and narrative attains its full meaning when it becomes a condition of temporal existence" (*Time* 1: 52).

23. Ricoeur explains that the act of emplotment combines two different temporal dimensions. The former is chronological and constitutes the episodic dimension of narrative: "It characterizes the story insofar as it is made up of events" (*Time* 1: 66). The second is what Ricoeur names the "configurational dimension," thanks to which the plot transforms the events into a story. "This configurational act consists of 'grasping together' the detailed actions. . . . It draws from this manifold of events the unity of one temporal whole" (*Time* 1: 66).

24. This observation is at the source of several negative comments on *Il Gattopardo.* According to Eugenio Montale, who wrote one of the first laudatory reviews of Lampedusa's novel, one of the few defects of the text was its lack of proportions. Montale particularly disliked the episode centered around Padre Pirrone, a secondary character who suddenly and for no necessary reason, according to Montale, becomes the main focus of a whole episode (3).

25. See for example the "come si usa da noi" ("as is done in Sicily") (113; 97), which comments upon the Sicilian habit of "promoting" a wild rabbit to the rank of hare for the formal dinner table because of the scarcity of game (Lucente, "Figure and Temporality" 207).

26. Examples of narratorial excursions into the extradiegetic future include the reference to the failure of Tancredi and Angelica's marriage (193); the bomb manufactured in Pittsburgh, Pennsylvania, which was to destroy Palazzo Ponteleone (264); the ironic notation about the "intimacy" that was to bind Austrians and Italians together in their opposing trenches in World War I (313); the revelation of the illness that would transform Angelica into a "larva miseranda" ("wretched specter") (313–14; 274); the allusion to modern trendy phraseology (174); urban development (223) and modern travel (121); and the mentioning of Sigmund Freud (134), Robert Koch (140), and Sergei Eisenstein (167).

27. Citing Louis O. Mink, Ricoeur explains that actions and events, although represented as occurring in the order of time, can be "surveyed as it were in a single glance as bound together in an order of significance, a representation of the *totum simul* which we can never more than partially achieve" (Mink, cited in Ricoeur, *Time* 1: 160).

28. Don Fabrizio's attempt to create a world of copies is demystified here by the narrator himself: "Ed il Principe, che aveva trovato Donnafugata immutata, venne invece trovato molto mutato lui . . . e da quel momento, invisibile, cominciò il declino del suo prestigio" ("And the Prince, who had found Donnafugata unchanged, was found very much changed himself . . . and from that moment, invisibly, began the decline of his prestige") (80; 69).

29. In Eduardo Saccone's words, the novel voices the desire "that denounces an absence rather than announcing a temptation—toward order, meaning, denied permanence: in short the privileges of divinity" (168).

30. "Attraverso le strette fessure delle palpebre gli occhi azzurro-torbido, gli occhi di sua madre, i suoi stessi occhi, lo fissavano ridenti" ("Dark blue eyes, the eyes of his mother, his own eyes, gazed laughingly at him through half-closed lids") (41; 35).

31. "Se vogliamo che tutto rimanga come è, bisogna che tutto cambi" ("If we want things to stay as they are, things will have to change") (42; 35).

32. On this point, see Lucente's discussion of *Il Gattopardo* as "a modern narrative that is at once perceptive and mystified, one in which the potentially disruptive functions of self-knowledge are contained only through the complementary and no less vigorous operations of *méconnaissance*" ("Figure and Temporality" 196).

33. Narrative symmetries between apparently different episodes are not limited to Father Pirrone's subplot. As Richard H. Lansing notes, Don Fabrizio's visit to the king is an "act of acknowledged submission to the monarchy," exactly as the tenants' visit to Don Fabrizio "constitutes a formal acknowledgement of social and economic dependence" (415). The parallel is so obvious that even the Prince realizes that his conversation with the peasants repeats his audiences with King Ferdinando (*Il Gattopardo* 59).

34. As Don Fabrizio is proud to observe, Concetta embodies, in her beauty and character, the traits of a "vera Salina" ("true Salina") (296; 258).

35. An obvious reminder of the dangers of interpretation is clear in the contrasting reports of the women's demonstration against their exclusion from the vote. The narrator describes them as "tre o quattro bagascette . . . beffeggiate via anche dai piú accesi liberali" ("three or four whores . . . jeered at even by the most advanced liberals") (134; 115), while the *Giornale di Trinacria* characterizes them as "gentili rappresentanti del bel sesso [che] . . . hanno sfilato nella piazza fra il generale consenso di quella patriottica popolazione" ("gentle representatives of the fair sex [who] . . . demonstrated in the main square amid general acclamation from the patriotic population") (134; 115).

36. As David Cowart points out, "form and content interweave as moments in a story about historical change—radical historical change—are illustrated with reference to radical changes in psychology, transportation, disease control, art, and later history" (137).

37. "Forgetting is produced by the disappearance or the retreat of the forces which keep alive, legitimate, and pass on our shared memories and beliefs. It thus appears, at first glance, as a disturbance, confusion or loss of an official, public memory, and in the final glance, as a factor in the production of meaning" (Bodei 5).

Chapter Three
Fiction and Women's History: Elsa Morante's *La Storia*

1. It was in the final phase of neoclassicism, Lionel Gossman explains, that the term *literature* became more closely associated with poetry, or with poetic and figurative writing, and took up the meaning of a corpus of sacred texts in which universal beauty and truth had been stored, and which was opposed to the world of historiography as faithful record of empirical reality. In an attempt to pinpoint the moment of separation between historical and poetic writing according to these criteria, Prosper de Barante identified in ancient Greece, before Herodotus, the moment in which the real was separated from the ideal, and the domain of the spirit from that of the material aspects of life (Gossman 5).

2. Recently, feminist historians have addressed this issue. Concerning women's history in France, Michelle Perrot points out that "[t]he 'profession' of the historian is a profession of men writing male history. The fields they cover—with political history in the forefront—are those of male action and power. . . . As history . . . is a highly esteemed branch of knowledge, for reasons of intellectual prestige but also of professional practice (for example, its role in the training of journalists, politicians or senior civil servants), it has remained a male preserve" ("Making History" 42, 54).

3. These questions that *La Storia* implicitly poses were particularly topical throughout the 1970s (*La Storia* appeared in 1974) thanks to the feminist debates following the political breakthrough of women's movements after 1968 (Perrot, "Making History" 43).

4. "La ricostruzione del passato," Gianna Pomata writes, "è un aspetto del modo complesso in cui un ordine sociale viene rappresentato e giustificato. È il paesaggio mentale in cui vengono ricostruite, a partire da tracce, le linee di formazione e di assestamento, o di sconvolgimento, del mondo che abbiamo ereditato. Questo paesaggio della mente è uno spazio di rappresentazione sociale. Come la scansione degli spazi cittadini, le facciate degli edifici pubblici, i monumenti, i nomi delle strade e delle piazze, mandano un messaggio sull'ordine e l'autorità sociale, così in ogni ricostruzione del passato è implicita una gerarchia di rilevanze, un'asserzione sulla dinamica fondamentale del mondo umano" ("The reconstruction of the past is an aspect of the complex manner in which a social order is represented and justified. It is the mental landscape in which we reconstruct—beginning from traces—the lines of formation and adjustment, or perturbation, of the world we have inherited. This mental landscape is a space of social representation. As the division of urban spaces, the facades of public buildings, the monuments and the names of streets and squares send a message regarding order and social authority, all reconstructions of the past imply a hierarchy of relevances and an assertion of the fundamental dynamics of the human world") ("La storia" 1434).

5. Traditional historical writing underwent serious criticism throughout the 1970s in Italy. Besides witnessing the rebirth of political movements for women's rights, the 1970s saw the development of social history under the influence of quantitative methods of analysis, and the birth of new research in historical demography by the *Annales* school and English Marxist scholars (J. Scott, "The Problem" 10).

6. "L'histoire des femmes," Perrot argues, "est, d'une certaine manière, celle de leur prise de parole" ("Women's history is, in a certain way, the history of their beginning to speak") (*Une Histoire* 4).

7. Perrot calls for an approach that pays attention to "words, gestures, images, places and objects that is derived both from literary analysis and from ethnography or even psychoanalysis, a multidisciplinary approach that should break down certain barriers without degenerating into empty talk" ("Making History" 50).

8. As Perrot asserts, "It is well known that records do not speak for themselves. There are no raw 'facts'; they are always 'processed'" ("Making History" 48).

9. As Paola Di Cori points out, feminist historians had to first of all determine "che cosa fosse un soggetto femminile, . . . come parlava, come era rappresentato, dove era possibile individuarlo" ("what a feminine subject was, . . . how she spoke, how she was represented, where one could possibly identify her") (98), and then face the forms of traditional historical representation and evaluate whether they were suitable for narrating women's experiences.

10. "On peut comparer la langue à une symphonie, dont la réalité est indépendante de la manière dont on l'exécute; les fautes que peuvent commettre les musiciens qui la jouent ne compromettent nullement cette réalité" ("Language can be compared to a symphony, the reality of which does not depend upon the manner in which this symphony is performed; the mistakes that the musicians may make as they are playing it do not compromise this reality at all") (Saussure 36).

11. "The Form of language is a systematic structure. It contains no individual elements as isolated components but incorporates them only in so far as 'eine Methode der Sprachbildung' can be discovered in them. The fixed mechanisms that, in their systematic and unified representation, constitute the form of language must enable it to produce an indefinite range of speech events corresponding to the conditions imposed by thought processes" (Chomsky 19–20).

12. "It is in and through language that man constitutes himself as a *subject,* because language alone establishes the concept of 'ego' in reality, in *its* reality which is that of the being" (Benveniste 224).

13. "This subject is a logical and even metaphysical postulate which assures the permanence and fullness of meaning. The transcendental ego is the guarantor of a meaning always already there" (Kristeva, "The Speaking Subject" 212).

14. See, for example, the narrator's comments when she explains that she herself would not have believed Useppe's extraordinary precocity if she had not shared, in some way, his own fate (106), and her reference to seeing Vilma among the old women who feed the stray cats at the Theater of Marcellus (480–81).

15. Some of the marks of the narrator's omniscience are utilized, as in *Il Gattopardo,* to highlight the narrator's subjective presence in her text, and, together with it, the time of her discourse as separated from that of the story. See, for example, her reference to the village of Dachau, which later, at the war's end, was to become famous for its concentration camp (15–16); her anticipation of Gunther's death (74; 63); and, especially, her reference to the distance separating the time of her own writing from the time of her characters' lives when she describes Nino's death (464).

16. See the narrator's telling, and patronizing, comment about Gunther: "Un po', difatti, il ragazzo era impaziente di avventura; ma un altro po' rimaneva, a sua stessa insaputa, un mammarolo" ("To some extent, in fact, he was impatient for adventure; but to some extent, also, unknown to himself, he remained a mamma's boy") (17; 15).

17. The revolutionary concept of a feminine historiography marked by a subjective framework was developed in the 1970s in Italy, especially in connection with the *gruppi di autocoscienza* ("self-consciousness groups"). Women talking to women about their experiences was also a way to give a voice to one's own subjectivity and elaborate the difference between external and internal time in a feminist perspective. As Di Cori observes, "La lettura e interpretazione della realtà è stata fatta interamente dipendere dalla propria soggettività e dal confronto di essa con quella delle altre donne—una attività che ha finito per attribuire alle esperienze soggettive i caratteri di vere e proprie entità fondatrici e depositarie uniche di verità storica" ("the reading and interpretation of reality was made to depend entirely upon one's own subjectivity and upon the comparison between one's subjectivity and that of other women. This activity has ended up attributing to subjective experiences the character of real founding entities, unique depositaries of historical truth") (101).

18. "Io, quanto a me, le rare e frammentarie notizie che ho potuto raccoglierne, le ho avute in gran parte da Ninnuzzu. . . . E cosí, la mia presente rievocazione del fatto rimane piuttosto vacante, e approssimativa" ("For myself, the scant and fragmentary information I have been able to gather came, to a large extent, from Ninnuzzu. . . . And so my present memoir of the event remains rather patchy and approximate") (412; 350).

19. "Conosco Nora solo da una sua fotografia, del tempo che era fidanzata" ("I know Nora only from a photograph taken in the days of her engagement") (53; 45).

20. As Perrot observes, oral records need to be incorporated into historical accounts: "For women, who have spoken a great deal more than they have written, and most of whose life is lived in a private sphere ignored by the written word, oral research is essential, hence most of the practitioners of this method are women. Accounts by women of their experience of historical events, the part they have played in them, their private family life or their 'life story' in general, illustrating the distinctiveness of women's experience—are all contributions of considerable value, provided the user bears in mind the fact that memory is a selective construction, by no means spontaneous, and that tape recordings provide only raw data, to be sifted and compared like other information" ("Making History" 50).

21. Significantly, the same image reappears, with ominous connotations, at the end of the novel, as it expresses Ida's maternal premonition of Useppe's death: "Ida . . . andava ascoltando un altro suono, del quale non aveva udito piú il simile dopo l'ultima sua passeggiata al Ghetto. Era, di nuovo, una specie di nenia ritmata che chiamava dal basso, e riesumava, nella sua dolcezza tentante, qualcosa di sanguinoso e di terribile" ("Ida . . . was listening to another sound, like something she hadn't heard since her last walk in the Ghetto. It was, again, a kind of cadenced dirge which called from below, and summed up, in its tempting sweetness, something bloody and terrible") (645; 545).

22. Lucia Re argues that in all of Morante's works there is a pervasive sense that the acquisition of sexual difference is regrettable: "This is due not to a puritanical devaluation of sexuality as a human phenomenon, but rather to the observation (now a staple concept of much feminist discourse) that the regimentation of the male/female polarity into sexual difference, its social and institutional appropriation, is more than the gateway to the definition of gender roles, and thus of women's inferiority in patriarchal societies. It also serves as a foundational oppositional structure on which all forms of violence and discrimination are predicated" (367–68). In this way, Useppe's ideal innocence represents what "humanity itself could be like were it to be free (or freed) of its obsession with the regimentation of difference" (Re 368).

23. As Lucente notes, "The straightest pathway into the other side of the story's titular dialectic, which is to say, into the fantasy world of the novel as *poesia,* is through the figure of *La Storia*'s most strikingly original and most engaging character, the child at once too strange and too beautiful for this world, Useppe" ("History" 248).

24. See the total isolation that characterizes, according to the *narratrice,* Useppe's epileptic seizures (451; 382), as well as his tendency to segregate himself from his schoolmates and the other children and their games (457; 388).

25. The reference to the monumental dimension of time, to a time that exists all at once or that never passes, appears again at the end of the novel. This time, however, it has lost all positive connotations, as it refers to Ida's descent into madness: "Lei pure, come il famoso Panda Minore della leggenda, stava sospesa in cima a un albero dove le carte temporali non avevano piú corso. Essa, in realtà, era morta insieme al suo pischelletto Useppe" ("She too, like the famous Lesser Panda of legend, was suspended at the top of a tree where temporal charters were no longer in effect. She, in reality, had died with her little Useppe") (649; 548).

26. "Giganti o nani, straccioni o paíni, decrepitudine o gioventú, per lui non faceva differenza. E né gli storti, né i gobbi, né i panzoni, né le scòrfane, per lui non erano meno carini di Settebellezze, solo che fossero tutti amici pari e sorridessero") ("Giants or dwarfs, beggars or dandies, decrepitude or youth, nothing made any difference to him. And neither the twisted nor the hunchback, the paunchy nor the scrawny: to him none was less lovely than the world's Paragon, provided all were friends equally and smiling") (557; 472).

27. On this topic, and particularly the questions: "Is women's writing different from men's? In what ways does their writing emphasize the fact that they are women?" see *New French Feminisms,* especially the essays by Xavière Gauthier and Hélène Cixous.

28. In *Ce sexe qui n'est pas un* (*This Sex Which Is Not One,* 1977), Luce Irigaray expands on the concept of "womanliness as masquerade" that Joan Rivière first proposed in 1929. Irigaray refers to women as alienated subjects who try to integrate themselves into the male script (Irigaray 84 and Suleiman 24).

29. "Essa non aveva mai avuto confidenza col proprio corpo. . . . Il suo corpo era cresciuto con lei come un estrane; . . . in compagnia del suo corpo si sentiva piú sola" ("She had never felt at ease in her own body. . . . Her body had grown up with her like an outside; . . . in the company of her body she felt more alone") (83; 72–73).

30. "[C]ol tempo, si avvezzò a quel grande rito serale, nutrimento necessario delle loro nozze. . . . Ida non comprendeva il godimento sessuale, che le rimase per sempre un mistero" ("[A]s time went on, she became accustomed to that great evening ritual, necessary nutrition of their marriage. . . . Iduzza didn't understand sexual pleasure, which remained a mystery to her always") (37; 31).

31. "[P]rophecy, creativity, and the feminine," James Mandrell writes, "are endowed with a positive value that counteracts the effects of history" (231).

32. A foreshortened rendition of two opposite historical constructions, one tragically cyclical, the other founded upon lawless change, emerges from Nora's and Giuseppe's unsophisticated historical views. For Nora, history is the theater of a fatal predestination: "gli ebrei sono un popolo predestinato dall'eternità all'odio vendicativo di tutti gli altri popoli; . . . la persecuzione si accanirà sempre su di loro, pure attraverso tregue apparenti, riproducendosi sempre in eterno, secondo il loro destino prescritto" ("the Jews are a people destined, since time began, to suffer the vindictive hatred of all other peoples; . . . even during apparent periods of truce, persecution will always dog them, eternally recurring, as their prescribed destiny") (24; 20). Giuseppe, on the other hand, is the Dionysian preacher of "la nuova storia" ("the new history") (25; 22), that imminent and implacable revolution fostering and guiding his anarchic faith.

33. It is, in Morante's words, the "senso del sacro" ("sense of the sacred"), the almost corporeal, animal wisdom that knows "il passato e il futuro di ogni destino" ("the past and future of every destiny") (21; 18). The term *sacred* has no positive attributes, as it refers to the universal power that creates, in order to destroy all living creatures. The sense of the sacred is the wisdom that allows Ida to "know" with terrible clarity about Useppe's death in the very moment in which it happens, even though she is not there with him.

Chapter Four
Transhistorical Narratives: The Apocalypse and the Carnival in Umberto Eco's *Il nome della rosa*

1. Corti rejects the generally accepted diachronic frame that places the dawn of the neo-avantgarde in the fall of 1956 with the first issue of *Il Verri,* and its sunset in the spring of 1969 with the last issue of *Il Quindici.* She distinguishes several different periods in the evolution of the neo-avantgarde, starting with its prehistory (1956–59) with *Il Verri* and the publication of Sanguineti's and Pagliarani's literary works, reaching its climax between 1959 and 1960 with the publication of *I Novissimi,* and revealing the often contradictory plurality of its positions with the Gruppo 63's polemical meetings (*Il viaggio* 113–14).

2. "Se l'artista cercasse di dominare il disordine della situazione presente rifacendosi ai moduli compromessi con la situazione entrata in crisi, in tal caso egli sarebbe veramente un mistificatore" ("An artist would be a mystifier if he tried to master the disorder of the present condition by relying on the very systems that are implicated with this condition of crisis") (Eco, "Del modo" 264). When the artist realizes that the system of communication is extraneous to the historical situation about which he wants to speak, Umberto Eco continues, he must also realize that he will be able to express this situation only through "l'invenzione di strutture formali che si facciano il *modello* di questa situazione" ("the invention of formal structures that will embody this situation and become its *model*") ("Del modo" 269).

3. In an interview published in the *Nouvel Observateur* in 1982, Eco made a similar point: "Je crois que le récit est une exigence fondamentale. 'Raconte-moi une histoire!' demande l'enfant. Or la littérature des vingt dernières années a mis en crise la narrativité. La demande du public n'a pas cessé pour autant et a été satisfaite ailleurs, par la télévision ou le cinéma" ("I believe that the story is a fundamental need. 'Tell me a story!' the child asks. Now, the literature of the last twenty years has put narrative in a state of crisis. However, the public has continued to request stories, and has been satisfied elsewhere by the television and the cinema") ("Le Tueur" 54).

4. Hayden White claims that narrative is "a meta-code, a human universal on the basis of which transcultural messages about the nature of a shared reality can be transmitted" (*The Content* 1).

5. In Frank Kermode's words, "No novel can avoid being in some sense what Aristotle calls 'a completed action.' This being so, all novels imitate a world of potentiality, even if it implies a philosophy disclaimed by their authors. They have a fixation on the eidetic imagery of beginning, middle, and end, potency and cause. Novels, then, have beginnings, ends and potentiality, even if the world has not" (138).

6. The apocalyptic model has wide-ranging implications. It is a theological model by way of Judeo-Christian eschatology, and also a political one by way of the "strong imperial ideology that continued up to the fall of the Holy Roman/Germanic Empire" (Ricoeur, *Time* 2: 23).

7. This is not true of all of the characters, of course. William does not subscribe to an apocalyptic worldview, yet he does evaluate its structuring potential and ideological significance. Aymaro of Alessandria fundamentally disagrees with Abo's apocalyptic predictions and censoring policies relating the transmission of knowledge. Aymaro believes that monasteries should overcome their isolation, and compromise with the new cultural and political realities in order to still exercise effective influence: "se sappiamo far bei libri fabbrichiamone per le università, e occupiamoci di quanto avviene giù a valle. . . . Apriamo la biblioteca ai testi in volgare, e saliranno quassù anche coloro che non scrivono più in latino" ("since we know how to make beautiful books, we should make them for the universities and concern ourselves with what is happening down in the valley. . . . We should open the library to texts in the vernacular, and those who no longer write in Latin will also come up here") (131; 141).

8. In the Semitic languages, the word for "seven" is traced to the representation of a perfect totality, the totality ordered and planned by God.

9. "Leggiamo l'inizio—ma quale? Ce ne sono tre, su tre registri diversi. . . . Qualcuno dice '*il 16 agosto 1968 mi fu messo tra le mani un libro. . . .*' Chi scrive è l' 'autore,' persona storica datata (presumibilmente Eco). . . . Il manoscritto del vecchio monaco tedesco ha inizio con un Prologo che comincia con le parole 'In principio erat Verbum,' facilmente riconoscibili come l'inizio del Vangelo di San Giovanni. La narrazione degli avvenimenti, fatta da Adso in prima persona . . . comincia con la frase 'Era una bella mattina di fine novembre,' inizio romanzesco per eccellenza che non a caso ritroviamo, nelle sue più comuni varianti, all'inizio del romanzo di Snoopy nello strip *Peanuts* di Charles Schultz" ("Let's read the beginning—but which one? There are three beginnings, with three different linguistic registers. . . . Someone says: 'On August 16, 1968, I was handed a book. . . .' The person who writes is 'the author,' a historically defined person (presumably Eco). . . . The manuscript by the old German monk starts with a Prologue that begins with the words: 'In the beginning was the Word,' easily recognizable as the beginning of the Gospel according to Saint John. Adso's first person narration . . . begins with the sentence 'It was a beautiful morning at the end of November,' the quintessential fictional beginning that we can find quite significantly, in its most common variations, at the beginning of Snoopy's adventures in the comic strip *Peanuts* by Charles Schultz") (De Lauretis, *Umberto Eco* 81–82).

10. "[N]on sono sicuro di non attribuirgli, a distanza di tempo, avventure e delitti che furono di altri, prima di lui e dopo di lui, e che ora nella mia mente stanca si appiattiscono a disegnare una sola immagine, per la forza appunto della immaginazione che, unendo il ricordo dell'oro a quello del monte, sa comporre l'idea di una montagna d'oro" ("I may even attribute to him adventures and crimes that belonged to others, before him and after him, and which now, in my tired mind, flatten out to form a single image. This, in fact, is the power of the imagination, which, combining the memory of gold with that of the mountain, can compose the idea of a golden mountain") (191; 219–20).

11. As Abo pessimistically comments: "Quante nostre abbazie, che duecento anni fa erano centro splendente di grandezza e santità, sono ora rifugio di infingardi. L'ordine è ancora potente, ma il fetore delle città cinge dappresso i nostri luoghi santi, il popolo di Dio è ora incline ai commerci e alle guerre di fazione, giù nei grandi centri abitati, dove non può avere albergo lo spirito della santità, non solo si parla . . . , ma già si scrive in volgare" ("How many of our abbeys, which two hundred years ago were resplendent with grandeur and sanctity, are now the refuge of the slothful? The order is still powerful, but the stink of the cities is encroaching upon our holy places, the people of God are now inclined to commerce and wars of faction; down below in the great settlements, where the spirit of sanctity can find no lodging, not only do they speak . . . in the vulgar tongue, but they are already writing in it") (44; 34).

12. "La bellezza del cosmo," William explains to Adso, "è data non solo dall'unità nella varietà, ma anche dalla varietà nell'unità" ("the beauty of the cosmos derives not only from unity in variety, but also from variety in unity") (24; 10).

13. Adso's experiences with William force him to revise his initial belief that "l'animo razionale . . . [si pasce] solo del vero, di cui . . . si sa già sin dall'inizio" ("the rational spirit . . . [feeds] only on the Truth, which . . . one knows from the outset") (23; 9).

14. "[È] ormai noto," William argues, "che diversi sono i nomi, che gli uomini impongono per designare i concetti, e uguali per tutti sono solo i concetti, segni delle cose. Così che certamente viene la parola *nomen* da *nomos,* ovvero legge, dato che appunto i *nomina* vengono dati dagli uomini *ad placitum,* e cioè per libera e collettiva convenzione" ("[I]t is now known that men impose different names to designate concepts, though only the concepts, signs of things, are the same for all. So that surely the word 'nomen' comes from 'nomos,' that is to say 'law,' since nomina are given by men ad placitum, in other words by free and collective accord") (357; 425).

15. "Io temo di non saper più distinguere" ("I fear I no longer know how to distinguish"), William confesses to Ubertino (65; 61).

16. Again, Eco's epistemological quest may be compared to Foucault's: "this sort of revolving door of rationality . . . refers us to its necessity, to its indispensability, and at the same time, to its intrinsic dangers" (Foucault, "Space" 249).

17. As William and Adso eventually find out, there was no set pattern organizing the sequence of the murders and, as William confesses to Adso: "Non v'era una trama, . . . e io l'ho scoperta per sbaglio. . . . Sono arrivato a Jorge attraverso uno schema apocalittico che sembrava reggere tutti i delitti, eppure era casuale. . . . Sono arrivato a Jorge inseguendo il disegno di una mente perversa e raziocinante, e non v'era alcun disegno" ("There was no plot, . . . and I discovered it by mistake. . . . I arrived at Jorge through an apocalyptic pattern that seemed to underlie all the crimes, and yet it was accidental. . . . I arrived at Jorge pursuing the plan of a perverse and rational mind, and there was no plan") (494–95; 599).

18. As this passage is a linguistic pastiche in which words are associated more for their phonic characteristics than their semantic meaning, an English translation would be impossible. William Weaver, who translated *Il nome della rosa,* omitted this passage from his translation.

19. Similarly, Adelmo's *marginalia* present an upside-down world: "Si trattava di un salterio ai margini del quale si delineava un mondo rovesciato rispetto a quello cui ci hanno abituati i nostri sensi. Come se al limite di un discorso che per definizione è il discorso della verità, si svolgesse profondamente legato a quello, per mirabili allusioni in aenigmate, un discorso menzognero su un universo posto a testa in giù, dove i cani fuggono davanti alla lepre e i cervi cacciano il leone" ("This was a psalter in whose margins was delineated a world reversed with respect to the one to which our senses have accustomed us. As if at the border of a discourse that is by definition the discourse of truth, there proceeded, closely linked to it, through wondrous allusion in aenigmate, a discourse of falsehood on a topsy-turvy universe, in which dogs flee before the hare, and deer hunt the lion") (84; 85).

20. It was through its illustrations, and not through its text, of course, that the Apocalypse became understandable and accessible to the vast majority of illiterate people.

21. Irony is undoubtedly at work in Eco's choice of Aristotle's lost book on comedy as the reason behind the abbey's murders. One of the founding fathers of patriarchy (Frentz 138), Aristotle's philosophical system is both hierarchical and dychotomized, significantly at odds with the displacing, polyphonic nature of the Carnival spirit (Lerner 208).

22. Dramatic historical events frame the genesis—both actual and fictional—of *Il nome della rosa.* Eco wrote his novel during the aftermath of the abduction and assassination of Christian Democrat leader Aldo Moro by the terrorist organization of the Red Brigades in 1978. In the novel's opening section entitled "Naturalmente, un manoscritto" ("Naturally, a manuscript"), a fictionalized Eco receives Vallet's book on August 16, 1968, six days before the Russian invasion of Prague.

Works Cited

Adorno, Theodor W. *Negative Dialectics.* Trans. E. B. Ashton. New York: Seabury, 1973.

———. "On the Fetish-Character in Music and the Regression of Listening." *The Essential Frankfurt School Reader.* Ed. Andrew Arato and Eike Gebhardt. Introd. Paul Piccone. New York: Urizen, 1978. 270–99.

Alicata, Mario. "Il principe di Lampedusa e il Risorgimento Siciliano." *Scritti letterari.* Ed. Natalino Sapegno. La Cultura: saggi di arte e di letteratura 14. Milan: Mondadori, 1968. 337–51.

Angeli, Gaetano. *Contro il leggersi romanzi dei giovani.* Verona: Moroni, 1821.

Aragon, Louis. "*Il Gattopardo* e *La Certosa.*" *Rinascita* 30 Mar. 1960: 223–26.

Aristotle. *Poetics.* Trans. and introd. Gerald F. Else. Ann Arbor: U of Michigan P, 1970.

Asor Rosa, Alberto. "Il linguaggio della pubblicità." *La fiera letteraria* 6 Oct. 1974: 7–8.

Austen, Jane. *Northanger Abbey.* 1818. Ed. and introd. Anne Henry Ehrenpreis. Harmondsworth: Penguin, 1972.

Bakhtin, M. M. *The Dialogic Imagination: Four Essays.* Ed. Michael Holquist. Trans. Caryl Emerson and Michael Holquist. Austin: U of Texas P, 1981.

———. Introduction. *Rabelais and His World.* By Bakhtin. Trans. Hélène Iswolsky. Bloomington: Indiana UP, 1984. 1–58.

Balestrini, Nanni, and Alfredo Giuliani, eds. *Gruppo 63: la nuova letteratura.* Panorami 4. Milan: Feltrinelli, 1964.

Barilli, Renato. "*Cahier de doléances* sull'ultima narrativa italiana." *Il Verri* 4 (1960): 90–111.

———. Rev. of *La Storia,* by Elsa Morante. *Il Verri* 7 (1974): 104–10.

———. "Le strutture del romanzo." *Gruppo 63: la nuova letteratura.* Ed. Nannni Balestrini and Alfredo Giuliani. Panorami 4. Milan: Feltrinelli, 1964. 25–47.

Barthes, Roland. "L'albero del crimine." *Almanacco Bompiani* (1971): 38–53.

———. "The Death of the Author." *Image, Music, Text.* Ed. and trans. Stephen Heath. Glasgow: Fontana, 1977. 142–48.

———. "Le Discours de l'histoire." *Social Science Information / Information sur les sciences sociales* 6.4 (1967): 65–75.

Barthes, Roland. "Introduction to the Structural Analysis of Narrative." *Image, Music, Text.* Ed. and trans. Stephen Heath. Glasgow: Fontana, 1977. 79–124.

———. "Textual Analysis of a Tale of Poe." *On Signs.* Ed. Marshall Blonsky. Oxford: Blackwell, 1985. 84–97.

Bassani, Giorgio. Introduction. *Il Gattopardo.* By Giuseppe Tomasi di Lampedusa. I Contemporanei 4. Milan: Feltrinelli, 1959. 7–13.

Baudrillard, Jean. "On Nihilism." *On the Beach* 6 (1984): 38–39.

Bazzoni, Giambattista. *Falco della Rupe, o la guerra di Musso.* Florence: Veroli, 1830.

Benveniste, Emile. *Problems in General Linguistics.* Trans. Mary Elizabeth Meek. Coral Gables, FL: U of Miami P, 1971.

Berengo, Marino. *Intellettuali e librai nella Milano della Restaurazione.* Turin: Einaudi, 1980.

Bermann, Sandra. Introduction. *On the Historical Novel.* By Alessandro Manzoni. Trans. Sandra Bermann. Lincoln: U of Nebraska P, 1984. 1–59.

Bernabò, Graziella. *Come leggere La Storia di Elsa Morante.* Come leggere 24. Milan: Mursia, 1991.

Best, Steven, and Douglas Kellner. *Postmodern Theory: Critical Interrogations.* Critical Perspectives. New York: Guilford, 1991.

Bianchetti, Giuseppe. "Discorso secondo." *Discorsi critici intorno alla questione se giovi di ammettere o no nella letteratura italiana il romanzo storico.* Treviso: Paluello, 1832. 73–114.

Biorci, Domenico. "Uno sguardo sulla letteratura, sul romanzo storico, e particolarmente sul racconto di Massimo D'Azeglio, *Ettore Fieramosca, o la disfida di Barletta.*" *Il Poligrafo* 15 (1833): 187–226.

Blanchot, Maurice. *Le Livre à venir.* Paris: Gallimard, 1959.

Blasucci, Luigi. "*Il Gattopardo.*" *Belfagor* 14 (1959): 117–21.

Bloom, Harold. *The Anxiety of Influence: A Theory of Poetry.* New York: Oxford UP, 1973.

Bocelli, Arnaldo. "La narrativa italiana." *Almanacco letterario Bompiani* (1959): 229–33.

Bodei, Remo. "Farewell to the Past: Historical Memory, Oblivion and Collective Identity." Paper presented at the University of California, Los Angeles. 28 May 1992.

Borsieri, Pietro. *Avventure letterarie di un giorno, o consigli di un galantuomo a vari scrittori. Manifesti romantici e altri scritti della polemica classico/romantica.* Ed. Carlo Calcaterra and Mario Scotti. Classici italiani 79. 2nd ed. Turin: UTET, 1979. 255–416.

Bosco, Umberto. "Preromanticismo e romanticismo." *Questioni e correnti di storia letteraria.* Ed. Umberto Bosco et al. Problemi ed orientamenti critici di lingua e di letteratura italiana 3. Milan: Marzorati, 1949. 597–657.

Braudel, Fernand. *On History.* Trans. Sarah Matthews. Chicago: U of Chicago P, 1980.

Calvino, Italo. "Il mare dell'oggettività." *Il Menabò* 2 (1960): 9–14.

———. Preface. *Il sentiero dei nidi di ragno.* By Calvino. Opere di Italo Calvino. Milan: Mondadori, 1993. v–xxv.

Cantoni, Remo. "Considerazioni sul realismo nella narrativa contemporanea." *Ulisse* 4 (1956/57): 968–77.

Caputo, Rino. "Un tema di politica culturale degli anni '60: *Il Gattopardo.*" *Studi novecenteschi* 4 (1975): 35–55.

Chomsky, Noam. *Cartesian Linguistics: A Chapter in the History of Rationalist Thought.* Studies in Language. New York: Harper, 1966.

Cixous, Hélène. "The Laugh of the Medusa." *New French Feminisms: An Anthology.* Ed. and introd. Elaine Marks and Isabelle de Courtivron. New York: Schocken, 1981. 245–64.

Cohn, Bernard S. "Anthropology and History in the 1980's: Toward a Rapprochement." *Journal of Interdisciplinary History* 12 (1981): 227–52.

Coleridge, S. T. *Lectures on Shakespeare and Other Old Poets and Dramatists.* Everyman Library. London: Dent, 1930.

Collingwood, R. G. *The Idea of History.* Ed. T. M. Knox. Oxford: Clarendon, 1946.

Corti, Maria. "È un'opera chiusa." *L'Espresso* 19 Oct. 1980: 108.

———. *An Introduction to Literary Semiotics.* Trans. Margherita Bogat and Allen Mandelbaum. Advances in Semiotics. Bloomington: Indiana UP, 1978.

———. *Il viaggio testuale: le ideologie e le strutture semiotiche.* Turin: Einaudi, 1978.

Cottignoli, Alfredo. "Tenca, Rovani, De Sanctis e il discorso manzoniano *Del romanzo storico.*" *Studi e problemi di critica testuale* 10 (1975): 155–65.

Cowart, David. *History and the Contemporary Novel.* Crosscurrents / Modern Critiques. 3rd ser. Carbondale: Southern Illinois UP, 1989.

Croce, Benedetto. "Marcel Proust: A Case of Decadent Historicism." *Benedetto Croce: Essays on Literature and Literary Criticism.* Trans. and introd. M. E. Moss. Albany: State U of New York P, 1990. 145–49.

Crovi, Raffaele. "Gli sperimentalisti." *Almanacco letterario Bompiani* (1959): 261–63.

Curtius, Ernst-Robert. *Europäische Literatur und lateinisches Mittelalter.* Bern: Francke, 1948.

Davin, Anna. "Redressing the Balance or Transforming the Art? The British Experience." *Retrieving Women's History: Changing Perceptions of the Role of Women in Politics and Society.* Ed. S. Jay Kleinberg. Studies in Development: Theory and Policy. Oxford: Berg/Unesco, 1988. 60–78.

Daw, Laurence. "The Apocalyptic Milieu of Pynchon's *Gravity's Rainbow.*" *Apocalyptic Visions Past and Present.* Proc. of Eighth and Ninth Annual Florida State University Conferences on Literature and Film. Ed. JoAnn James and William J. Cloonan. Tallahassee: Florida State UP, 1988. 91–98.

De Castris, Leone. *La polemica sul romanzo storico.* Bari: Cressati, 1959.

De Certeau, Michel. *The Writing of History.* Trans. Tom Conley. European Perspectives. New York: Columbia UP, 1988.

De Lauretis, Teresa. "Il principio Franti." *Saggi su Il nome della rosa.* Ed. Renato Giovannoli. Milan: Bompiani, 1985. 45–55.

———. *Umberto Eco.* Il Castoro 79. Florence: La Nuova Italia, 1981.

Deleuze, Gilles. *The Logic of Sense.* Trans. Mark Lester and Charles Stivale. Ed. Constantin V. Boundas. New York: Columbia UP, 1990.

Derla, Luigi. *Il realismo storico di Alessandro Manzoni.* Milan: Istituto Editoriale Cisalpino, 1965.

De Rosa, Giuseppe. "*Il Gattopardo.*" *La civiltà cattolica* Apr. 1959: 169–82.

Derrida, Jacques. "La Loi du genre / The Law of Genre." *Glyph: Textual Studies* 7 (1980): 176–232.

De Sanctis, Francesco. "Del romanzo storico e i *Promessi sposi.*" *Manzoni.* Ed. Carlo Muscetta and Dario Puccini. Gli Struzzi 276. Turin: Einaudi, 1983. 348–50.

Di Cori, Paola. "Prospettive e soggetti nella storia delle donne: alla ricerca di radici comuni." *La ricerca delle donne: studi femministi in Italia.* Ed. Maria Cristina Marcuzzo and Anna Rossi-Doria. Soggetto donna 2. Turin: Rosenberg, 1987. 96–122.

Eagleton, Terry. *Marxism and Literary Criticism.* Berkeley: U of California P, 1976.

Eco, Umberto. *Apocalittici e integrati: comunicazioni di massa e teorie della cultura di massa.* 4th ed. Milan: Bompiani, 1984.

———. "Del modo di formare come impegno sulla realtà." *Opera aperta: forma e indeterminazione nelle poetiche contemporanee.* Milan: Bompiani, 1976. 235–90.

———. "The Frames of Comic 'Freedom.'" *Carnival!* Ed. Thomas A. Sebeok and Marcia E. Erickson. Approaches to Semiotics 64. Berlin: Mouton, 1984. 1–9.

———. "La generazione di Nettuno." *Gruppo 63: la nuova letteratura.* Ed. Nanni Balestrini and Alfredo Giuliani. Panorami 4. Milan: Feltrinelli, 1964. 407–16.

———. "L'industria aristotelica." *Almanacco Bompiani* (1971): 5–11.

———. *The Name of the Rose.* Trans. William Weaver. New York: Warner, 1986.

———. *Il nome della rosa.* 1980. Milan: Bompiani, 1988.

———. *Opera aperta: forma e indeterminazione nelle poetiche contemporanee.* Milan: Bompiani, 1976.

———. "Palinsesto su Beato." *Beato di Liébana: miniature del Beato de Fernando I y Sancha.* Introd. Luis Vásquez de Parga Iglesias. Parma: Franco Maria Ricci, 1973. 21–80.

———. "Postille a *Il nome della rosa.*" *Il nome della rosa.* By Eco. Milan: Bompiani, 1988. 507–33.

———. *Postscript to The Name of the Rose.* Trans. William Weaver. San Diego: Harcourt, 1984.

———. *Trattato di semiotica generale.* Il campo semiotico: studi Bompiani 12. Milan: Bompiani, 1975.

———. Interview. "Le Tueur, l'abbé, et le sémioticien." *Nouvel Observateur* Nov. 1982: 52–54.

Eco, Umberto, and Cesare Sughi. "Questo Almanacco." *Almanacco Bompiani* (1971): 3–4.

Eliot, T. S. "Tradition and the Individual Talent." *Selected Prose of T. S. Eliot.* Ed. Frank Kermode. New York: Harcourt, 1975. 37–44.

Erlich, Victor. *Russian Formalism: History, Doctrine.* Slavistic Printings and Reprintings 4. 2nd rev. ed. The Hague: Mouton, 1965.

Ferretti, Gian Carlo. *Il best-seller all'italiana: fortune e formule del romanzo "di qualità."* 2nd ed. Rome: Laterza, 1983.

Forster, E. M. *Aspects of the Novel, and Related Writings.* The Abinger Ed. of E. M. Forster 12. London: Edward Arnold, 1974.

Fortini, Franco. "Contro *Il Gattopardo.*" *Saggi italiani.* Strumenti di studio. Bari: De Donato, 1974. 242–51.

Foucault, Michel. *The Order of Things: An Archaeology of the Human Sciences.* World of Man. New York: Vintage-Random, 1973.

———. "Space, Knowledge, and Power." *The Foucault Reader.* Ed. Paul Rabinow. New York: Pantheon, 1984. 239–56.

———. "What Is an Author?" *The Foucault Reader.* Ed. Paul Rabinow. New York: Pantheon, 1984. 101–20.

Fowler, Alastair. "The Life and Death of Literary Forms." *New Directions in Literary History.* Ed. Ralph Cohen. Baltimore: Johns Hopkins UP, 1974. 77–94.

Frentz, Thomas. "Resurrecting the Feminine in *The Name of the Rose.*" *Pre/Text: A Journal of Rhetorical Theory* 9 (1988): 123–45.

Fubini, Mario. *Critica e poesia.* L'Ippogrifo 3. Rome: Bonacci, 1973.

Garosci, Aldo. "Romanzo, storia e società." *Ulisse* 4 (1956/57): 1010–19.

Gauthier, Xavière. "Is There Such a Thing as Women's Writing?" *New French Feminisms: An Anthology.* Ed. Elaine Marks and Isabelle de Courtivron. New York: Schocken, 1981. 161–64.

Genette, Gérard. "Genres, 'types,' modes." *Poétique* 32 (1977): 399–421.

———. *Palimpsestes: La Littérature au second degré.* Points: Essays 257. Paris: Seuil, 1982.

Giannantonio, Pompeo. "Lucia e il personaggio femminile nel romanzo europeo dell'Ottocento." *Critica letteraria* 39 (1983): 213–36.

Gilmour, David. *The Last Leopard: A Life of Giuseppe Tomasi di Lampedusa.* London: Collins Harvill, 1988.

Girard, René. *The Scapegoat.* Trans. Yvonne Freccero. Baltimore: Johns Hopkins UP, 1986.

Giuliani, Alfredo. Preface. *I Novissimi: poesie per gli anni Sessanta.* Biblioteca del Verri: collana di poesia. Turin: Einaudi, 1972. 3–12.

Głowińsky, Michał. "Les Genres littéraires." *Théorie littéraire: Problèmes et perspectives.* Paris: PUF, 1989. 81–94.

———. "Theoretical Foundations of Historical Poetics." *New Literary History* 7 (1976): 237–45.

Golden, Leon. "Eco's Reconstruction of Aristotle's Theory of Comedy in *The Name of the Rose.*" *Classical and Modern Literature* 6 (1986): 239–49.

Gossman, Lionel. "Narrative Form as a Cognitive Instrument." *The Writing of History: Literary Form and Historical Understanding.* Ed. Robert H. Canary and Henry Kozicki. Madison: U of Wisconsin P, 1978. 3–39.

Guglielmi, Angelo. "Avanguardia e sperimentalismo." *Gruppo 63: la nuova letteratura.* Ed. Nanni Balestrini and Alfredo Giuliani. Panorami 4. Milan: Feltrinelli, 1964. 15–24.

———. "Il nuovo 'realismo.'" *Avanguardia e sperimentalismo.* Materiali 1. Milan: Feltrinelli, 1964. 9–18.

Guiducci, Armanda. "La problematica politico-sociale nella nostra narrativa." *Ulisse* 4 (1956/57): 987–97.

Guillén, Claudio. *Literature as System: Essays Toward the Theory of Literary History.* Princeton, NJ: Princeton UP, 1971.

Halbwachs, Maurice. *La memoria collettiva.* Ed. Paolo Jedlowski. Milan: Unicopli, 1968.

Hawkes, Terence. *Structuralism and Semiotics.* Berkeley: U of California P, 1977.

Hutcheon, Linda. *A Poetics of Postmodernism: History, Theory, Fiction.* New York: Routledge, 1988.

Irigaray, Luce. *This Sex Which Is Not One.* Trans. Catherine Porter and Carolyn Burke. Ithaca, NY: Cornell UP, 1985.

Jameson, Fredric. *The Ideologies of Theory: Essays 1971–1986.* Vol. 2. Theory and History of Literature 49. Minneapolis: U of Minnesota P, 1988. 2 vols.

———. *The Political Unconscious: Narrative as a Socially Symbolic Act.* Ithaca, NY: Cornell UP, 1981.

Jauss, Hans-Robert. "Littérature médiévale et théorie des genres." *Poétique* 1 (1970): 79–101.

Kermode, Frank. *The Sense of an Ending: Studies in the Theory of Fiction.* Max Flexner Lectures 1965. London: Oxford UP, 1967.

Krauss, Werner. *Essays zur französischen Literatur.* Berlin: Aufbau-Verlag, 1968.

Kristeva, Julia. "The Bounded Text." *Desire in Language: A Semiotic Approach to Literature and Art.* Ed. Leon S. Roudiez. Trans. Thomas Gora, Alice Jardine, and Leon S. Roudiez. New York: Columbia UP, 1980. 34–63.

———. "Oscillation du 'pouvoir' au 'refus.'" *New French Feminisms: An Anthology.* Ed. Elaine Marks and Isabelle de Courtivron. New York: Schocken, 1981. 165–67.

———. *Revolution in Poetic Language.* Trans. Margaret Waller. Introd. Leon S. Roudiez. New York: Columbia UP, 1984.

Kristeva, Julia. "Semiotics: A Critical Science and/or a Critique of Science." *The Kristeva Reader.* Ed. and introd. Toril Moi. New York: Columbia UP, 1986. 74–88.

———. "The Speaking Subject." *On Signs.* Ed. Marshall Blonsky. Oxford: Blackwell, 1985. 210–20.

———. *Le Texte du roman: Approche sémiologique d'une structure discursive transformationnelle.* Approaches to Semiotics 6. The Hague: Mouton, 1970.

———. "Women's Time." *The Kristeva Reader.* Ed. and introd. Toril Moi. New York: Columbia UP, 1986. 187–213.

———. "Word, Dialogue and Novel." *The Kristeva Reader.* Ed. and introd. Toril Moi. New York: Columbia UP, 1986. 34–61.

Lacan, Jacques. *Ecrits.* Le Champ Freudien. Paris: Seuil, 1966.

Lansing, Richard H. "The Structure of Meaning in Lampedusa's *Il Gattopardo.*" *PMLA* 93 (1978): 409–22.

Lerner, Gerda. *The Creation of Patriarchy.* New York: Oxford UP, 1986.

Levin, Harry. "Literature as an Institution." *Accents* 6 (1946): 159–68.

Lucente, Gregory. "Figure and Temporality in a Historical Novel." *Beautiful Fables: Self-Consciousness in Italian Narrative from Manzoni to Calvino.* Baltimore: Johns Hopkins UP, 1986. 196–221.

———. "History and the Trial of Poetry: Everyday Life in Morante's *La Storia.*" *Beautiful Fables: Self-Consciousness in Italian Narrative from Manzoni to Calvino.* Baltimore: Johns Hopkins UP, 1986. 246–65.

———. "*Scrivere o fare . . . o altro:* Social Commitment and Ideologies of Representation in the Debates over Lampedusa's *Il Gattopardo* and Morante's *La Storia.*" *Italica* 61 (1984): 220–51.

Lukács, Georg. *The Historical Novel.* Trans. Hannah Mitchell and Stanley Mitchell. New York: Humanities, 1965.

———. "Narrate or Describe?" *Writer and Critic and Other Essays.* Ed. Arthur D. Kahn. London: Merlin, 1970. 110–48.

———. "Realism in the Balance." *Aesthetics and Politics.* Trans. Ronald Taylor. London: NLB, 1977. 28–67.

Manacorda, Giuliano. *Storia della letteratura italiana contemporanea 1940–1975.* Nuova biblioteca di cultura 166. 4th rev. ed. Rome: Editori Riuniti, 1977.

Mandrell, James. "The Prophetic Voice in Garro, Morante and Allende." *Comparative Literature* 42 (1990): 227–46.

Manzoni, Alessandro. *The Betrothed.* Trans. Bruce Penman. London: Penguin, 1972.

———. *Carteggio di Alessandro Manzoni.* Ed. G. Sforza and G. Gallavresi. Vol. 2. Milan: Hoepli, 1912.

———. *On the Historical Novel.* Introd. and trans. Sandra Bermann. Lincoln: U of Nebraska P, 1984.

———. *Tutte le opere di Alessandro Manzoni.* Ed. Alberto Chiari and Fausto Ghisalberti. 7 vols. Milan: Mondadori, 1957–70.

Marx, Karl, and Friedrich Engels. *Scritti sull'arte.* Bari: Laterza, 1967.

Matthiessen, F. O. *American Renaissance: Art and Expression in the Age of Emerson and Whitman.* New York: Oxford UP, 1941.

Mazzini, Giuseppe. "Del dramma storico." *Scritti letterari editi ed inediti di Giuseppe Mazzini.* Vol 1. Imola: Galeati, 1906. 255–329.

———. Rev. of "Del romanzo in generale, ed anche dei *Promessi sposi* di Alessandro Manzoni," by Paride Zaiotti. *Scritti letterari editi ed inediti di Giuseppe Mazzini.* Vol 1. Imola: Galeati, 1906. 31–41.

———. "D'una letteratura europea." *Scritti letterari editi ed inediti di Giuseppe Mazzini.* Vol 1. Imola: Galeati, 1906. 177–222.

Mazzoni, Guido. *L'Ottocento.* Ed. Aldo Vallone. Storia letteraria d'Italia. 2nd. rev. ed. Milan: Vallardi, 1973.

McGann, Jerome. *The Beauty of Inflections: Literary Investigations in Historical Method and Theory.* Oxford: Clarendon, 1988.

Meyers, Geoffrey. "Symbol and Structure in *The Leopard.*" *Italian Quarterly* 9 (1965): 50–70.

Miller, J. Hillis. *Fiction and Repetition: Seven English Novels.* Cambridge, MA: Harvard UP, 1982.

Mink, Louis O. "The Autonomy of Historical Understanding." *Philosophical Analysis and History.* Ed. William H. Dray. Sources in Contemporary Philosophy. New York: Harper, 1966. 160–92.

———. "Narrative Form as a Cognitive Instrument." *The Writing of History: Literary Form and Historical Understanding.* Ed. Robert H. Canary and Henry Kozicki. Madison: U of Wisconsin P, 1978. 129–49.

Mitchell, Juliet. Introduction. *Feminine Sexuality: Jacques Lacan and the Ecole Freudienne.* Ed. Juliet Mitchell and Jacqueline Rose. Trans. Jacqueline Rose. New York: Norton; New York: Pantheon, 1985. 1–26.

Moi, Toril. Introduction. "Women's Time." *The Kristeva Reader.* Ed. Toril Moi. New York: Columbia UP, 1986. 187–88.

Montale, Eugenio. "*Il Gattopardo.*" *Corriere della sera* [Milan] 12 Dec. 1958: 3.

Montani, Giuseppe. Rev. of *Cabrino Fondulo,* by Vincenzo Lancetti, *Alessio,* by Angelica Palli, and *Novelle storiche corse,* by Francesco Ottaviano Renucci. *Antologia* 27.80 (1827): 75–96.

Morante, Elsa. *History: A Novel.* Trans. William Weaver. New York: Knopf, 1977.

———. *La Storia.* Gli Struzzi 58. Turin: Einaudi, 1974.

———. "Sul romanzo." *Opere.* Ed. Carlo Cecchi and Cesare Garboli. Vol. 2. I Meridiani. Milan: Mondadori, 1990. 1497–1520. 2 vols.

Morawski, Kalikst. *Il romanzo storico italiano nell'epoca del Risorgimento.* Warsaw: Zakład Narodowy Imienia Ossolińskich, 1970.

Moscheni, Costanza. *Dei moderni romanzi: memoria di Costanza Moscheni.* Lucca: Tipografia di Jacopo Balatresi, 1828.

Negri, Renzo. "Il discorso *Del romanzo storico* nel trittico narrativo manzoniano." *Forum Italicum* 11 (1977): 307–29.

O'Neill, Tom. "Ants and Flags: Tomasi di Lampedusa's *Gattopardo.*" *The Italianist* 13 (1993): 180–208.

Orlandi, Ferdinando. "Dissertazione sopra il romanzo storico." *Dissertazioni storico-critiche sopra il Romanticismo e il Classicismo.* Florence: Magheri, 1839. 101–41.

Ortner, Sherry. "Is Female to Male as Nature Is to Culture?" *Woman, Culture and Society.* Ed. M. Z. Rosaldo and L. Lamphere. Stanford: Stanford UP, 1974. 67–87.

Pampaloni, Geno. "Destra e sinistra in letteratura." *Comunità* May/June 1959: 88–90.

———. "*Il Gattopardo* (o anche: *les lendemains qui ne chantent pas*)." *Comunità* Feb. 1959: 78–85.

Pascoli, Giovanni. "Il fanciullino." *Prose di Giovanni Pascoli.* Vol. 1. Introd. Augusto Vicinelli. 3rd ed. Milan: Mondadori, 1956. 5–56. 2 vols.

Pasolini, Pier Paolo. "La libertà stilistica." *Officina* 9–10 (1957): 341–46.

———. "Il neo-sperimentalismo." *Officina* 5 (1956): 169–82.

Passerini, Luisa. *Storia e soggettività: le fonti orali, la memoria.* Biblioteca di storia 35. Scandicci: La Nuova Italia, 1988.

Pellico, Silvio. "Lettere di Giulia Willet pubblicate da Orinitia Romagnuoli." *Il Conciliatore: foglio scientifico-letterario.* Ed. Vittore Branca. Vol. 2. Florence: Le Monnier, 1953. 15–20. 3 vols.

Perelman, Chaïm. *The New Rhetoric and the Humanities: Essays on Rhetoric and Its Applications.* Synthese Library 140. Dordrecht: Reidel, 1979.

Perrot, Michelle. *Une Histoire des femmes est-elle possible?* Paris: Rivages, 1984.

———. "Making History: Women in France." *Retrieving Women's History: Changing Perceptions of the Role of Women in Politics and Society.* Ed. S. Jay Kleinberg. Studies in Development: Theory and Policy. Oxford: Berg/Unesco, 1988. 41–59.

Piccioni, Leone. *La narrativa italiana tra romanzo e racconti.* Milan: Mondadori, 1959.

Pomata, Gianna. "Commento alla relazione di Paola Di Cori." *La ricerca delle donne: studi femministi in Italia.* Ed. Maria Cristina Marcuzzo and Anna Rossi-Doria. Soggetto donna 2. Turin: Rosenberg, 1987. 112–22.

———. "La storia delle donne: una questione di confine." *Gli strumenti della ricerca.* Ed. Giovanni de Luna. Vol. 10, bk. 2. Florence: La Nuova Italia, 1983. 1434–69. 10 vols.

Proust, Marcel. *In Search of Lost Time.* Vol. 1. Trans. C. K. Scott Moncrieff and Terence Kilmartin. Rev. D. J. Enright. London: Chatto, 1992. 6 vols.

Ragusa, Olga. "Stendhal, Tomasi di Lampedusa and the Novel." *Comparative Literature Studies* 10 (1973): 195–228.

Re, Lucia. "Utopian Longing and the Constraints of Racial and Sexual Difference in Elsa Morante's *La Storia.*" *Italica* 70 (1993): 361–75.

Ricoeur, Paul. *The Contribution of French Historiography to the Theory of History.* The Zaharoff Lecture 1978–79. Oxford: Clarendon, 1980.

———. *The Reality of the Historical Past.* The Aquinas Lecture 1984. Milwaukee: Marquette UP, 1984.

———. *Time and Narrative.* Trans. Kathleen McLaughlin and David Pellauer. 3 vols. Chicago: Chicago UP, 1984–85.

Robey, David. "Umberto Eco." *Writers and Society in Contemporary Italy.* Ed. Michael Caesar and Peter Hainsworth. New York: St. Martin, 1984. 63–87.

Romagnoli, Sergio. "Il romanzo storico." *Storia della letteratura italiana.* Ed. Emilio Cecchi and Natalino Sapegno. Vol. 8. Milan: Garzanti, 1968. 7–87. 9 vols.

Romanò, Angelo. "Al di qua e al di là dal neorealismo." *Discorso degli anni Cinquanta.* Il Tornasole. Milan: Mondadori, 1965. 169–76.

Rose, Jacqueline. Introduction. *Feminine Sexuality: Jacques Lacan and the Ecole Freudienne.* Ed. Juliet Mitchell and Jacqueline Rose.

Trans. Jacqueline Rose. New York: Norton; New York: Pantheon, 1985. 27–57.

Rosso, Stefano. "Postmodern Italy: Notes on the 'Crisis of Reason,' 'Weak Thought,' and *The Name of the Rose.*" *Exploring Postmodernism.* Selected Papers Presented at a Workshop on Postmodernism at the 11th Intl. Comp. Lit. Cong., Paris, 20–24 Aug. 1985. Ed. Matei Calinescu and Douwe Fokkema. Amsterdam: Benjamins, 1987. 79–92.

Saccone, Eduardo. "Nobility and Literature: Questions on Tomasi di Lampedusa." *MLN* 106 (1991): 159–78.

Salfi, Francesco. Rev. of *I promessi sposi,* by Alessandro Manzoni. *Revue Encyclopédique* 38 (1828): 376–89.

Salinari, Carlo. "*Il Gattopardo.*" *Vie nuove* 10 Jan. 1959: 46.

Samonà, Giuseppe Paolo. *Il Gattopardo, i racconti, Lampedusa.* Biblioteca di cultura 121. Florence: La Nuova Italia, 1974.

Sanguineti, Edoardo. "Il dibattito in occasione del primo incontro del gruppo a Palermo." *Gruppo 63: la nuova letteratura.* Ed. Nanni Balestrini and Alfredo Giuliani. Panorami 4. Milan: Feltrinelli, 1964.

Saussure, Ferdinand de. *Cours de linguistigue générale.* Ed. Tullio de Mauro. Paris: Payot, 1972.

Savini, Marta. *Riviste ottocentesche e storia della critica.* Biblioteca di cultura 50. Rome: Bulzoni, 1974.

Schiavoni, Franco. "Faith, Reason and Desire." *Meanjin* 43 (1984): 573–81.

Scott, Joan Wallach. "Gender: A Useful Category of Historical Analysis." *The American Historical Review* 91 (1986): 1053–75.

———. "The Problem of Invisibility." *Retrieving Women's History: Changing Perceptions of the Role of Women in Politics and Society.* Ed. S. Jay Kleinberg. Studies in Development: Theory and Policy. Oxford: Berg/Unesco, 1988. 5–29.

Selig, Karl-Ludwig. "*Il Gattopardo:* Observations on Enumeration and Some Other Aspects of the Text." *Teaching Language Through Literature* 26 (1986): 36–41.

Spagnoletti, Giacinto. "Scrivere 'alla Morante.'" *La fiera letteraria* 6 Oct 1974: 12–13.

Steinmetz, Horst. "Genres and Literary History." *General Problems of Literary History: Proceedings of the 10th Congress of the International Comparative Literature Association, New York 1982.* Ed. Anna Balakian et al. Vol. 1. New York: Garland, 1985. 251–55. 3 vols.

Suleiman, Susan. *Subversive Intent: Gender, Politics and the Avant-Garde.* Cambridge, MA: Harvard UP, 1990.

Tenca, Carlo. *Saggi critici di una storia delle letteratura italiana e altri scritti.* Ed. Gianluigi Berardi. Milan: Sansoni, 1969.

Titta Rosa, Giuseppe, ed. *Colloqui col Manzoni.* Milan: Ceschina, 1954.

Todorov, Tzvetan. *The Fantastic: A Structural Approach to a Literary Genre.* Trans. Richard Howard. Ithaca, NY: Cornell UP, 1975.

———. "The Origin of Genres." *New Literary History* 8 (1976): 159–70.

Tomasi di Lampedusa, Giuseppe. *Il Gattopardo.* I Contemporanei 4. Milan: Feltrinelli, 1959.

———. *The Leopard.* Trans. Archibald Colquhoun. New York: Avon, 1975.

Tommaseo, Niccolò. "Del romanzo storico." *Antologia* 39.117 (1830): 40–63.

———. *Il duca d'Atene.* Milan: Sanvito, 1858.

———. Rev. of *I Lombardi alla prima crociata,* by Tommaso Grossi. *Antologia* 24.70 (1826): 3–30.

———. Rev. of *Sibilla Odaleta,* by Carlo Varese. *Antologia* 29.87 (1828): 87–93.

Toynbee, Philip. "Experiment and the Future of the Novel." *The London Magazine* 3.5 (1956): 48–56.

Trombatore, Gaetano. "Considerazioni sulla narrativa siciliana." *Belfagor* 20 (1965): 1–10.

Uzielli, Sansone. "Del romanzo storico, e di Walter Scott. Articolo II." *Antologia* 13.39 (1824): 118–44.

Varese, Carlo. *La fidanzata ligure.* Paris: Baudry, 1832.

———. *Preziosa di Sanluri ossia i montanari sardi.* Milan: Stella, 1832.

———. *Sibilla Odaleta: episodio delle guerre d'Italia.* Paris: Baudry 1832.

Vattimo, Gianni. *Le avventure della differenza: che cosa significa pensare dopo Nietzsche e Heidegger.* Saggi blu. Milan: Garzanti, 1980.

———. "Bottle, Net, Truth, Revolution, Terrorism, Philosophy." *Denver Quarterly* 16.4 (1982): 24–34.

Vassalli, Sebastiano. *La chimera.* Turin: Einaudi, 1990.

Veyne, Paul. *Writing History: Essay on Epistemology.* Trans. Mina Moore-Rinvolucri. Middletown, CT: Wesleyan UP, 1984.

Rev. of *Viaggi di Francesco Petrarca in Francia, in Germania ed in Italia descritti dal professore Ambrogio Levati,* by Levati. *Biblioteca italiana* 23 (1821): 145–69.

Vico, Giambattista. *The New Science of Giambattista Vico.* Trans. Thomas Goddart Bergin and Max Harold Fisch. Ithaca, NY: Cornell UP, 1968.

Viëtor, Karl. "L'Histoire des genres littéraires." *Poétique* 32 (1977): 490–506.

Vitello, Andrea. *Giuseppe Tomasi di Lampedusa.* La Diagonale 17. Palermo: Sellerio, 1987.

Vittori, Fiorenza. "Struttura e problematica del discorso manzoniano *Del romanzo storico.*" *Italianistica* 6 (1977): 19–42.

Vittorini, Elio. "Vittorini confessa: scrivo i libri ma penso ad altro." *Il Giorno* [Milan] 24 Feb. 1959: 9.

Wachtel, Nathan. *The Vision of the Vanquished: The Spanish Conquest of Peru through Indian Eyes, 1350–1570.* New York: Barnes, 1977.

Wellek, René. *Concepts of Criticism: Essays.* Ed. Stephen G. Nichols, Jr. New Haven: Yale UP, 1963.

Wellek, René, and Austin Warren. *Theory of Literature.* 3rd ed. New York: Harcourt, 1977.

White, Allon. "Hysteria and the End of Carnival." *The Violence of Representation: Literature and the History of Violence.* Ed. Nancy Armstrong and Leonard Tennenhouse. London: Routledge, 1989. 157–70.

White, Hayden. *The Content of the Form: Narrative Discourse and Historical Representation.* Baltimore: Johns Hopkins UP, 1987.

———. "The Historical Text as Literary Artifact." *The Writing of History: Literary Form and Historical Understanding.* Ed. Robert H. Canary and Henri Kozicki. Madison: U of Wisconsin P, 1978. 41–62.

———. *Metahistory: The Historical Imagination in Nineteenth-Century Europe.* Baltimore: Johns Hopkins UP, 1973.

Zaiotti, Paride. "Del romanzo in generale, ed anche dei *Promessi sposi,* romanzo di Alessandro Manzoni." Parts 1 and 2. *Biblioteca italiana* 47 (1827): 322–72; 48 (1827): 32–81.

———. "De' romanzi storici." *Biblioteca italiana* 58 (1830): 145–92.

Index

Works by Alessandro Manzoni, Giuseppe Tomasi di Lampedusa, Elsa Morante, and Umberto Eco are listed by title.